$\mathcal{S} \cap \cap$ /

D0081669

THE IRAQ WARS AND AMERICA'S MILITARY REVOLUTION

Many saw the United States' decisive victory in Desert Storm (1991) as not only the vindication of American defense policy since Vietnam but also as a confirmation of a revolution in military affairs (RMA). Just as information age technologies were revolutionizing civilian life, the Gulf War appeared to reflect similarly profound changes in warfare. A debate has raged ever since about a contemporary RMA and its implications for American defense policy. Addressing these issues, *The Iraq Wars and America's Military Revolution* is a comprehensive study of the Iraq Wars in the context of the RMA debate. Focusing on the creation of a reconnaissance-strike complex and conceptions of parallel or nonlinear warfare, Keith L. Shimko finds a persuasive case for a contemporary RMA while recognizing its limitations as well as promises. The RMA's implications for American defense policy are more ambiguous because the military lessons of the Iraq Wars need to be placed in the context of judgments about national interests and predictions of future strategic environments.

Keith L. Shimko is associate professor of political science at Purdue University, where he has taught since 1989. His teaching and research interests are in the areas of international relations and security. Professor Shimko is the author of *Images and Arms Control*, which received the Quincy Wright Award in 1992, and three editions of *International Relations: Perspectives and Controversies*. He has also taught at the University of Hamburg, where he was a guest professor in the Institute for Peace Research and Security Policy in 2002–2003.

The Iraq Wars and America's Military Revolution

Keith L. Shimko

Purdue University

CAMBRIDGE UNIVERSITY PRESS

CAMBRIDGE UNIVERSITY PRESS
Cambridge, New York, Melbourne, Madrid, Cape Town, Singapore,
São Paulo, Delhi, Dubai, Tokyo

Cambridge University Press
32 Avenue of the Americas, New York, NY 10013-2473, USA

www.cambridge.org
Information on this title: www.cambridge.org/9780521128841

First published 2010

Printed in the United States of America

A catalog record for this publication is available from the British Library.

Library of Congress Cataloging in Publication data

Shimko, Keith L., 1962–
The Iraq wars and America's military revolution / Keith L. Shimko.
    p.   cm.
Includes bibliographical references and index.
ISBN 978-0-521-12884-1 (pbk.)
1. Military art and science – Technological innovations – History – 21st century.
2. Military art and science – Technological innovations – History – 20th century.
3. Iraq War, 2003 – Technology.   4. Afghan War, 2001 – Technology.
5. Persian Gulf War, 1991 – Technology.   6. United States – Military policy.   I. Title.
U43.U4S55   2010
355'.070973 – dc22   2010010983

ISBN 978-0-521-11151-5 Hardback
ISBN 978-0-521-12884-1 Paperback

In memory of my mother and father, Riitta Shimko (1939–2002) and Leonard Shimko (1936–2006).

CONTENTS

ACKNOWLEDGMENTS

This project began as a study of the possible impact of the revolution in military affairs on NATO when I was a guest professor at the University of Hamburg's Institute for Security Policy and Peace Research for the 2002–2003 academic year. While at Hamburg I shifted my focus as I became convinced, especially after the March 2003 invasion of Iraq, that anyone interested in the RMA needed to be focusing on the Iraq Wars. Although my research on the RMA and NATO never bore any fruit in terms of publications, my time in Hamburg was both enjoyable and intellectually productive in giving me time to start thinking about the RMA in broader terms. I remain grateful to Goetz Neuneck as well as the Institute's other faculty and graduate students for making my stay so worthwhile and stimulating.

This manuscript on the RMA and the Iraq Wars has benefited from the insights of many at different stages. Jeanne Olofson – scholar, soldier, and deaconess – provided valuable feedback on the initial book prospectus. Professor Robert Gray of Franklin and Marshall College read both the prospectus and the draft manuscript, making several important suggestions for improving the final product. Christopher Olofson read the manuscript with extreme care, saving me from numerous substantive and stylistic errors. I am grateful to Ed Parsons, formerly of Cambridge University Press, for his early support and enthusiasm for the project. I would like to offer special thanks to one of the manuscript's reviewers for Cambridge, Professor Jasen Castillo of Texas A&M University. In his reviews and subsequent discussions, Professor Castillo offered the model of constructive academic criticism.

On a more personal note, I would like to dedicate this book to the memory of my parents, Riitta and Leonard Shimko, both of whom passed away way too soon. My satisfaction with having finally completed the book is diminished only by my sadness that neither of them is here to see it.

I MILITARY REVOLUTIONS AND THE IRAQ WARS

1991, A New Kind of War?

The conduct and outcome of the first Iraq War in 1991 came as something of a revelation to the majority of Americans who had little reason to follow the previous decade's advances in military technologies and innovations in war-fighting doctrine. It was, in the words of Colin Gray, "a flash in the sky of strategic consciousness."[1] The war's conduct was unusual in that weeks of relentless bombing preceded engagement with Iraqi ground forces, leaving many wondering when the real war would begin. In the absence of actual ground combat by the coalition, pressure mounted to let the American people know exactly how Kuwait was going to be liberated. Generals Colin Powell and Norman Schwarzkopf agreed on the need to provide more information about the war's progress and the plan for victory. At a news conference a week into the war, they explained the coalition's actions and strategy. Powell described the plan to defeat the Iraqi army in vivid terms: "Our strategy to go after the enemy is very, very simple. First we're going to cut it off and then we are going to kill it."[2] Powell and Schwarzkopf arrived at the press conference armed with visual aids. After showing footage of a lone car crossing a bridge through crosshairs, Schwarzkopf declared the driver the "luckiest person in Iraq" as a guided bomb raced toward the bridge, hitting it dead-on just as the car appeared to reach safety on the other side. The assembled press corps giggled. This was only the beginning of a steady stream of such images. Government buildings, critical infrastructure, Iraqi planes, and their bunkers and munitions depots were destroyed with a deadly precision reminiscent of video games. Whether such images accurately

[1] Quoted in Lusaz Kamienski, "Comparing the Nuclear and Information RMAs," *Strategic Insight* Vol. 2, No. 4 (April 4, 2003). Accessed at: www.ccc.nps.navy.mil/si/apr03/strategy2.asp.

[2] Stephen Budiansky, *Air Power: The Men, Machines, and Ideas That Revolutionized War from Kitty Hawk to Iraq* (New York: Penguin, 2004), p. 423.

reflected the air war as a whole is another matter. As portrayed at the time, however, the war was clearly not a repeat of World War II. There were no fleets of aircraft dropping thousands of bombs and razing entire cities. This was not aerial bombing as most people remembered or imagined it. This imagery contributed to a sense that this was a different kind of war, an impression only magnified by the war's unexpectedly lopsided result. Despite dire prewar predictions of coalition casualties in the thousands, only 147 American and 99 other coalition soldiers were killed in action.[3]

Not everyone, however, was completely surprised. For at least a decade before the war, many in the Department of Defense and wider strategic community had been talking about a contemporary "revolution in military affairs" (RMA), a change in warfare that might prove as profound as the introduction of gunpowder weapons in the fourteenth century. Just as advances in information technology were transforming economic and civilian life, so too did many expect a similarly revolutionary transformation of warfare. These arguments progressed on two levels. On a theoretical level, there was speculation about the future of warfare in general that transcended any immediate national concerns. On a more practical level, predictions of an RMA were associated with a policy agenda emphasizing the exploitation of technological advances to preserve and even improve the United States' long-term strategic position. Many of those advancing this agenda were instrumental in shaping the 1991 Iraq War plan, which they saw as a proving ground, a large-scale test and demonstration of their vision of a transformed military applying new technology in innovative ways to achieve victory in war. Success in 1991 was taken as vindication of previous defense policy decisions as well as a green light to continue along the same path. The Iraq War brought these ideas and policy agendas, which were already familiar to readers of military journals, into full public view.

Whether or not observers accepted or even cared about predictions of an emergent RMA, it was difficult to analyze the 1991 Iraq War without using language suggesting that significant, even revolutionary, military changes were underway. Robert Citino thinks the war revealed "a *quantum* leap in the quick flow of information, always the thorniest command and control issue."[4] Stephen Budiansky cites the *Gulf War Air Power Survey*'s conclusion that "*never* has an air force found itself in the position of preparing the battlefield to the extent" witnessed in the Gulf War.

---

[3] Alastair Finlan, *The Gulf War, 1991* (New York: Routledge, 2003), p. 85. Although there is some minor variation in these numbers, the general point that American and coalition casualties were very low by any standard is uncontested.

[4] Robert Citino, *Blitzkrieg to Desert Storm: The Evolution of Operational Warfare* (Lawrence, KS: University of Kansas Press, 2004), p. 290, emphasis added.

He deemed this "not an idle boast."[5] Military historian John Keegan argues that "since 1991 there has been a *revolution* in accuracy, promising the results sought by air forces since the dawn of strategic bombing."[6] John House agrees: "*for the first time*, airpower at least approached the effectiveness that its advocates preached for generations."[7] George and Meredith Friedman attribute "the success of the bombing campaign in the Persian Gulf . . . [to] the *radical* revision of bombing probabilities."[8] Max Boot echoes these assessments: "precision guided weapons . . . made possible a *quantum leap* in bombing accuracy over the unguided projectiles of World War II." And even though he is somewhat skeptical of more grandiose predictions about a contemporary RMA, Boot concedes, "something *extraordinary* happened on the night of January 17–18, 1991. It was the opening night not only of Operation Desert Storm but, arguably, of *a whole new era of warfare*."[9] These are typical observations. The same adjectives tend to reappear in almost any discussion of the 1991 Iraq War – "revolutionary," "for the first time," "radical," "unprecedented," "quantum leap," and "extraordinary." Language suggesting revolutionary change pervades descriptions even in the absence of explicit references to an RMA. None of this proves that the 1991 Iraq War marked the beginning of a new RMA, but at a minimum there appears to be near-universal agreement that something important was changing.

Revolutions and Military Revolutions

People like to talk about revolutions, military and otherwise, because they are dramatic events that immediately attract attention. It would be easy to compile a long list of supposed social, political, economic, technological, medical, scientific, and intellectual revolutions. But unfortunately, the term *revolution* is more commonly used than defined. It is often employed with the implicit assumption that people already know what it means. One is tempted to draw parallels with the U.S. Supreme Court's identification of pornography as something difficult to define in the abstract but easy to recognize when encountered. Although it may be impossible to devise definitive criteria for identifying revolutions, we can at least sketch

---

[5] Budiansky, *Air Power*, p. 423, emphasis added.
[6] John Keegan, *The Iraq War* (New York: Vintage, 2004), p. 142.
[7] John M. House, *Combined Arms Warfare in the Twentieth Century* (Lawrence, KS: University of Kansas Press, 2001), p. 269, emphasis added.
[8] George and Meredith Friedman, *The Future of War: Power, Technology and American Dominance in the 21st Century* (New York: Crown, 1996), p. 269, emphasis added.
[9] Max Boot, *War Made New: Technology, Warfare and the Course of History, 1500 to Today* (New York: Gotham Books, 2006), pp. 321 and 322, emphasis added.

some general guidelines for distinguishing revolutionary change that will help in thinking about a possible revolution in military affairs.

Revolutions are generally thought to involve some combination of wide-ranging, unusually significant, and/or rapid change. Theda Skocpol, for example, defines social revolutions as "rapid, basic transformations of a society's state and class structures."[10] Thus, we can think of revolutions in terms of the *scope, magnitude,* and *speed* of change they entail. Those revolutions universally accepted as such often display all three elements of revolutionary change. The Russian Revolution is a case in point. It was certainly wide in scope, affecting almost every facet of Russian life as the political order was upended, the economic system transformed, and social relations reconfigured. The magnitude of these changes was unusually significant: the creation of the Bolshevik dictatorship was no mere tinkering with the previous order. And the pace of change was rapid, taking just a few years. But there are also "revolutions" for which the term is used colloquially. The so-called Reagan Revolution, which entailed some relatively modest policy revisions (e.g., reduced marginal tax rates and less regulation), hardly seems worthy of the description in comparison to something like the Russian Revolution.

Of the possible elements of revolutionary change, speed may be the most problematic, particularly since *revolution* is easily juxtaposed with *evolution,* which conveys a sense of gradualism. There is little consistency on this point. While the Russian Revolution remade an entire social, political, and economic order in a short period, the Industrial Revolution did the same over a century or more. Although there is no denying the change associated with the Industrial Revolution, it is difficult to consider it rapid unless one adopts a very broad historical perspective in which several generations is not a very long time. Still, no one advocates relabeling the Industrial *Revolution* as industrial *evolution.* This suggests that speed is the most dispensable characteristic of revolutions. We are probably fortunate that debates over the RMA tend not to dwell on the issue of speed. At least implicitly, most seem to accept Andrew Liaropoulos's conclusion that "the 'revolution' in Revolution in Military Affairs should not be taken to mean the change will necessarily occur rapidly, but just that the change will be profound."[11]

While speed may not constitute an essential element of revolutions, significant change undoubtedly does. One can imagine a revolution that takes some time to unfold, but not a revolution without major change. The analytical and empirical challenge is identifying these changes and judging

---

[10] Theda Skocpol, *States and Social Revolutions: A Comparative Analysis of France, Russia and China* (Cambridge: Cambridge University Press, 1979), p. 4.

[11] Andrew N. Liaropoulos, "Revolutions in Warfare: Theoretical Paradigms and Historical Evidence – the Napoleonic and First World War Revolutions," *The Journal of Military History* Vol. 70 (April 2006), p. 370.

whether they constitute a "basic transformation," to use Skocpol's terminology. In cases such as the Russian Revolution the answer is so evidently in the affirmative that the question need not be asked explicitly. Most cases are not as clear-cut. Barry Watts makes the valuable if somewhat obvious point that "there is no field of human endeavor in which we possess precise, unambiguous, cut-and-dry criteria for distinguishing evolutionary change from revolutionary change." Largely as a result of the "inherent imprecision of our conceptual categories," we need to recognize that "such classifications are always to some degree arbitrary."[12] But by focusing on the scope, magnitude, and, to a lesser degree, speed of change as potential elements of any revolution, we can at least begin to frame the issues in the debate about a contemporary RMA.

The concept of military revolutions is not new. Historians, especially those specializing in the military history of early modern Europe, began using the term in the 1950s to describe several periods of military innovation between the fourteenth and seventeenth centuries.[13] Histories of technology and warfare, for example, routinely discuss the development of gunpowder weapons, particularly early cannons, during this period under the general rubric of a gunpowder or artillery revolution.[14] The military reforms Napoleon instituted in the wake of the French Revolution are commonly referred to as the Napoleonic Revolution. More recently, references to the post–World War II nuclear revolution have become standard.[15] None of this has been uncontroversial. The precise nature of military revolutions was as much a matter of contention as their identification. Some observers identify only three military revolutions in all of history while others claim as many as ten in just the last 600 years. But the general notion that certain periods can usefully be described as revolutionary because they stand out from the normal pattern of military

---

[12] Barry Watts, *Six Decades of Guided Munitions and Battle Networks: Progress and Prospects* (Washington, DC: Center for Strategic and Budgetary Assessments, 2007), pp. 65 and 258.

[13] Michael Roberts is sometimes credited with introducing the concept of military revolutions in his book *The Military Revolution* (Belfast, 1956). See also Clifford Rogers, ed., *The Military Revolution Debate: Readings on the Military Transformation of Early Modern Europe* (Westview: Boulder, CO, 1995); Geoffrey Parker, *The Military Revolution: Military Innovation and the Rise of the West* (Cambridge: Cambridge University Press, 1988); Brian M. Downing, *The Military Revolution and Political Change: The Origins of Democracy and Autocracy in Early Modern Europe* (Princeton: Princeton University Press, 1992); and William H. McNeill's classic *The Pursuit of Power: Technology, Armed Force, and Society Since 1000* (Chicago: University of Chicago Press, 1982).

[14] See Geoffrey Parker, "The Gunpowder Revolution," in Geoffrey Parker, ed., *Warfare: The Triumph of the West* (Cambridge: Cambridge University Press, 1995), pp. 106–19; and Bruce D. Porter, *War and the Rise of the State: The Military Foundations of Modern Politics* (New York: Free Press, 1994), pp. 31–2, 37, 53, 65.

[15] See Robert Jervis, *The Meaning of the Nuclear Revolution* (Ithaca: Cornell University Press, 1990).

innovation was widely, if not universally, accepted long before the debate about a possible contemporary revolution.

The current debate is usually traced to the late 1970s and early 1980s, when Soviet military theorists began to warn that emerging technologies were creating military capabilities that might erode Soviet advantages vis-à-vis the United States and NATO in Europe. The Soviets were, for example, well aware of the United States' use of laser-guided munitions in the final years of the Vietnam War. They were particularly alarmed by the military lessons of wars in the Middle East between Israel and its Soviet-armed neighbors in which radar detection and guided munitions combined to produce shockingly high military losses on both sides, illustrating the lethality of new technologies and weapons. The Soviets feared that their forces in Europe were becoming increasingly vulnerable to these emerging technologies. Within the larger context of the information revolution, these developments convinced some Soviet theorists that a "military-technical revolution" was in the offing. And when they considered who was likely to be the major beneficiary of this revolution, they feared it was the United States, not the Soviet Union.[16]

As similar ideas took hold in the West, the concept of a "revolution in military affairs" replaced the Soviet military-technical revolution, reflecting a belief that Soviet conceptualizations exaggerated the importance of technology in relation to other elements of military change. No one questioned that technological advances were a significant component of the changes underway, but they were only part of the equation. Technological change does not automatically bring about an RMA; it merely creates the opportunity. New weapons and technologies usually need to be accompanied by military doctrine and organizational reform for their revolutionary potential to be realized. This basic insight is often illustrated with reference to the German *blitzkrieg* of World War II. The key to the *blitzkrieg*'s success was not Germany's possession of weapons that others lacked. Germany was not the only country with radios, airplanes, a mechanized infantry, and tanks. What set the Germans apart from competitors were their ideas about how these weapons could be combined and military units reorganized to take full advantage of them on the battlefield.[17]

---

[16] Jacob W. Kipp, "The Labor of Sisyphus: Forecasting the Revolution in Military Affairs During Russia's Time of Crisis," in Thierry Gongora and Harald von Riekoff, eds., *Toward a Revolution in Military Affairs? Defense and Security at the Dawn of the Twenty-first Century* (Westport, CT: Greenwood Press, 2000), pp. 87–93. Also, Williamson Murray and MacGregor Knox, "Thinking about Revolutions in Warfare," in MacGregor Knox and Williamson Murray, eds., *The Dynamics of Military Revolution, 1300–2050* (Cambridge: Cambridge University Press, 2001), pp. 2–4.

[17] See James S. Corum, *Roots of Blitzkrieg: Hand Von Seekt and German Military Reform* (Lawrence, KS: University of Kansas Press, 1994); Robert Citino, *The Path to Blitzkrieg: Doctrine and Training in the German Army, 1920–1939* (Boulder, CO; Lynne Rienner,

Thomas Graves notes that "despite a vast literature on the RMA idea over the last decade, there has never been a clear consensus on the meaning and definition of a true 'Revolution in Military Affairs.'"[18] Part of the problem is that as the concept became more popular, definitions have proliferated. It is as though each analyst wants to use his or her unique definition rather than rely on someone else's. This tendency toward definition proliferation is common in the social sciences. Matters have been further complicated by the appearance of concepts in the 1980s and 1990s whose relationship to the RMA was not always clear. In addition to "military-technical revolutions" and RMAs, one encounters "revolutions in strategic affairs," "net-centric warfare," "information warfare," "fourth-generation warfare," "military transformation," and so on. Yet, despite the apparent conceptual confusion, there is enough common ground in the most commonly accepted definitions to provide a working conceptualization of a revolution in military affairs.

Claiming that "more is definitely less when it comes to definitions," Colin Gray opts for brevity, defining an RMA "as a radical change in the character or conduct of war."[19] According to Clifford Rogers, "an RMA is simply a revolutionary change in how war is fought."[20] Andrew Krepinevich is slightly less succinct: "What is a military revolution? It is what occurs when the application of new technologies into a significant number of military systems combines with innovative operational concepts and organizational adaptation in a way that fundamentally alters the character and conduct of conflict. It does so by producing a dramatic increase – often an order of magnitude or greater – in the combat potential and military effectiveness of armed forces."[21] Andrew Marshall, the influential Director of the Office of Net Assessment in the U.S. Department of Defense (for whom Krepinevich once worked) defines an RMA as "a major change in the nature of warfare brought about by the innovative application of new technologies which, combined with dramatic changes in military doctrine and operational and organizational

1999); Robert Citino, *The Quest for Decisive Victory: From Stalemate to Blitzkrieg in Europe, 1899–1940* (Lawrence, KS: University of Kansas Press, 2002); Williamson Murray, "May 1940: Contingency and Frailty of the German RMA," in MacGregor Knox and Williamson Murray, eds., *The Dynamics of Military Revolution, 1300–2050* (Cambridge: Cambridge University Press, 2001), pp. 154–74; and Williamson Murray and Alan Millett, *A War to Be Won: Fighting the Second World War* (Cambridge: Harvard University Press, 2001), especially chapters 2 and 3.

18 Thomas C. Graves, "Al Qaeda, RMA and the Future of Warfare," U.S. Army War College, Unpublished M.A. Thesis, 2008, p. 5.

19 Colin Gray, *Another Bloody Century: Future Warfare* (London: Phoenix), p. 105.

20 Clifford J. Rogers, "'Military Revolutions' and 'Revolutions in Military Affairs': A Historian's Perspective," in Thierry Gongora and Harald von Riekoff, eds., *Toward a Revolution in Military Affairs?* (Westport, CT: Greenwood Press, 2000), p. 22.

21 Andrew F. Krepinevich, "Cavalry to Computer: The Pattern of Military Revolutions," *The National Interest* (Fall 1994), p. 30.

concepts, fundamentally alters the character and conduct of military operations."[22]

Military historians MacGregor Knox and Williamson Murray adopt a similar definition while drawing a useful distinction between *military revolutions* and *revolutions in military affairs*. Pointing to such examples as the Napoleonic and Industrial revolutions, they conceptualize *military revolutions* broadly as fundamental "upheavals" whose effects extended well beyond the battlefield and military organizations. In addition to the more narrow effects on warfare, military revolutions bring "systemic changes in politics and society. They [are] uncontrollable, unpredictable and unforeseeable.... [they] recast society and the state as well as military organizations." In contrast, Knox and Murray prefer to evaluate contemporary changes in terms of a more modest *revolution in military affairs* entailing "the assembly of a complex mix of tactical, organizational, doctrinal and technological innovations in order to implement a new conceptual approach to warfare or to a specialized sub-branch of warfare."[23] Although revolutions in military affairs are more limited in significance and scope, they may ultimately be subsumed within a larger military revolution. Futurists Heidi and Alvin Toffler, for example, discuss the changes of warfare associated with the information revolution as an integral component of a larger process of social and political change on par with the agricultural revolution, when people ceased being hunter-gatherers to engage in fixed farming and animal husbandry, and the industrial revolution.[24]

Richard Hundley offers a slightly different definition of an RMA as a "paradigm shift in the nature and conduct of military operations that either renders obsolete or irrelevant one or more of the core competencies of a dominant player, creates one or more new core competencies in some major new dimension of warfare, or does both." On first reading this sounds quite different from other definitions, but on closer inspection there is common ground since "core competencies" result from the same combination of technological, doctrinal, and organizational changes that other RMA theorists emphasize. As Hundley explains, "although not all RMAs are technology driven, those that are usually brought about by combinations of technologies rather than by individual ones and involve

---

[22] Cited in Thierry Gongora and Harald von Riekoff, eds., *Toward a Revolution in Military Affairs? Defense and Security Policy at the Dawn of the 21st Century* (New York: Greenwood Press, 2000), p. 1.

[23] Knox and Murray, "Thinking about Revolutions in Warfare," pp. 6–7 and 12. Also, Williamson Murray, "Thinking about Revolutions in Military Affairs," *Joint Force Quarterly* (Summer 1997), pp. 69–76.

[24] See Alvin Toffler, *The Third Wave* (New York: Bantam Books, 1984). More focused on the relevance of this thesis for warfare is Alvin and Heidi Toffler, *War and Anti-War: Survival at the Dawn of the 21st Century* (New York: Little, Brown and Co., 1993), especially pp. 64–81.

essential doctrinal and organizational changes along with new technologies."[25] Hundley's approach is interesting in suggesting that RMAs may *but need not necessarily* result in fundamental changes in existing military practices (i.e., core competencies). Existing core competencies may endure (or even be enhanced) in an RMA consisting largely of fundamentally new core competencies in other aspects of warfare. This conceptualization is useful in allowing us to think about an RMA involving both critical elements of continuity in some dimensions of warfare as well as revolutionary change in others.

To avoid a point of confusion often evident in discussions of a contemporary RMA, it is important to emphasize the distinction between the *nature* of war, which RMAs do not alter, and the *character* of war, which they do affect. Colin Gray is emphatic: "Some confused theorists would have us believe that war can change its nature. Let us stamp out this nonsense immediately." In the tradition of Clausewitz, Gray notes that "war is organized violence threatened or waged for political purposes. That is its nature. If the behavior under scrutiny is other than that just defined, it is not war." The introduction of gunpowder, for example, did not change the *nature* of warfare but rather the manner in which it was conducted, its character. Similarly, contemporary RMA theorists claim that changes in military technology, doctrine, and organization are changing how wars are fought, not the fact that they remain organized violence waged for political purposes. The Iraq Wars did not reflect any change in the nature of warfare. If there was any change, it was in how the wars were conducted. RMA theorists recognize the distinction between "war's permanent nature but changing character."[26]

The Contemporary Debate

If we are in the midst of an RMA, what is the nature of the revolution? What aspects of warfare are being revolutionized? How are the character and conduct of warfare changing? Although proponents of an RMA offer somewhat different answers to these questions, there is a common intellectual foundation that unites most claims of a contemporary RMA. The shared assumption is that just as the rise of industrialism in the late nineteenth and early twentieth centuries profoundly changed the conduct of war, so too will the transition from industrial to information-based economies and societies. Kipp is representative in viewing the "defining feature of the RMA" as "the shift from mass industrial warfare to information warfare."[27]

[25] Richard O. Hundley, *Past Revolutions, Future Transformations* (Santa Monica, CA: RAND, 1999), p. 9.
[26] Gray, *Another Bloody Century*, pp. 30 and 33.
[27] Kipp, "The Labor of Sisyphus," p. 93.

To understand why many saw the 1991 Gulf War as the critical turn-ing point in this transition, imagine video of F-117s attacking targets in downtown Baghdad on the war's first night playing alongside footage of allied bombing raids on Hamburg or Tokyo during World War II. Pre-sented with such a contrast it would be difficult to avoid the conclusion that one was witnessing two very different kinds of warfare. The leveling of German and Japanese cities was in many respects the culmination of industrial era warfare – wildly indiscriminate and massively destructive. Perhaps no one conveys the essence of industrial war better than Bruce Porter. Discussing the relentless killing on the western front during World War I, he observes that:

Even as the essence of the Industrial Revolution was an exponential increase in the productive capacity of the individual laborer, the crux of the machine gun was its multiplication in the killing capacity of the individual soldier. . . . While the machine guns spewed out death at the Somme and Passchendaele, the armaments factories of the Great War spewed out ten thousand standardized items of war material and munitions – all the technological and organizational genius of the industrial age culminating in the mass production of mass destruction.[28]

It was the combination of modern nationalism, industrialism, and techno-logical limitations that produced a form of warfare whose defining char-acteristic was mass. Nationalism motivated people by the tens of millions; factory assembly lines churned out a seemingly inexhaustible supply of guns, bullets, shells, and bombs; and the inaccuracy of weapons required their use in large numbers to hit and destroy specific targets. The result was modern total war in which entire societies were mobilized, targeted, and nearly destroyed. Implicitly or explicitly, claims of a contemporary RMA see nothing less than the demise of the era of total war and the end of industrialism's "mass production of mass destruction."

Jeffrey Cooper is among those who frame the RMA explicitly in these terms. Explaining that the Napoleonic Revolution began a "150 year period . . . of military expansion with the shift to mass armies, continental or global scope of operations, and dependence on attrition warfare," he suggests that a contemporary RMA "may mark the closing of that era of warfare dominated by large military forces and equally large scopes of military operations. This RMA may usher in a new period of military contraction and a return to wars fought for limited objectives by valuable forces too precious to waste in mass, attrition-style warfare."[29] George and Meredith Friedman echo these themes, predicting that "for the first time in five hundred years, we are about to see a dramatic decrease in

---

[28] Porter, *War and the Rise of the State*, pp. 149–50.
[29] Jeffrey R. Cooper, "Another View of the Revolution in Military Affairs," in John Arquilla and David Ronfeldt, eds., *In Athena's Camp: Preparing for Conflict in the Information Age* (Santa Monica, CA: RAND, 1997), pp. 112–13.

the size of land forces, without a decrease in military effectiveness . . . with precision-guided munitions, the number of men involved in arms factories and armies will decline precipitously." Perhaps more importantly, on the battlefield "the level of devastation will decline as well. The relatively light damage to Iraq in the six-week bombing campaign, compared, for example, to the damage to Hanoi in the Christmas bombing, is foretaste of a more moderate sort of war."[30]

Along similar lines, J. Marshall Beier points to the emergence (or re-emergence) of normative constraints on targeting civilians as a critical element of the new RMA representing a repudiation of the logic of total war:

The present moment marks an important historical reversal. For nearly two centuries, the gains of a much longer historical trend toward discrimination between combatants and non-combatants have been eroded . . . But since the end of the Cold War, claims of discriminancy on behalf of PGMs and their operational use have given rise to a disciplining effect upon offensive war operations, with domestic and international support increasingly averse to any significant danger to non-combatants.[31]

The blurring of the distinction between combatants and civilians in twentieth-century warfare was partly a consequence of limited surveillance and targeting technologies. As Patrick Morgan explains, "force has been a blunt instrument because military resources have made it so. To compensate for difficulty in finding and hitting targets, military forces have often resorted to saturating the target area or using large explosions." The result was a mode of warfare "difficult to encompass within systems of law or morality."[32]

In such analyses one sees the dominant leitmotif of arguments for a contemporary RMA: new technologies combined with proper doctrine and organization are force multipliers allowing fewer soldiers armed with fewer weapons to be equally effective, applying force in a manner that is less destructive and reduces collateral damage and noncombatant casualties. For RMA advocates this is a reversal of the trends that defined industrial war and thus represents a change in the character of warfare that deserves to be considered revolutionary.

For some observers, the juxtaposition of coalition air attacks on Baghdad and allied raids on axis cities provides a particularly apt illustration of an RMA in which technological advances have had their most profound effect on aerial bombing. Most RMA advocates see technological

---

[30] Friedman and Friedman, *The Future of War*, p. 393.
[31] J. Marshall Beier, "Discriminating Tastes: 'Smart' Bombs, Non-Combatants, and Notions of Legitimacy in Warfare," *Security Dialogue* Vol. 34, No. 4 (December 2003), p. 413.
[32] Patrick M. Morgan, "The Impact of the Revolution in Military Affairs," *The Journal of Strategic Studies* Vol. 23, No. 1 (March 2000), p. 141.

change impacting almost every aspect of military power, but one school of thought highlights its disproportionate effect on air forces, portraying the RMA as fundamentally an air power revolution. Precision targeting has not only rendered obliteration bombing a relic of the past, but also enabled militaries to apply aerial power in ways that generations of air theorists could only dream of. Benjamin Lambeth is one of the most forceful exponents of the air power RMA thesis, emphasizing how "recent developments have dramatically increased the *relative* combat potential of air power in comparison to that of other force elements."[33] This shift is the result of new technologies that permit attacks on a wide range of strategic targets with limited collateral damage and civilian casualties, even in densely populated urban environments. According to Lambeth,

American air power has been transformed...to a point where it has finally become truly strategic in its potential effects. That was not the case before the advent of stealth technology, highly accurate strike capability, and substantially improved availability of battlefield information. Earlier air campaigns were of limited effectiveness at the operational and strategic levels because they simply involved too many aircraft and too high a loss rate to achieve too few results.... air power now permits the attainment of strategic results through simultaneity rather than through the classical sequence of methodical plodding from tactical goals through operational level goals to strategic goals at an exorbitant cost in lives, forces and national treasure.[34]

Similarly, Richard Hallion argues that "the combination of the lethality of modern air weapons, coupled with the freedom of maneuver, range, precision, and sustainability of air attack, has revolutionized war."[35] Consequently, "today, air power is the dominant form of military power. Does this mean that all future wars will be won solely by air power? Not at all. But what this does mean is that air power has clearly proven its ability not merely to be decisive in war.... but to be the *determinant of victory* in war."[36] Clifford Rogers reaches a similar conclusion: "we may finally have reached the stage that airpower enthusiasts from Douhet onward have constantly, if heretofore inaccurately, proclaimed: the point at which airpower surpasses land power as the *primary* determinant of victory or defeat in warfare."[37]

Other assessments of the RMA are a bit more tempered and specific in identifying how warfare is changing. Elliot Cohen, a coauthor of the *Gulf*

[33] Benjamin S. Lambeth, *The Transformation of American Air Power* (Ithaca: Cornell University Press, 2000), p. 297.
[34] Ibid., pp. 298 and 302.
[35] Richard P. Hallion, *Storm Over Iraq: Air Power and the Gulf War* (Washington, DC: Smithsonian Institution, 1997), p. 254.
[36] Ibid., p. 264.
[37] Clifford J. Rogers, "'Military Revolutions' and 'Revolutions in Military Affairs,'" p. 31.

War Air Power Survey (GWAPS), offers a cautious though nonetheless positive analysis of the RMA, seeing a number of "reason[s] to think that a major change – call it transformation or not – in warfare has occurred."[38] In making the case for a contemporary RMA, Cohen points to changes in the composition of military forces, a series of increasingly lopsided battle outcomes, and new "processes of battle."[39]

Although "war remains a rough and dirty business," Cohen notes that "the forces that wage it are fundamentally unlike their predecessors." Most obviously, the modern soldier is a "far more lethal creature" as a result of new technologies: "not only are his weapons much better," but "with radio, laser designators and precision navigation, he can bring down vast amounts of firepower from aircraft, artillery and missiles."[40] Less obviously, soldiers are increasingly elite professionals as opposed to the mass conscripts that filled the ranks of industrial age armies. Given the complex technologies and weapons of the RMA, "only in very special circumstances (Israel being the most notable case) can conscript armies prove competitive in large-scale warfare." This explains why the wealthiest nations with access to advanced technologies "have either shifted to volunteer militaries, or simply gotten out of the business of having sophisticated armies." As a result of the RMA, the average soldier "is no longer what he was, a mass consumable of war, but rather a highly-trained specialist."[41]

In terms of battle outcomes, Cohen is struck by how easily nations equipped with RMA technologies and weapons prevailed over their opponents. This was most evident in the United States' wars against Iraq. Even though "the discrepancy between advanced military powers and others has yielded victories that were easily anticipated," the results "were far more lopsided than had been expected." Adding to the mix NATO's war against Kosovo in 1999 and Israel's war with Syria in 1982, Cohen thinks that the "sequence of lopsided successes . . . over a period of 20 years, and indeed the growth in disproportionableness of such outcomes requires explanation."[42] Here, Cohen reflects the commonly held view that because "RMAs frequently bestow an enormous and immediate military advantage on the first nation to exploit them in combat," extremely one-sided results are *prima facie* grounds for suspecting that an RMA is underway.[43]

---

[38] Eliot A. Cohen, "Change and Transformation in Military Affairs," *Journal of Strategic Studies*, Vol. 27, No. 3 (September 2004), p. 407.

[39] Ibid., p. 403.

[40] Ibid., pp. 403 and 404.

[41] Ibid., p. 404.

[42] Ibid., p. 404.

[43] Hundley, *Past Revolutions, Future Transformations*, p. 13.

Whether the processes of battle are changing is, Cohen admits, "more difficult to judge." Although the "combat experiences of fear and adrenaline-induced excitement have not changed" and "much of the central activity of combat looks as it ever did," Cohen sees important changes in how war is waged. "At the highest level of combat," he argues, "the modern commander operates in a communication environment that is very different from before" in having the advantage of "a vast increase in the amount of reliable information at command posts in the field, and the networking of information within units, in a theater, and even globally."[44] In this sense, the RMA involves a substantial reduction, though by no means the elimination, of the proverbial fog of war. More importantly, "modern warfare is increasingly warfare without fronts. The combination of long-range air power, equally long-range missile and rocket fires, and special operations forces has gradually eroded the idea of front lines and more or less secure rear areas, except, perhaps, on a continental scale."[45] Morgan agrees with Cohen, arguing that "for a country with a full range of RMA capabilities, strategy will likely turn on pinning down an opponent throughout an entire theater or his entire country, not concentrating at one isolated point for penetrating attacks and breakthroughs."[46] Of course, theorists have made such predictions since aircraft first held out the promise of jumping over the front to attack targets in the rear. Although the concept has a long lineage in military thought, RMA theorists contend that stealth, communications, surveillance, and precision-targeting technologies have finally made it possible to realize the potential of deep battle. This ability to reliably and simultaneously strike a wide range of tactical, operational, and strategic targets over a very large battle space is perhaps the most commonly cited way in which the RMA is changing what Cohen labels the "processes of battle."

Differences clearly exist among those who think we are witnessing a new RMA. Although everyone agrees, for example, that advances in air power are an important component of the RMA, few go so far as to declare it the *primary* determinant of victory in war. A more common approach, exemplified by Cohen, sees air power's increasing effectiveness as a critical *component* of a multifaceted RMA driven by a combination of surveillance, communications, and targeting technologies. Differences among RMA proponents center on matters of emphasis and nuance within a common conceptual framework within which it becomes "possible to envision war and lesser military actions as more precise in terms

[44] Cohen, "Change and Transformation in Military Affairs," pp. 405–6.
[45] Ibid., p. 405.
[46] Morgan, "The Impact of the Revolution in Military Affairs," p. 139.

of damage.... [and] war as controlled and precise, even among great powers, would be a radical change."[47]

RMA Skepticism

Not everyone accepts that new technologies are altering the character of warfare. The central question is whether even radical improvements in communication, surveillance, and targeting capabilities have been translated into revolutionary changes in how wars are fought. Beginning with an assumption that "a true military revolution would have to *overthrow the existing military order*," Howard J. Marsh is among the skeptics hesitant to accept claims of an RMA largely because "recent advances in technology have, for the most part, been harnessed to twentieth-century doctrinal thought."[48] While videos presented at Gulf War press conferences may have been vivid, and the comparison between the bombing of Hamburg and Baghdad dramatic, such evidence may be misleading, creating a superficial impression of revolutionary change while underlying military fundamentals remain undisturbed. Avi Kober explains that "military analysts have offered two competing interpretations of the Iraq War [2003]." RMA proponents offer an interpretation along the lines discussed previously, while skeptics portray "the Gulf War, Afghanistan and the Iraq War as rather orthodox theater warfare."[49] No one has been more adamant and effective in advancing the latter position than Stephen Biddle.

Biddle's analysis of the RMA derives from his effort to explain battlefield success and failure in what he labels the "modern system," a conceptual framework that emerged in the early twentieth century as militaries tried to address "the central problem of modern warfare: how to conduct meaningful military actions in the face of radical firepower."[50] This tremendous increase in firepower, most evident on the Western front in World War I, resulted from industrial age productivity and weapons that filled the battle space with vast quantities of flying metal, making advances *en masse* or in organized formations suicidal. The stagnant, continuous front and its trenches were manifestations of the tactical and operational dilemmas of radical firepower. Biddle explains how attempts

---

[47] Morgan, "The Impact of the Revolution in Military Affairs," p. 141.
[48] Howard J. Marsh, "Emerging Technologies and Military Affairs," in Thierry Gongora and Harald von Riekoff, eds., *Toward a Revolution in Military Affairs? Defense and Security at the Dawn of the Twenty-first Century* (Westport, CT: Greenwood Press, 2000), p. 61, emphasis added.
[49] Avi Kober, "Does the Iraq War Reflect a Phase Change in Warfare?" *Defense & Security Analysis*, Vol. 21, No. 2 (June 2005), p. 121.
[50] Stephen Biddle, *Military Power: Explaining Victory and Defeat in Modern Battle* (Princeton: Princeton University Press, 2004), p. 28.

to solve this problem eventually resulted in "a process of convergent evolution . . . [that] produced a stable and essentially transformational body of ideas on the methods needed to operate effectively in the face of radically lethal modern weapons." These methods would form the basis of modern system and become the "fundamental property of modern warfare."[51]

As the belligerents in World War I quickly discovered, radical firepower made massed forces in the open increasingly vulnerable to devastating attacks. Waves of soldiers slaughtered as they emerged from their trenches to advance on enemy positions were a testament to the severity of the problem. In this environment, battlefield movement required new ways to avoid and/or suppress enemy firepower. Firepower avoidance entailed organizing and moving forces in smaller units, exploiting cover and concealment while moving across the battlefield. Dispersion and maneuver replaced massed frontal assaults. Firepower suppression required intricate coordination between maneuvering units and supporting artillery. The result was "a tactical system wherein a brief 'hurricane barrage' suppresses defenses while small units work their way forward independently, using local terrain for cover and providing supplementary suppressive fires of their own to keep defenders' heads down."[52] This system brings together all the critical elements of successful offense when confronted with massive volumes of lethal firepower: "cover, concealment, dispersion, small-unit independent maneuver, suppression and combined arms integration."[53] Defense also changed along the same lines, emphasizing "depth, reserves, and counterattack" rather than fixed (and thus vulnerable) defensive positions.[54]

In terms of explaining victory and defeat in battle, Biddle concludes that skillful implementation of the modern system of force employment is more important than either technological or numerical superiority. Although more soldiers and better weapons are helpful, they do not compensate for poor force employment. Mastering this modern system, however, is difficult. The dispersion of forces required for defense in-depth and small infantry unit maneuver on offense "complicates command and control, increases the burdens on junior leaders, and challenges morale among troops who feel dangerously isolated." The coordination of infantry movement and artillery fire (i.e., maneuver and firepower) and effective conduct of combined arms warfare is also a complex technological and organizational task. Not every military is able or willing to implement the modern system. Authoritarian regimes in particular

51 Ibid., pp. 28 and 31.
52 Ibid., p. 37.
53 Ibid., p. 35.
54 Ibid., p. 46.

may be hesitant to permit the "extensive independent decision making by junior officers and senior enlisted personnel" it requires.[55] For these regimes, fears of political survival often outweigh considerations of military effectiveness.[56] Biddle ultimately provides a wealth of empirical and experimental evidence to support his conclusion that skillful force employment is the best predictor of battlefield success.

Biddle evaluates claims of a contemporary RMA primarily in the context of examining whether new technologies are altering the modern system by increasing the importance of technological superiority relative to force employment in battle. Although he offers no explicit definition, Biddle appears to share Marsh's view that an RMA would have to overthrow the modern system of warfare. In judging whether advances in surveillance and communications are revolutionizing warfare, for example, Biddle sets the standard for an RMA by asking if "new information technology made the modern system *obsolete*?"[57] A negative answer rules out the possibility of an RMA. The same basic question is posed for all the technologies supposedly driving the RMA. This framing clearly sets a very high bar: there is no RMA as long as the modern system as Biddle defines it endures.

Biddle recognizes that revolutionary change is theoretically possible: the modern system, he concedes, is "not eternal." Because "the modern system itself was a response to a particular complex of technological changes in the mid to late nineteenth century ... it can be overturned by some comparably sweeping technological changes."[58] This would require, however, technological advances that dwarf anything seen thus far. According to Biddle, "the key requirement" for overturning the modern system is "the capacity to make terrain *irrelevant*" and to "see and destroy *anything* on the Earth's surface *regardless of cover or concealment or intermingling*." It is not enough that advances dramatically increase the ability to see and destroy targets: a new RMA requires surveillance and targeting technologies that would make it impossible to conceal and/or protect militarily relevant targets anywhere in any setting. Complete transparency and total vulnerability are the prerequisites for displacing the modern system. This is obviously not the case today, and in something of an understatement Biddle predicts dryly that this is "unlikely to happen soon."[59]

The implications of Biddle's analysis for debates over the RMA are clear. In his view, an RMA must end the modern system of warfare, for

[55] Ibid., p. 49.
[56] See, for example, James T. Quinlivan, "Coup-Proofing: Its Practice and Consequences in the Middle East," *International Security* Vol. 24, No. 2 (Fall 1999), pp. 131–65.
[57] Biddle, *Military Power*, p. 62.
[58] Ibid., p. 72.
[59] Ibid., pp. 72–3.

anything less is not a revolution. In his analysis there is no such thing as an RMA *within* the context of the modern system. As long as the basic tactical and operational elements of the system – that is, independent small unit movement, the coordination of firepower and maneuver, combined arms warfare and the necessity/possibility of concealment and cover – remain critical to success in battle, there is no revolutionary change. This approach leads Biddle to reject the commonly held view of Germany's *blitzkrieg* as a revolution in combined arms warfare. From Biddle's perspective, the *blitzkrieg* was merely a more effective implementation of the modern system that emerged nearly two decades prior.[60] The Germans may have exploited new technologies and combined them in innovative ways, but they fought battles according to preexisting concepts embodied in the modern system.

It is important to note that Biddle's modern system deals almost exclusively with the tactical and operational aspects of conventional *land* warfare. He says, for example, nothing about naval warfare. And more significantly for contemporary RMA debates, he deals "only tangentially with the use of air power as anything but an adjunct to ground operations."[61] Particularly telling is the absence of any discussion of strategic bombing. From Biddle's account of military power in the modern system one would never know that hundreds of thousands of civilians were killed from the air in the past century in an effort to erode an adversary's ability or willingness to fight. Because strategic bombing was a defining element of twentieth-century total war, this omission seems almost inexplicable.[62] But because the scope of Biddle's analysis is limited to the determinants of victory and defeat in conventional land battle, it is not surprising that the use of air power beyond the battlefield falls outside his purview. Anything not related to land combat receives either short shrift or no shrift at all. Biddle's modern system could be more accurately relabeled as the modern system of ground combat tactics and operations. Although there is certainly nothing wrong with focusing on this undoubtedly important

[60] Stephen Biddle, "Past as Prologue: Assessing Theories of Future War," *Security Studies* Vol. 8 (Autumn 1998), pp. 32–44. See also Michael Horowitz and Stephen Rosen, "Evolution or Revolution," *The Journal of Strategic Studies* Vol. 28, No. 3 (June 2005), pp. 441–2.

[61] Eliot A. Cohen, "Biddle on Military Power," *The Journal of Strategic Studies* Vol. 28, No. 3 (June 2005), p. 414. Martin Van Creveld, offers the same criticism in "Less Than Meets the Eye," *The Journal of Strategic Studies* Vol. 28, No. 3 (June 2005), p. 449.

[62] The literature on strategic bombing is voluminous, but the best place to start is Tami Davis Biddle's *Rhetoric and Reality in Air Warfare: The Evolution of British and American Ideas about Strategic Bombing, 1914–1945* (Princeton: Princeton University Press, 2004). See also Conrad Crane, *Bombs, Cities and Civilians: American Airpower Strategy in World War II* (Lawrence, KS: University of Kansas Press, 1993) and Jorg Friedrich, *The Fire: The Bombing of Germany, 1940–45* (New York: Columbia University Press, 2006).

aspect of warfare, in limiting the scope of his analysis, Biddle inevitably restricts the breadth of his conclusions.

In the final analysis, Biddle sees less than meets the eye in dramatic quasi-video game imagery often taken as evidence of an RMA. Appearances are deceiving because seemingly revolutionary technologies are used to pursue fairly traditional or orthodox war-fighting strategies. A new RMA would need to significantly alter the tactical and operational requirements for successful conventional land warfare or eliminate the need for ground combat altogether. There is no evidence that this is happening. Technology may be enhancing the effectiveness of militaries conducting modern system operations, but it is not changing the system itself. The emergence of the modern system in the early twentieth century may have been an RMA, but there has been no revolutionary change since the end of World War I. "The modern system," according to Biddle, "works by exploiting properties of military technology that have *changed little since 1918* and are changing only slowly today."[63] One is almost taken aback by such a boldly counter-intuitive claim. Considering the range of military technologies that have appeared since 1918 – thoroughly mechanized armies, jet fighters, stealth bombers, radar detection, laser designation, satellite surveillance, and GPS guidance, to name just a few – it seems to fly in the face of common sense to portray the last century in terms of military continuity and stasis. Can it really be, RMA proponents would ask, that a century of perhaps the greatest and most rapid scientific and technological advances in all of human history has produced no radical or revolutionary changes in the character of warfare?

Thinking about a New RMA

Biddle's analysis raises a number of critical empirical and conceptual questions central to the RMA debate. Is he correct, for example, that recent technological advances have failed to alter the modern system? And even if Biddle is correct that the elements of successful ground combat are the same today as they were in 1918, does this necessarily imply the absence of revolutionary change in other equally significant components of modern warfare? Or rephrasing the question slightly, should we equate land battle tactics and operations with the character of warfare more generally? Conceptually, one also needs to ask whether obsolescence of the modern system is the appropriate standard, or should we admit the possibility of RMAs even *within* the system's broad outlines?

These questions highlight the critical issues that drive the RMA debate – disagreements about the magnitude and scope of military change. In

---

[63] Ibid., p. 52, emphasis added.

arguing that new technologies have failed to overturn the modern system, Biddle essentially rejects claims that contemporary changes rise to the level of a revolutionary transformation. For Biddle, technologies that could lead to a genuine revolution remain a distant prospect. To date, the magnitude of change has been insufficient to qualify as an RMA, and this will likely remain the case for the foreseeable future. Indeed, his requirement that cover and concealment of any sort become impossible (as opposed to increasingly difficult) is so demanding that it is unlikely to ever be met. One wonders whether any historical RMA could satisfy similarly stringent criteria. The typical interpretation of the gunpowder revolution, for example, is that it shifted the military advantage toward the offense as common modes of fortification grew increasingly vulnerable. Gunpowder weapons made defense more difficult, not impossible. More elaborate fortifications could still provide adequate protection.[64] If the obsolescence of defensive fortifications was the requirement for an RMA in the fourteenth century, there would have been no gunpowder "revolution."

Biddle's focus on conventional land combat and criticisms that he ignores such things as strategic bombing reminds us that war is a multi-faceted phenomenon, involving a broad range of tasks from logistics to command and control to land, sea, and air combat. There is no reason to assume that RMAs will entail equally radical changes across the entire scope of military operations. Some elements of the existing military order may be unaffected, others reinforced, and still others completely transformed. It is conceivable, for example, that technological advances might revolutionize intelligence gathering, command and control, and air power while having much less of an impact on conventional land warfare. Revolutions need not revolutionize everything. Hundley's approach to RMAs is particularly useful in this respect. In his view, an RMA "*either* renders obsolete or irrelevant one or more of the core competencies of a dominant player, creates one or more new core competencies in some major new dimension of warfare, or does both." From this perspective, obsolescence of the modern system would not be a prerequisite for an RMA that created new "core competencies" in other areas. Similarly, Jeffrey Cooper argues that "truly innovative developments often do not only enhance the ability to execute existing tasks, but also attempt to perform new functions."[65] This suggests that a contemporary RMA may very well enhance the ability to implement the modern system while simultaneously creating revolutionary possibilities in other dimensions of warfare.

---

[64] Martin Van Creveld, *Technology and War: From 2000 b.c. to Present* (New York: Free Press, 1989), pp. 101–4, and Parker, "The Gunpowder Revolution."
[65] Cooper, "Another View of the Revolution in Military Affairs," p. 119.

The Iraq Wars

The current RMA is probably unprecedented in being the first to be so extensively analyzed as it is supposedly unfolding. Largely because the concept is so new, historical RMAs have been identified only in retrospect, not contemporaneously. Such hindsight offers some analytical benefits the current debate necessarily lacks. One advantage is a measure of detachment. Today, for example, there is no longer anyone around with a vested personal or organizational interest in whether or not Germany's *blitzkrieg* was revolutionary. The policy and political consequences of such a judgment are inconsequential, though it remains important for debates about the nature of RMAs. Questions about a contemporary RMA cannot be so easily divorced from policy and political concerns. Even the most cursory glance at military journals reveals how deeply RMA debates are entangled in struggles over the future of American defense policy, which inevitably involves competition over priorities and resources.

Hindsight also allows us to view RMAs in their entirety. It is easier to provide a satisfying analysis of an RMA's dynamics and consequences after it has run its course. Even those who think we are witnessing a new RMA recognize that there is no way of knowing whether we are at its very beginning or further along. There is even the possibility that the pace of technological change has reached a point where the very notion of distinct RMAs that can be isolated from the normal pattern of military change and innovation is no longer tenable. We may be entering a period involving a rapid succession of RMAs. But in the absence of hindsight, any analysis of a new RMA must deal with significant uncertainty. There are good reasons why "history offers few examples of contemporary observers who correctly assessed an ongoing revolution, but many examples of false prophets."[66] None of this should preclude efforts to address the critical questions raised in the current RMA debate. Although it may be some time before we have sufficient evidence for final judgments, there is no shortage of information for initial assessments. We simply need to recognize that our conclusions on many issues will of necessity be provisional.

All agree that RMAs are characterized by significant changes in the conduct of warfare. Whatever the changes in military technology, doctrine, and/or organizations, if they do not significantly alter how wars are fought, there is no RMA. As a result, claims of an RMA must be evaluated or tested first and foremost against the realities of war. For a contemporary RMA, any evaluation must begin with the 1991 Iraq War. If future historians ultimately conclude that the late twentieth and early twenty-first centuries ushered in a new era in warfare, the 1991 Iraq War

---

[66] Jeremy Shapiro, "Information and War: Is It a Revolution?" in Zalamy Khalilzad and John White, eds., *Strategic Appraisal: The Changing Role of Information in War* (Santa Monica, CA: RAND), pp. 114–15.

will surely be singled out as the turning point. But even those who see the war as a critical juncture disagree about whether it represents the end of one age or the beginning of another.

According to Admiral William Owens, one of the RMA's leading military theorists, the 1991 Iraq War "was not a new kind of war, but the last of the old ones."[67] For Owens, the war had more in common with the industrial age wars of massive firepower than the nimble precision attacks that will supposedly characterize information-age wars. Certainly, aspects of the war were new, but continuities with the past outweighed elements of the future. Delbert Thiessen stresses continuity with the past in more vivid terms: "The Persian Gulf War was perhaps the last Clausewitzian war ever to be fought. It was so classic that General George Patton from the tank war of WW II could have been briefed in an hour and taken over command."[68] Max Boot agrees. Although noting that the 1991 Iraq War was an "advertisement for the power of precision weaponry" that fueled a "heated debate in the halls of the Pentagon about 'the RMA,'" he thinks it still "fit the traditional firepower-intensive mode: more than five weeks of relentless bombing was followed by a massive ground onslaught."[69] In this view, information technologies had yet to produce a genuinely information-age war – they merely allowed the United States to wage an industrial age war with greater ferocity and efficiency.

Others see the first 1991 Iraq War as the first conflict of the information age. Prone to sweeping generalizations, Heidi and Alvin Toffler claim that "Saddam never understood that an entirely new war-form was about to change the entire nature of warfare."[70] More cautious analysts offered similar assessments. Cohen, for example, argues that "it took the 1991 Gulf War to convince a broad spectrum of officers that very large changes in the conduct of war *had occurred*."[71] Michael Ignatieff was also more impressed by the war's novelty: "in Desert Storm in 1991, American technology gave a ruthless and stunning demonstration of how far the RMA had transformed the American way of war."[72] And Norman Davis characterizes the war as the first information-age war, going so far as to

---

[67] Mike Davis, "War-Mart: Revolution in Warfare Slouches Toward Baghdad – It's All in the Network," *San Francisco Chronicle* (March 9, 2003), p. D1.

[68] Delbert Thiessen, *Bittersweet Destiny: The Stormy Evolution of Human Behavior* (Edison, NJ: Transaction Publishers, 1996), p. 388.

[69] Max Boot, *War Made New*, p. 8.

[70] Heidi and Alvin Toffler, *War and Anti-War*, p. 66.

[71] Eliot Cohen, "Technology and Warfare," in John Baylis, James Wirtz, Colin S. Gray, and Eliot Cohen, eds., *Strategy in the Contemporary World* (Oxford: Oxford University Press, 2007), p. 148, emphasis added.

[72] Michael Ignatieff, "The New American Way of War," *The New York Review of Books* Vol. 27, No. 12 (July 20, 2000), p. 14.

claim that "the 1991 Persian Gulf War was the prototype of this future kind of war."[73]

Whether one sees the 1991 Iraq War as the last old or the first new war is not the critical issue. Either way, it provides the starting point for evaluating claims of a contemporary RMA. But it is only the beginning. A single war seldom provides convincing evidence of an RMA, though in 1991 some more enthusiastic RMA theorists thought it did. The case for the RMA must also be analyzed in the context of all that has transpired since. In the almost two decades since the war's end the United States has been involved in a series of military operations that may have reinforced or undermined the lessons of 1991. The United States' humanitarian intervention in Somalia, for example, may have lasted only a few months and involved a fraction of the forces committed to Desert Storm, but it may have revealed important limitations of the RMA that would become even more evident later. Similarly, NATO's war on Serbia in 1999 may have been restricted to aerial attacks over only a few weeks, but it also might offer valuable clues about the nature of a possible RMA. On an analytical level, these conflicts may be just as important as the Gulf War. The significance of conflicts is not always related to their size. Looking at a variety of war types and military missions is essential for assessing the scope of the RMA. Just as RMAs do not revolutionize every *aspect* of war, there is reason to assume that they will fundamentally change every *type* of war. The notion that an RMAs impact may vary by conflict type is reflected in Michael Sheehan's question, "Does the RMA influence all forms of war or simply large-scale conventional inter-state war?"[74] Answering this critical question, of course, requires us to look at something other than large-scale conventional wars.

Although other conflicts may be analytically significant, there is little doubt that the Iraq Wars remain central to the debate over the RMA. As of the spring of 2009, the United States had been at war with or in Iraq for six of the previous eighteen years. Including its role in enforcing no-fly zones between the wars, the United States has been militarily involved in Iraq continuously for almost two decades. By almost any measure, including most obviously the commitment of troops and resources, the United States' other military engagements during that period pale in comparison. As a result, it is hard to deny the singular significance of the Iraq Wars for analyzing claims of a new RMA. At the end of the day, few

73 Norman Davis, "An Information-Based Revolution in Military Affairs," *Strategic Review* (Winter 1996), p. 85.
74 Michael Sheehan, "The Changing Character of War," in John Baylis, Steve Smith, and Patricia Owens, eds., *The Globalization of World Politics* (Oxford: Oxford University Press, 2007), p. 218.

would disagree that the Iraq Wars are exhibit A in any case for or against a contemporary RMA.

Although it is common to discuss the American military experience in Iraq in terms of two wars, it is analytically more useful to think in terms of three. Two of these wars were waged *against* Iraq and the regime of Saddam Hussein, while the other has been waged *in* Iraq against a very different set of opponents. The first Iraq War, often referred to as the Gulf War or Persian Gulf War, was waged over six weeks in January and February of 1991. The chain of events leading to the war began with the Iraqi invasion and conquest of Kuwait in August 1990. After six months of diplomacy and military preparations, the United States eventually led a broad international coalition under the auspices of the United Nations to expel Iraqi forces and liberate Kuwait. There is nothing novel or controversial in identifying this as the first Iraq War.

For most, the second Iraq War began with the invasion in March 2003 and continues to this day. Indeed, the U.S. military classifies everything after the initial invasion as part of the same operation, Operation Iraqi Freedom. This includes not only the defeat of the Iraqi army and over-throw of Saddam Hussein but also the conflicts that emerged gradually over subsequent months. It has all been part of the same long war. From a military perspective, however, one wonders whether it makes sense to view everything that has happened since 2003 as a single conflict. Certainly there were important continuities, most significantly the involve-ment of the United States in fighting on the territory of Iraq. But changes in the war beginning in the summer of 2003 were critical and altered the character of the conflict. The most important of these changes was in the identity and nature of the opponent. Rather than fighting a regime with a traditional military, the opponent became a complicated mix of regime loyalists, Al-Qaeda, insurgents, and sectarian militants. These opponents waged a different kind of war. Instead of a high-intensity interstate war in the open desert, the United States and its allies were forced to fight a low-intensity war against a largely urban insurgency. Thus, by the fall of 2003, the enemy, the fighting, and the military challenges were different. If we want to extract the military lessons, it makes more sense to view the war in Iraq after the summer of 2003 as separate and distinct from the war against Iraq in March 2003.

Although United States' wars and military missions over the course of almost two decades provide a fairly rich and diverse body of evidence on which to evaluate claims of an RMA, we need to remain cognizant of evidentiary limitations. Most significantly, as Cohen reminds us, all of these wars "involved the wildly disproportionate forces of the United States and its allies against far smaller opponents." There are undoubt-edly valuable lessons to be learned from these conflicts. But what we are lacking is a war pitting the United States against a genuinely peer military competitor equipped with comparable technologies and weapons. It is difficult to imagine what such a conflict would look like based on those we have experienced. The wars waged since 1991 can "serve as indicators . . . but not proof of some larger change." Cohen suggests, however, that a final judgment on the RMA may "require evidence gathered in a much larger conflict."[75] Perhaps fortunately, this evidence is still lacking.

Conclusion: Theory, Policy, and a Contemporary RMA

Despite the lack of consensus on the wisdom or likely consequences of the Iraq Wars, all agree that their political and strategic legacies for the United States, the Middle East, and the larger international order will be profound. But in addition to their political and strategic significance, the Iraq Wars are also defining military events on at least two levels that reflect the policy and theoretical dimensions of the RMA debate. First, from a policy perspective, the Iraq Wars tested the American military's ability to carry out the full spectrum of missions it is likely to encounter in the years ahead – high-intensity interstate warfare, postconflict stability operations and counterinsurgency campaigns. Given the extent of the military involvement in Iraq and elsewhere over the past twenty years, we know enough about the United States' military performance to start drawing some policy-relevant lessons even if the final political/strategic outcome in Iraq (and Afghanistan) remains in doubt. Indeed, the American military has already begun to draw lessons that will (and should) shape the future direction of defense policy. Second, from a theoretical perspective, it is also possible to see the Iraq Wars as turning points in military history, marking the beginning of a "revolution in military affairs." Advances in intelligence gathering and dissemination went a long way toward lifting the "fog of war." Laser and satellite guidance allowed the United States to restrict the scope of collateral damage while assuring that targets were hit with a high degree of certainty and accuracy. A wide range of interrelated new technologies and weapons changed what was possible in war. Although others have dealt extensively with the political and strategic aspects of the Iraq Wars, this book addresses their military significance by focusing on two questions that have been at the center of the current RMA debate: What are the military lessons of the Iraq Wars for the future of American defense policy? Should the Iraq Wars be seen as a fundamental turning point in the history of warfare?

---

[75] Cohen, "Technology and Warfare," p. 149.

2 FROM VIETNAM TO IRAQ – THE REBIRTH OF AMERICAN MILITARY POWER AND THE ORIGINS OF AN RMA

The First Iraq War

Even those inclined to view the 1991 Iraq War as a turning point in the history of warfare concede that this is a matter of legitimate debate, a proposition about which reasonable analysts can disagree. That the war was a turning point for the American military, however, seems almost incontestable. As American and coalition forces gathered in the Arabian Desert in the winter of 1991 to do battle with Iraq, memories of Vietnam and the self-doubt the war engendered were never far from the surface. The outcome in Vietnam had shaken the U.S. military to its core, and the recovery over the subsequent decade and a half had been difficult and sometimes painful. Some may have seen the 1991 Iraq War as a test of abstract theories of changing warfare, but for the American military the stakes were less esoteric. The war provided an opportunity for institutional redemption, a chance to finally exorcise the ghosts and demons of Vietnam. It was certainly a surprising opportunity, and not merely because of the near universal failure to anticipate the Iraqi invasion of Kuwait. Throughout much the 1980s, the United States viewed Iraq as something of an ally, a bulwark against the spread of Iranian fundamentalism and influence. The unexpected nature of the 1991 Iraq War reminds us that nations and their militaries do not always enjoy the luxury of fighting the opponents for whom they prepared and trained. The F-117 stealth fighters that played such a crucial role in the war were not originally intended to take on the Iraqi Air Force. The multimillion dollar Tomahawk cruise missiles launched from ships in the Persian Gulf were not acquired to attack the Baath Party headquarters in downtown Baghdad. And the Airborne Warning and Control System (AWACS) and the Joint Surveillance Target Attack Radar System (JSTARS) planes that patrolled the skies over Iraq were not developed to track the movement of Iraqi ground and air forces. While these weapons and technologies certainly came in very handy against Iraq, they were designed, developed, and justified with very different enemies and wars in mind. The military's road from Vietnam may have ultimately winded its way to Baghdad, but this was not the intended destination when the journey began.

To understand the forces that shaped the military that went to war in 1991 as well as the debate over the RMA, one needs to begin with the American experience in Vietnam. As Thomas Ricks notes, "the modern U.S. army," the one that defeated Iraq in 1991 and 2003 and is viewed by many as embodying a contemporary RMA, "was born in the ashes of that war."[1] This image of a military phoenix rising from the ashes of traumatic defeat serves as a prominent leitmotif of analyses of American military policy in the 1970s and 1980s. Frederick Kagan echoes Ricks: "we simply cannot understand how the armed forces reached their current state of excellence and strain without a careful consideration of their rebirth after failure."[2] This "regenerative process," as Boot characterizes it, was driven by powerful intellectual, technological, political, and strategic forces.[3] These included a desire to learn the lessons of a lost war, the appearance of technologies with the potential to solve some of the enduring problems of warfare, and the coupling of these technologies with new doctrines to deal with specific strategic and military challenges. And this rebirth of American military coincided with, and was taken as evidence of, a contemporary RMA. The regeneration of American military power and possible transformation of warfare itself were part and parcel of the same process.

The First Glimmers of Revolution

Identifying the specific starting point of an RMA is rarely easy. Analysts can agree that an RMA is underway while debating exactly when it started. Isolating the origins of RMAs is always somewhat arbitrary. Take, for example, the nuclear revolution, which would appear to be a relatively straightforward case. Most would probably say the nuclear revolution began in the summer of 1945 with the first successful test in the New Mexico desert and the use of atomic weapons against Japan a few weeks later. But it would not be entirely unreasonable to argue that the nuclear revolution began in 1942 with the first self-sustaining nuclear reaction under Enrico Fermi's direction in his University of Chicago laboratory. The starting date chosen is largely irrelevant to the significant

[1] Thomas Ricks, *Fiasco: The American Military Adventure in Iraq* (New York: Penguin, 2005), p. 130.
[2] Frederick Kagan, *Finding the Target* (New York: Encounter Books, 2007), p. 5.
[3] Boot, *War Made New*, p. 322.

debates about the nuclear revolution and its impact, but someone trying to tell the story of the nuclear age has to start somewhere. Similarly, if we think of the current RMA as a reflection of a larger information revolution, we might be tempted to trace its origins all the way back to the 1930s when the computer, the iconic machine of the age, first appeared. But the history of an RMA is not the same as a history of the basic technologies associated with it. What matters most is not when the underlying technologies first appeared, but rather when they started to affect the conduct of warfare in significant ways.

It was in Vietnam that the United States first employed some of the earliest versions of the weapons associated with the contemporary RMA that would be improved and refined in the decades leading up to the Iraq Wars. During the early phases of the Vietnam War, bombing raids against targets in North Vietnam had to address the same problem that had plagued all such missions since the advent of airpower: the difficulty of hitting and destroying relatively small targets with bombs dropped from moving planes thousands of feet in the air, a task made even more difficult if the planes themselves were trying to evade enemy fire. The crux of the problem was that once munitions were fired, released, or launched there was no way to control their course: the only force guiding them to their targets was gravity. This basic shortcoming had remained unchanged since the Germans first pushed bombs out of their Zeppelins onto London half a century earlier. As Kenneth Werrell observes, "American airmen entered the Vietnam conflict armed primarily with free-fall bombs ('dumb bombs') that were no different from those used in World War I."[4] The solution to this problem also remained unchanged: as compensation for their inaccuracy many bombs needed to be dropped to increase the chances of hitting the targets. And as has been the case throughout the history of airpower, most of the bombs landed on something other than their intended targets.

The quest for more accurate bombs is as old as airpower itself. Some of these efforts focused on better aiming devices for regular gravity bombs such as the Norden bombsight the United States employed during World War II. Under favorable conditions, the bombsight did improve accuracy somewhat, but in the real world, conditions were rarely favorable and the accuracy was much less impressive than promised.[5] More ambitious programs sought the development of guided munitions whose course could be controlled after release. Barry Watts' excellent study traces this history all the way back to fanciful proposals for pilotless planes in

---

[4] Kenneth P. Werrell, "Did USAF Technology Fail in Vietnam: Three Case Studies," *Airpower Journal* (Spring 1998), p. 93.
[5] Budiansky, *Air Power*, pp. 173–6.

World War I and more serious programs developing radio-guided bombs during World War II.[6] The results of these early efforts were disappointing. Even the infamous German V-2 rockets, using a guidance mechanism incorporating gyroscopes, usually missed their targets by very large margins. Efforts to develop guided munitions languished somewhat in the two decades after World War II, in part because of the increased focus on the strategic nuclear weapons that did not need to be terribly precise. Although experimental guided munitions were combat tested in Vietnam as early as the mid-1960s, it was not until operations Linebacker I and II in 1972 that guided weapons began to come into their own.[7] Although only a small percentage of the ordnance utilized during these operations was guided (in this case, the laser-guided Paveway I), their contribution was significant, knocking out targets such as bridges and generators that had survived previous raids with nonguided weapons.[8] According to one extensive survey, the laser-guided bombs of Linebacker were "about 16 times more effective than a visually released conventional bomb."[9] But well beyond their role in the Linebacker, the appearance and use of guided weapons represented a critical juncture in the evolution of modern warfare that foreshadowed the wars to come, including the Iraq Wars. Winslow Wheeler, who headed the Government Accounting Office's assessment of the Desert Storm air campaign, recalls that he "first started hearing about revolutions in warfare after some guided munitions hit a bridge in the Vietnam War."[10] Benjamin Lambeth highlights the larger significance of the Linebacker bombing raids conducted with laser-guided munitions:

[D]uring Linebacker... *and for the first time in the history of air warfare,* the more effective Paveway I LGBs were used to telling effect by the Air Force against the Paul Doumer bridge in the heart of the Hanoi complex.... In a precursor to Desert Storm's later proof of air power's ability to achieve the effects of mass with relatively few sorties, the use of laser-guided weapons during Linebacker enabled U.S. planners to achieve lethal effects against once-indestructible targets... With the improvement achievable in accuracy, destroying hard structures

---

[6] Barry Watts, *Six Decades of Guided Munitions and Battle Networks.* There is also some useful discussion on early attempts to develop guided munitions in Crane, *Bombs, Cities and Civilians.*

[7] See ibid., pp. 93–6, for a brief overview. Another good brief discussion of guided weapons in the Vietnam War is Richard P. Hallion, *Storm Over Iraq* (Washington, DC: Smithsonian Institution, 1997), pp. 303–5 (Appendix E).

[8] According to Hallion, over 21,000 laser-guided bombs were used in Vietnam; see Hallion (1992), p. 21.

[9] Herman Gilster, *The Air War in Southeast Asia: Case Studies of Selected Campaigns* (Maxwell Air Force Base, Alabama: Air University Press, 1993), p. 98.

[10] Quoted in David Isenberg, "U.S. Warfare Equation 'Full of Baloney,'" *Asia Times Online* (October 28, 2003). Accessed at: www.atimes.com/atimes/Middle_East/EJ28Ak03.html.

such as bridges with consistency and minimal effort became *the new hallmark of American conventional airpower*.[11]

The results of Linebacker "vanquished official doubts about the effectiveness and reliability of precision weapons."[12] This was one of the considerations that led Malcolm Currie, the Director of Defense Research and Engineering, to testify before Congress in 1974 that "a remarkable series of technological developments have brought us to the threshold of what will become a true revolution in conventional warfare."[13]

For an admittedly imperfect historical parallel one might recall the Battle of Cambrai (1917) during World War I, the first time tanks were used in significant numbers on the battlefield. After years of stalemated trench warfare that consumed hundreds of thousands of lives in futile attempts to move the stationary continuous front, the British used 324 tanks to make what passed for tremendous movement at the time. In only a few hours, "the attackers had advanced to a depth of almost four miles, at almost no cost in casualties."[14] Compared to the plodding slaughter fests that characterized the Western front before 1917, this was remarkable. Although British gains were quickly reversed by a German counterattack, Cambrai is important because it marked the beginning of mechanized warfare. The prospect of setting the front into motion was not fully realized until two decades later when the Germans combined tanks with radio and aircraft in the *blitzkrieg*. The significance of Cambrai lay in the promise demonstrated, not the immediate results achieved. Similarly, even though the laser-guided bombs of Linebacker did not dramatically alter the course of the Vietnam War, they provided an early indication of the ways in which new weapons and technologies might transform the conduct of war, even if observers at the time had little inkling of what was to come.

Critical turning points are not always recognized as such at the time. With a few exceptions already noted, the success of guided munitions in Linebacker did not exactly spark widespread predictions of a new way of

[11] Benjamin Lambeth, *The Transformation of American Air Power*, pp. 39–40, emphasis added. For more on Linebacker I (May 10–October 23, 1972) and Linebacker II (December 18–29, 1972), see Mark Clodfelter, *The Limits of Air Power: The American Bombing of North Vietnam* (New York: Free Press, 1989), pp. 166–76 and 194–202. Clodfelter, somewhat oddly, makes no mention of the new laser-guided weapons. Robert Pape also discusses the two Linebacker operations without mention of the laser-guided weapons in *Bombing to Win: Airpower and Coercion in War* (Ithaca: Cornell University Press, 1998), pp. 195–205. An additional source is Wayne Thompson, *To Hanoi and Back: The U.S. Air Force and North Vietnam, 1966–1973* (Washington, DC: Smithsonian Institution Press, 2000), pp. 219–54.
[12] Budiansky, *Air Power*, p. 407.
[13] Quoted in Lawrence Freedman, *The Revolution in Strategic Affairs* (London: Oxford University Press, 1998), p. 22.
[14] John Keegan, *The First World War* (New York: Knopf, 1998), p. 370.

war, perhaps because the raids came toward the end of a war being lost. But even before Linebacker there were some who saw the seeds of a new military future. As early as 1969, General William Westmoreland claimed that "the Army has undergone in Vietnam a quiet revolution in ground warfare." Looking into the future he saw "combat areas that are under 24 hour real or near real time surveillance of all types ... and battle-fields on which we can destroy anything we locate through instant com-munications and the almost instantaneous application of highly lethal firepower." Within "no more than 10 years" he anticipated "an Army built into and around an area control system that exploits the advanced technology of communications, sensors, fire detection, and the required automatic data processing."[15] Although Westmoreland's ten-year predic-tion may have been overly optimistic, his vision could easily be mistaken for that of a net-centric war theorist from the 1990s.

After Vietnam: Constraints and Challenges

The years immediately following defeat in Vietnam were among the most difficult in the history of the U.S. military. The sheer trauma of defeat was hard to shake. Images of people desperately trying to claw their way onto the last helicopters taking off from the roof of the American embassy in Saigon during the war's last days were vivid and fresh reminders of a humiliating defeat. The less than enthusiastic welcome offered to return-ing troops only exacerbated the sting. A generation of young military officers, including Colin Powell, Norman Schwarzkopf, and others who would gradually work their way up the ranks and later play instrumental roles in the Iraq Wars was deeply affected by the failure in Vietnam and understandably determined to avoid a repetition. "Never again" was a refrain as common within the military as it was among civilian opponents of the war, though agreement with the general lesson masked significant disagreement about its meaning.[16] Did the lessons involve learning to fight insurgencies more effectively or trying to avoid such conflicts altogether? In addition to deciphering mantras such as "never again" and deter-mining the lessons of Vietnam, the generation who came of age during Vietnam faced the task of reviving an institution battered by more than a decade of an increasingly unpopular and ultimately unsuccessful war. There was not much time for licking wounds. This learning and rebuild-ing would have to proceed in the face of new constraints and pressing strategic/military challenges.

---

[15] Quoted in Loren Baritz, *Backfire: A History of How American Culture Led Us into Vietnam and Made US Fight the Way We Did* (Baltimore: Johns Hopkins University Press, 1985), p. 50.

[16] See Earl Ravenal, *Never Again: Learning from America's Foreign Policy Failures* (Philadelphia: Temple University Press, 1980).

In addition to dealing with the consequences of defeat, the military was still coming to grips with the transition to the all-volunteer force (AVF). After years of study and mounting opposition to the draft, President Nixon ended military conscription in July 1973. Conscription had been the foundation of the nation's military manpower since the beginning of World War II and throughout the Cold War. The basic framework of the selective service system remained intact, but draft-age men were no longer even required to register. In an emergency it would take some time to get the system up and running again.[17] Military opinion on the AVF was divided. While discipline problems during the Vietnam War illustrated some of the problems of relying on draftees, many worried that a purely volunteer system could not possibly meet the manpower needs of a global power with wide-ranging international commitments. No comparably sized military anywhere in the world relied on volunteers alone to fill its ranks. Even those who thought a volunteer military might be sufficient for peacetime needs feared it would be inadequate in wartime, when it would be much more difficult to lure soldiers with promises of pay and other benefits. Although the AVF would eventually overcome its birth pangs and win over most skeptics, its success was not completely apparent until the mid-1980s. In the late 1970s, adjusting the AVF remained a major challenge for an institution still coming to grips with its recent defeat.[18]

New fiscal constraints accompanied the potential manpower limitations of the AVF. The effects of the drawdown at the end of the Vietnam War combined with a prevailing antimilitary sentiment were reflected in reduced military expenditures in the immediate postwar period. In 1976 defense expenditures were about a third less than at the peak of the Vietnam War. The Ford and Carter administrations were relatively lean years for the military. The more severe fiscal constraints, however, were temporary. There was a slight improvement in defense spending after the 1979 Soviet invasion of Afghanistan followed by much more substantial increases in the Reagan administration. Still, the general atmosphere of fiscal austerity combined with concerns about the adequacy of manpower created a sense that the military needed to think of ways to use its human and financial resources more efficiently, to do more with less.

Manpower and money were not the military's only concerns in the wake of Vietnam. The war also highlighted the American public's sensitivity to casualties: as casualties mounted, support for the war declined. There was, of course, nothing new about such concerns. Even in World War II, which was as popular as any war in American history, images

---

[17] President Carter revived draft registration after the 1979 Soviet invasion of Afghanistan and remains in place to this day. Despite campaign promises to the contrary, President Reagan continued draft registration.

[18] On the AVF, see Bernard Rostker, *I Want You! The Evolution of the All Volunteer Force* (Santa Monica, CA: RAND, 2006).

of Americans killed in the Pacific theater were carefully censored for fear that they would erode morale and support for the war on the home front. The post-Vietnam concern that a reluctance to place Americans in harm's way might preclude the use of force in the years ahead was merely the most recent manifestation of this sentiment. The belief in the public's casualty sensitivity may have been exacerbated by the war, but it certainly did not originate with Vietnam.[19] Thus, from the perspective of military planners, not only did they have to deal with manpower and fiscal constraints but also social-political currents that were increasingly demanding that military actions be conducted with minimal casualties.

The end of Vietnam War, however, did not provide any strategic pause in which to overcome constraints. The Soviet military threat did not disappear during the decade the United States was preoccupied in Vietnam. In fact, despite President Nixon's pursuit of détente, the Soviet threat appeared greater than ever. The Soviet Union's influence throughout the Third World grew as its involvement in regional conflicts continued unabated. Whatever nuclear advantages the United States enjoyed before the Vietnam War began had evaporated: by the late 1970s it was faced with the reality of Soviet nuclear parity. Some even feared the emergence of Soviet nuclear superiority fueled by Soviet beliefs that, contrary to the doctrine of mutual assured destruction, a nuclear war could be fought and won with a preemptive strike on American nuclear forces.[20] Conservative critics within Nixon's own party, including Ronald Reagan, charged that détente had lulled the United States into a sense of complacency while Soviet military power grew and Soviet influence expanded. In addition to concerns about Soviet expansion and nuclear policy, many saw the growth of Soviet conventional power in Europe as the most pressing military challenge. Lambeth explains that "while the United States was bogged down in Southeast Asia between 1965 and 1975, the Soviet Union, encouraged and abetted by Washington's embroilment in Vietnam.... upgraded [its] forward-deployed conventional forces into a daunting juggernaut overshadowing Western Europe."[21] Relying on U.S. Department of Defense figures, John House notes that "the Warsaw Pact outnumbered NATO in just about everything," including tanks,

[19] Recent research has called into question many of the commonly accepted assumptions about the American public's sensitivity to casualties. This remains a contentious scholarly debate. See, for example, Peter Feaver and Christopher Gelpi, *Choosing Your Battles: American Civil–Military Relations and the Use of Force* (Princeton: Princeton University Press, 2004), especially Chapter 4. What matters here, however, is the belief that the American public was increasingly sensitive to casualties, not whether this was in fact the case. It is the perception that mattered, not its accuracy.

[20] The classic statement of this view was Richard Pipes, "Why the Soviet Union Thinks It Could Fight and Win a Nuclear War." *Commentary* Vol. 64, No. 1 (July 1977), pp. 21–34.

[21] Lambeth, *The Transformation of American Air Power*, p. 54.

artillery, armored personnel carriers, antitank guided munitions, and tactical aircraft.[22]

The Soviet conventional edge was not small: in most of these weapons the Soviet advantage was on the order of two- or three-to-one. Soviet numerical superiority was so great that many analysts feared the margin exceeded what was necessary for a successful attack. At the point of attack the Soviet Union could bring "overwhelming force" to bear as "hordes of tanks, mechanized infantry loaded in BMP armored personnel carriers and massive concentrations of artillery" would break through NATO's defenses in short order.[23] NATO would be overwhelmed, and perhaps overrun, before reserve forces were mobilized and reinforcements arrived from the United States. Although some viewed such scenarios as wildly implausible and dependent on an exaggerated view of Soviet capabilities, many analysts inside and outside the military took the possibility of a successful Soviet attack on NATO very seriously.[24] Frederick Kagan is almost certainly correct in pointing to the "general consensus that NATO would be hard pressed to stop such an attack with conventional forces."[25] These fears provided part of the motivation for the controversial deployment of new intermediate-range nuclear missiles in Western Europe in the early 1980s, though reliance on nuclear weapons to deter a Soviet attack did not sit well with the European public.

Thus, the most immediate challenge facing the U.S. military was countering Soviet conventional superiority in Europe within post-Vietnam constraints – that is, adjusting to the AVF, smaller budgets, and the American public's casualty aversion. But no matter how daunting the task, it was preferable to the challenge of fighting insurgents and guerillas in the towns and jungles of Vietnam. Although no one liked the outcome of Vietnam, "the end of U.S. involvement in Southeast Asia allowed the army to return to a mission with which it was more comfortable: preparing for large-scale conventional warfare with the Soviet Union."[26] It is no secret that the American military possesses what Jeffrey Record describes

---

[22] House, *Combined Arms Warfare in the Twentieth Century*, p. 230.
[23] Citino, *From Blitzkrieg to Desert Storm*, p. 269. This scenario was the basis of General John Hakett's bestselling book *The Third World War, August 1985* (New York: Macmillan, 1982). BMP carriers would provide Soviet forces with some measure of protection against radiation as well as chemical and biological weapons. The "BMP" refers to vehicle's designation in Russian.
[24] Barry R. Posen was among those who questioned more alarmist assessments of the NATO/WARSAW PACT balance. See, for example, Posen's "Measuring the European Conventional Balance: Coping with Complexity in Threat Assessment," *International Security* Vol. 9, No. 3 (Winter 1984/85), pp. 47–88, and "Is NATO Decisively Outnumbers?" *International Security* Vol. 12, No. 4 (Spring 1988), pp. 186–202. Another dissent was Tom Gervasi, *The Myth of Soviet Military Supremacy* (New York: Harper and Row, 1986).
[25] Kagan, *Finding the Target*, p. 5.
[26] Citino, *From Blitzkrieg to Desert Storm*, p. 265.

as a "historical aversion to counterinsurgency."[27] The frustrations of Vietnam only magnified this aversion. Learning the lessons of Vietnam did not entail preparing to fight counterinsurgencies more effectively. John A. Nagl notes that the post-Vietnam army returned to its "conventional warfare comfort zone" as it "intentionally turned away from the painful memories of Vietnam to the kind of wars it knew how to fight and win." As just one sign of this shift in focus, "the Command and General Staff College cut the forty-hour Low Intensity Conflict curriculum to just nine hours in 1979."[28] The renewed emphasis on the Soviet threat was clearly welcome because "after the uncertainties of the Vietnamese bush, it was a much more comfortable place to be for a mechanized western army."[29] But a greater level of comfort with the mission did not automatically produce any immediate solution to the problem of Soviet military superiority in Europe. The military may have preferred the question, but the answer was not clear.

Countering Soviet Superiority

On paper, the Soviet conventional advantage in Europe was impressive. How this would have translated into battlefield performance and success in the event of an invasion is something the world never found out. But at the time there were two general options available to the United States – proceed with a military buildup to match Soviet forces or find a way to counter Soviet capabilities by identifying and exploiting weaknesses. Those who doubted the United States could or should match the Soviet Union's manpower and hardware were drawn to the later strategy. One of those thinking along these lines was Andrew Marshall. A relatively secretive figure, Marshall was involved in military strategy throughout the Cold War. After working at the RAND Corporation since 1949 alongside such strategic heavyweights as Herman Kahn and Albert Wohlstetter, Marshall came to Washington in 1973 at Nixon's behest to head the Department of Defense's newly created Office of Net Assessment (ONA), a position he would hold for almost three decades under six presidents. In this capacity, he would play a critical role in shaping American defense policy and become one of the leading figures in the debate over the RMA.

The ONA was envisaged as sort of in-house think tank on military and strategic issues. Understandably, during the 1970s and 1980s, Marshall's ONA focused on analyzing Soviet military capabilities and strategy. Marshall was aware that assessing the relative military power was more

[27] Jeffrey Record, "Why the Strong Lose," *Parameters* (Winter 2005), p. 26.
[28] John A. Nagl, *Learning to Eat Soup with a Knife: Counterinsurgency Lessons from Malaya and Vietnam* (Chicago: University of Chicago Press, 2002), p. 206.
[29] Citino, *From Blitzkrieg to Desert Storm*, p. 265.

complicated than counting and comparing soldiers and weapons. Although it is useful to know whether one's opponent has more tanks and artillery, this is only a part of a more complicated analysis. Numerical advantage is not always a reliable predictor of success in war, in part because the requirements of offense and defense are rarely identical. Focusing on simplistic quantitative measures of military power can encourage the mistaken view that the only solution to quantitative imbalances is to eliminate them: if a potential opponent has more tanks, one needs to compensate by building more tanks. But this kind of *symmetrical* response was not always desirable. It was not that Marshall was unconcerned about Soviet conventional advantages. The question was what to do about them. Rather than playing to the Soviet Union's strengths by mimicking its arsenal, Marshall preferred to identify and exploit Soviet weaknesses in pursuit of an *asymmetrical* response. The Soviet strength was in large armies equipped with all the trappings of modern industrial wars of attrition. Not only was it unlikely that the United States and NATO could match Soviet numbers, but doing so might be unwise even if possible. What the United States needed was not the same numbers of everything but rather a *force multiplier*, something that it would make its numerically inferior forces more effective than Soviet forces. The United States needed to identify the Soviet Union's Achilles heel, which Marshall thought was technology, particularly information technology. Bruce Berkowitz explains:

A totalitarian country like the Soviet Union had to control the flow of information. The Soviet regime was so worried about the threat of *samizdat* [an underground dissident press] that in 1971 the average Soviet citizen could not get near a Xerox machine, never mind a computer. This was a weakness that would help destroy the Soviet Union.... Marshall could see that as long as the Communists remained communists, the Soviets would never catch up. The United States, said Marshall, had to figure out a way to use this advantage.[30]

Exploiting the United States' superior technology to compensate for the Soviet Union's larger forces became known as the "offset strategy," though there is some disagreement about who coined the phrase. As William Perry and Ashton Carter explain, "Harold Brown [Secretary of Defense in the Carter administration] called this the 'offset strategy' because ... new weapons would give qualitative advantages to American forces to offset the quantitative advantages that Soviet forces enjoyed." This all dovetailed nicely with emerging Toffleresque notions of profound changes in war accompanying the information revolution. In Marshall's view, the Soviet Union excelled at producing huge quantities of weapons

---

[30] Bruce Berkowitz, *The New Face of War: How War Will Be Fought in the 21st Century* (New York: Free Press, 2003), p. 35.

ideally suited to a form of warfare that was in its way out anyway. Carter and Perry note that "the Defense Department still pursues this strategy of using information technology to achieve a decisive edge on the battle-field." The terminology, however, has changed slightly: "today it is not called the offset strategy; instead it has achieved the status of a 'revolution in military affairs,' and is the subject of study and of admiration (or fear) by military forces around the world."[31]

Although Berkowitz claims that Soviet leaders "did not appreciate" the threat that information-age technologies posed to their regime, some Soviet military strategists were acutely aware of the dangers for the Soviet Union's military position. In fact, they may have realized the danger before many in the West recognized the opportunity. As Murray and Knox explain, "the appearance in the 1970s of striking new technologies within the American armed forces... suggested to Soviet thinkers that a further technological revolution was taking place that had potentially decisive implications for the Soviet Union.... from the Soviet perspective this was a particularly frightening prospect."[32] As a result, "Soviet military leaders.... [tried] to warn their political masters of the dangers of falling further behind."[33] The Soviet discussion of an impending "military-technical revolution" was infused with concerns about the long-term implications for the Soviet Union. On this issue at least, Andrew Marshall and some of his counterparts in the Soviet Union were seeing the future in much the same way. But Marshall and others were quick to emphasize that Soviet power needed to be offset by more than new technologies. The United States would also need better soldiers and better military doctrine. It was the combination of improved training, new technologies, and an innovative war-fighting doctrine that would compensate for Soviet numerical advantages. The offset strategy needed to be multi-dimensional.

A Revolution in Training

Even the most ardent technophiles knew that technology alone was an answer to nothing. Although new technologies and weapons were integral to any offset strategy, they were only part of a larger project of rebuilding American military power. Superior technology is never a guarantee of military success. Looking back on the experience in Vietnam, for example, the military recognized performance problems that had little or nothing to do with technological inadequacies. Vietnam revealed

---

[31] Ashton B. Carter and William J. Perry, *Preventive Defense: A New National Security Strategy for the United States* (Washington, DC: Brookings Institution, 1999), p. 180.

[32] Knox and Murray, "Thinking About Revolutions in Warfare," p. 3.

[33] Freedman, *The Revolution in Strategic Affairs*, p. 27.

deficiencies in military basics that needed to be addressed before the potential of new technologies and weapons could even begin to be realized. A highly technological military would require a highly professional and well-trained force capable of using the new weapons effectively. If anything, as technologies progressed and weapons systems became more complex, even higher levels of training and professionalism would be required. As Freedman notes, "the stress on high quality weaponry has reduced the importance of numbers, while at the same time putting a premium on high-quality troops."[34] Thus, as the military looked backward to the deficiencies of Vietnam and forward to countering the Soviet threat, there was a renewed emphasis on the "ancient verities that stood the test of time – training, discipline and professionalism."[35]

The Air Force was among the first to implement training reforms in light of Vietnam. Of particular concern was poor pilot performance in air-to-air combat missions over North Vietnam and the success of surface-to-air attacks against American forces. Air Force studies indicated that a pilot's first ten missions were the most dangerous and the chances of survival increased substantially thereafter. The problems of poor air combat performance and unacceptable loss rates in early missions were traced to the same cause: inadequate training. As a result, beginning in 1975 (and continuing to this day) the Air Force instituted the so-called Red Flag training exercises incorporating aircrews from other branches as well as NATO and regional allies. Red Flag training exercises last six weeks and expose pilots and crews to realistic battle scenarios against a full range of threats to test and hone essential aerial combat skills. The creation of "aggressor squadrons" was a particularly critical innovation increasing the realism and intensity of the Red Flag exercises. Aggressor squadrons were composed of American pilots and crews trained to emulate the tactics and techniques of likely opponents. As one would expect, throughout the late 1970s and 1980s, the aggressor squadrons acted as stand-ins for Soviet air forces to prepare American and allied aircrews for a showdown with the Soviet Union in Europe. Although there were some unavoidable limits in creating realistic war scenarios (e.g., limited access to Soviet aircraft and military hardware), such exercises constituted a "revolution in training" driven by the recognition that the Air Force "may have concentrated too extensively on improving the machine and have not spent enough effort on the man who must fly it or on the training which he must have to make the machine an exploitable advantage."[36]

Similar efforts to improve training were underway in the U.S. Army, the most notable development being the creation of the National Training

---

[34] Ibid., p. 15.
[35] Murray and Scales, *The Iraq War*, p. 48.
[36] The quote is from a Tactical Air Command journal and is taken from Lambeth, *The Transformation of American Air Power*, p. 62. Lambeth also provides a good discussion of Red Flag and other changes in Air Force training in pp. 59–71.

Center (NTC) at Fort Irwin in California's Mojave Dessert in 1981. As with Red Flag for the Air Force, "the new training center represented the capstone achievement of the 'training revolution' that had taken place in the Army since the end of the Vietnam conflict." The renewed emphasis on training was particularly critical as the Army adjusted to the AVF and reoriented itself away from Vietnam to focus on the Soviet threat in Europe, where it needed to be prepared to win despite being outnumbered. Once again the goal was realism in training: "At the National Training Center, soldiers ... were trained for war in a setting as close as possible to the reality of combat. Training exercises for armor and mechanized infantry battalion task forces included highly realistic live-fire exercises and force-on-force engagements." Just as the Red Flag exercises included an enemy in aggressor squadrons, training at the NTC incorporated mock opposition forces consisting of American and allied troops "of superior numbers, all of whom had been schooled in Warsaw Pact doctrine, tactics and strategy."[37]

It is a cliché that military officers would rather have great soldiers with poor weapons than poor soldiers with great weapons. The renewed emphasis on the basics of military training reflected this familiar sentiment. Of course, militaries would rather not have to choose: the ideal was to have both, the best weapons employed by professional and exceptionally well-trained soldiers. This was the American military's goal in the aftermath of Vietnam. In this sense, high-quality professional training was just as much a force multiplier as high technology weapons. By all accounts this post-Vietnam revolution in training was a tremendous success. Frederick Kagan reflects the consensus in arguing that as a result of the more intensive and realistic training embodied in Red Flag and at the NTC "the air power services and the Army ... create[d] an American military able for the first time in its history to take to the field on very short notice with a superb standard of training and a good deal of experience in highly realistic simulated combat."[38] While technology and weapons often receive most of the attention, quality training was an equally important element not only of the offset strategy but also the larger revolution in military affairs that many saw emerging in the 1980s.

A Revolution in Technology

Although Bruce Berkowitz is probably exaggerating when he claims that "information technology has become so important in defining military power that it overwhelms almost everything else," he is on firmer ground

---

[37] Anne W. Chapman, *The Origins and Development of the National Training Center, 1976–1984* (Fort Monroe, VA: United States Army Training and Doctrine Command, 1992), p. 1.
[38] Kagan, *Finding the Target*, p. 52.

in claiming that "no one has felt the effects of the Information Revolution more than the world's military forces."[39] Few would quibble with the later observation, particularly when talking about the American military, which has led the way in exploiting information-age technologies. Indeed, from a military perspective the information revolution could not have come at a more opportune moment for the United States. Just as the United States needed to find a way to counter Soviet advantages in quantitative measures of military power, information-age technologies provided a foundation for radical improvements in weapons capabilities. It was not a matter of any single technology but rather a bundle of simultaneous technological advances. Stephen Cimbala makes the point nicely, referring to "the *conjunction of breakthroughs* in electronics, communications and cybernetics [that] impacted every aspect of American life, including military affairs."[40] For those concerned primarily with the challenges posed by Soviet military power, these breakthroughs could be significant technological force multipliers, a means of countering Soviet advantages with fewer but better soldiers and weapons. Others more generally interested in the future of warfare generally viewed these same breakthroughs as offering the potential for a revolution in military affairs.

The range of technologies pursued and the diversity of weapons developed in the 1970s and 1980s was such that any attempt to catalog them all would devolve into an unwieldy laundry list of military hardware and specifications. Rather than focusing on the technologies and weapons themselves, it is better to begin by thinking in terms of the enduring problems of warfare they help solve or at least minimize. Two such problems stand out. The first is what Clausewitz famously referred to as the "fog of war," or the ambiguity and incomplete information that inevitably plagues military operations at all levels: strategic, operational, and tactical. The second is the problem of target acquisition, or the ability of munitions to actually hit, and thus disable or destroy, objects of military significance. These are problems as old as war itself. Although few thought information technologies could completely eliminate these problems, American defense planners and RMA enthusiasts believed they could substantially reduce the fog of war and dramatically improve target acquisition.

The fog of war results largely from the absence of accurate information, either an inability to acquire the needed information in the first place or a failure to get it to those who need it in a timely fashion. Given that the basic problem is informational, it should come as no surprise that the technologies of the information age might be particularly valuable for

[39] Berkowitz, *The New Face of War*, p. 2.
[40] Stephen J. Cimbala, "Transformation in Concept and Policy," *Joint Force Quarterly* (July 2005), p. 28, emphasis added.

reducing the fog of war. The technologies have the potential for dealing with both components of the fog of war – the acquisition of information, or intelligence gathering, as well as its dissemination. Although there is a tendency to focus on new weapon systems, it is in the realm of intelligence and communications that we may be seeing the most significant advances. As Elinor Sloan argues, "more than precision munitions or the contribution of any particular military platform, it is the potential of new military technologies to reduce the 'fog of war' that could change the way wars are fought."[41] More exuberant RMA proponents went so far as to predict the *elimination* of the fog of war, an unnecessary and unrealistic prediction that merely sets up a straw man easily ridiculed by RMA skeptics. More sober analysts talked about *reducing* the fog of war, recognizing that uncertainties such as the enemy intentions and motivations would never be eliminated by technology. Whatever the disagreements on how much the fog of war could be reduced, there was consensus that information technologies were the driving force behind the RMA, in part because many of the weapons associated with RMA are dependent on information. Precision-guided munitions, after all, require equally precise intelligence regarding the identity and location of targets.

On the information gathering side of the fog of war equation, the critical advances were in a wide range of sensors and their platforms promising dramatically improved battle space awareness – that is, knowledge about the location and movement of friendly and hostile forces over the entire area in which fighting is taking place. Advances in computing, microelectronics, and miniaturization improved the full spectrum of sensors – for example, optical, thermal-infrared, laser, and radar – at all levels. Night vision sensors, for example, improved to the point where the range of vision in complete darkness matched the range of a soldier's weapon. But the most significant advances in terms of increasing battle space awareness were in wide-area sensors on aerial and space platforms – that is, manned aircraft, unmanned aerial vehicles (UAVs), and satellites. Many of these systems were in early stages of development and deployment during the 1991 Iraq War but much further long by 2003.[42]

For increasing battle space awareness, the two most important systems were those that could identify and track friendly and hostile forces in the air and on the ground over a wide area. The problem of tracking aerial forces was solved first with the development and deployment of the AWACS in the late 1970s. A radar-based sensing system aboard highly modified Boeing 707s, AWACS provides the ability to look down on an

[41] Elinor Sloan, *The Revolution in Military Affairs* (Montreal: McGill-Queens University Press, 2002), p. 6.

[42] Perhaps the best (and very accessible) overview of developments in sensor and communications technology is provided in Michael O'Hanlon, *Technological Change and the Future of Warfare* (Washington, DC: Brookings Institution, 2000), pp. 32–67.

aerial battle space over a range of approximately 250 miles to identify and track friendly and hostile forces in the air. One benefit of such a system is the ability to see deep into enemy territory, which made it particularly attractive to NATO as it contemplated possible war with the Soviet Union. Never used for that purpose, AWACS has nonetheless proven useful in every major American military engagement since its delivery.[43] In 1991, AWACS was joined by the JSTARS that could do on the ground what AWACS did in the air – that is, identify and track the location and movement of friendly and hostile forces over a range of 150 miles.[44] Although these ranges might not seem impressive at first glance, they would enable one AWACS in tandem with one JSTARS to cover a ground and aerial battle space the size of France in a single eight-hour shift (with the important proviso, of course, that they were allowed to operate unmolested). It is easy to see why many thought a significant reduction in the fog of war was in the offing.

UAVs have joined AWACS and JSTARS as critical surveillance tools. Attempts to develop unmanned or remotely piloted aerial devices go as far back as World War I. In the United States, efforts to develop unmanned surveillance capabilities were spurred in part by the downing of spy planes over the Soviet Union and Cuba in the early 1960s. Remotely piloted Firebee drones (another commonly used name for UAVs) were utilized extensively for surveillance during the Vietnam War. But it was during the 1980s that UAVs really started to come of age. As microprocessors got ever smaller while their power increased exponentially, UAVs became cheaper, smaller, and more effective. The potential benefits of UAVs had been clear for some time. Much smaller than planes, they are more difficult to detect and target: it is much easier for an opponent to attack a Boeing 707 than a UAV a fraction its size. UAVs are much less expensive than surveillance planes, making them more expendable. And because by definition UAVs have no crews, they can be sent into dangerous environments without placing people in harm's way. Although many of the technical specifications remain secret, modern UAVs offer unprecedented surveillance capabilities. By the mid-1990s, for example, UAVs were equipped with optical sensors (video cameras) with a resolution of approximately four inches from six miles away and a mere half inch from half a mile.[45] In the past two decades there has been a proliferation of UAVs with different capabilities. The Pioneer played a prominent role in the 1991

---

[43] Other countries, including Great Britain, France, Japan, Saudi Arabia, and Israel also have AWACS capabilities.

[44] JSTARS was still considered experimental and in development when two were rushed to help in the 1991 Iraq War. It was not until 1996 that the system would be approved for large-scale production, which meant fourteen at the time. Indeed, it was the performance of JSTARS in 1991 to created pressure to speed up deployment.

[45] O'Hanlon, *Technological Change and the Future of Warfare*, p. 34.

Iraq War while the Predator, perhaps the most well known of all UAVs, was widely used in 2003 and after. UAVs have typically been used for surveillance, but newer versions are equipped with munitions that allow them to play combat/attack roles. Although pilots are not thrilled at the prospect, some even see a future where UAVs replace manned bombers and fighters.

The fog of war is also reduced with space-based intelligence assets. This includes traditional but increasingly capable spy satellites whose telescopes can detect objects as small as six inches from 150 miles above the earth's surface. The most significant and novel space-based intelligence asset reducing the fog of war is the Global Positioning System (GPS). Developed, deployed, and controlled by the Department of Defense, GPS is a worldwide radio navigation system consisting of at least twenty-four satellites that allows anyone possessing a GPS receiver to determine his position, velocity, and the local time. The system has a wide range of civilian, commercial, and scientific uses. Anyone with an Onstar navigation system in his car enjoys the benefits of GPS. The system's purpose, however, was and remains primarily military. This can be seen in the system's two levels of service and information: the Standard Positioning Service (SPS) available to all free of charge and the Precise Positioning Service (PPS), whose more granular data is tightly controlled by the Department of Defense. Fully aware of its military value, the United States has always protected its ability to deny potential enemies access to the most militarily useful aspects of GPS. As the official website of the U.S. Navigation Center indicates, "the U.S. Government . . . maintains the capability to prevent hostile use of GPS . . . while retaining a military advantage in a theater of operations without disrupting or degrading civilian uses outside the theater of operations."[46] In terms of increasing battle space awareness, the primary benefit of GPS is that it allows forces to determine their positions and navigate with great accuracy even when the local terrain (e.g., a wide open desert) offers few useful landmarks while allowing commanders to keep track of their location and movement.

The ability to gather information is only part of the solution to the fog of war. It is not enough that forces are able to use GPS to ascertain their position – they need to communicate their location to others and vice versa, and this information needs to be shared while it is still accurate and relevant. Battle space awareness, or reducing the fog of war, requires the timely dissemination of information, not merely its acquisition. The ability to communicate rapidly and transmit large amounts of data is perhaps the defining feature of the information age: entire book manuscripts and movies can be transmitted over the Internet in a matter of seconds. Although no one doubted that the sheer quantity of raw intelligence

---

[46] See www.navcen.uscg.gov/GPS/.

and dissemination points in complex battle operations posed significant challenges, the general optimism regarding improved communications is reflected in O'Hanlon's observation that "these areas of defense operation probably offer the greatest potential for huge strides in coming years as a result of technological progress."[47]

Identifying and tracking enemy targets is not that helpful unless they can be attacked, disabled, or destroyed. Militaries have struggled with this problem for as long as they have fought wars, often facing painful trade-offs and adopting less than optimal solutions. For example, there is usually an inverse relationship between distance and accuracy because the likelihood of hitting a target diminishes as distance from it increases. The obvious solution is to get closer to the target: soldiers have to advance or bombers must fly lower. But this creates a new problem. While proximity increases accuracy, it also increases vulnerability. The likelihood of hitting targets can be also improved by increasing the number of projectiles fired toward the target. Firing more bullets or artillery shells or dropping more bombs represents a statistical solution to the problem of inaccuracy. This is also not an ideal solution because it wastes resources and increases the risk of collateral damage. The basic problem encountered throughout military history is that the path of projectiles, be they arrows, spears, bullets, artillery shells, rockets, or bombs has been dictated by the laws of gravity. Projectiles are shot or dropped in the direction of their targets and then gravity determines where and what they hit.

Recognizing the shortcoming of such munitions, militaries have long searched for ways to guide projectiles to desired targets. Early examples of guided munitions include heat-seeking missiles that, for example, can attack enemy aircraft by homing in on the heat generated by their engines. Technological advances in the 1970s and 1980s would finally bring the grail of precision and accuracy within reach. Laser-guided munitions of the kind used on Vietnam were the first major development. Although they represented a substantial improvement, laser-guided munitions have significant shortcomings: clouds, fog, and other adverse weather conditions can seriously degrade performance, and forces need to be close enough to the target to aim the laser guiding the munitions. An alternative that does not suffer from similar problems is satellite guidance. Satellite-guided weapons can operate in all weather conditions and from much greater distances. Because the technological challenges were greater, however, the development of satellite-guided munitions lagged a bit behind those guided by laser. Taken together, advances in these critical guidance technologies would lead to significant improvements in the ability to attack targets reliably from greater distances.

---

[47] O'Hanlon, *Technological Change and the Future of Warfare*, p. 52.

Even technologies that do not appear at first glance to be information-related can, upon closer inspection, be viewed in these terms. Stealth technologies are a case in point. During the 1970s and 1980s, a number of technological advances made it possible to design weapons platforms that were difficult to detect with available sensor technology. These technologies were applied primarily to combat aircraft, most notably to F-117 fighters and B-2 bombers, so they could evade detection and carry out aerial attacks against heavily defended targets. There was nothing new about the desire of military forces to avoid detection: attempts to avoid radar detection are as old as radar itself. The F-117 and B-2 were not even the first stealth military aircraft. In the late 1950s and early 1960s, for example, the U-2 and SR-71 "Blackbird" spy planes incorporated features that supposedly reduced their radar signature, though their effectiveness remains a matter of debate.[48] There was no such debate regarding the F-117 and B-2. Advances in aircraft design and composite construction materials permitted the development of genuinely "low observable" aircraft. This reduced observability highlights the informational nature of the technologies. One needs to remember that there are two sides of the coin when it comes to creating an information advantage in war – maximizing one's knowledge of the battle space while minimizing an opponent's. The goal is to reduce one's own fog while increasing the opponent's. AWACS, JSTARS, UAVs, and spy satellites are examples of surveillance systems that create an advantage by increasing available information. Stealth is an example of technology that creates an advantage by denying information. Fighters and bombers that can avoid detection effectively keep critical information from opponents. This creates an advantage for those possessing stealth and a disadvantage for opponents who do not.

It is important to view these technological advances in surveillance, communications, and target acquisition organically. The over-arching goal was not to develop individual systems performing isolated tasks. On their own, none of these capabilities was particularly useful. This is why, as Cimbala noted, we need to think in terms of a "conjunction of breakthroughs" allowing the creation of ever more effective "surveillance-strike complexes" or "guided munitions battle networks."[49] New technologies and weapons provided the foundation for an all-encompassing military architecture whose overall effectiveness would be greater than the sum of its parts. It was this conjunction of technological advances that could be leveraged to solve strategic military challenges the United States faced in the 1980s and perhaps even change the face of modern warfare.

---

[48] Michael Brown, *Flying Blind: The Politics of the U.S. Strategic Bomber Program* (Ithaca: Cornell University Press, 1992), p. 273.

[49] These terms are used in Watts, *Six Decades of Guided Munitions and Battle Network*.

A Revolution in Doctrine

In addition to well-trained forces equipped with the best weapons, militaries need some idea of how these forces are supposed to use their weapons to achieve victory in war: in other words, a military doctrine. Barry Posen provides a basic conceptualization of military doctrine as a "subcomponent of grand strategy that deals explicitly with military means. Two questions are important: *What* means shall be employed? And *how* shall they be employed?" Military doctrine involves a "set of prescriptions... specifying how military forces should be structured and employed to respond to recognized threats and opportunities," or, as Kagan phrases it, "a clear, reasonable, and well-articulated notion of how to fight."[50]

If the main military threat confronting the United States was the growing conventional imbalance in Europe, the major doctrinal challenge was discerning how well-trained but outnumbered troops with superior technology and weapons could counter the threat. In Posen's terms: What military means would be employed and how? How would NATO fight and defeat the Soviet Union in the event of war in Europe? This was the dilemma that consumed the U.S. Army's Training and Doctrine Command (TRADOC) in the late 1970s and early 1980s. The eventual doctrine that took shape became known as AirLand Battle. The goal of AirLand Battle was not merely to resist a Soviet advance at the point of attack but to pursue an aggressive counteroffense consisting of coordinated, rapid, and simultaneous land and aerial assaults on the full range of front and rear echelon Soviet forces and assets over an expanded battle space, hopefully without any resort to nuclear weapons. What became known as "deep battle" or the "extended battlefield" was the defining feature of the doctrine. NATO wanted to reach well behind the line of engagement to prevent the arrival of Soviet follow-on forces, which might comprise as much as three quarters of Soviet forces. On some level there is nothing terribly novel about this. In another era this might have been referred to as interdiction. The difference was that technological advances had improved radically the prospects for such an approach and opened up new opportunities for a much wider range of attacks. Warren Chin probably provides the best and most succinct description of the intersection of technology and doctrine in AirLand Battle:

Although the idea of deep battle and deep operations was hardly new, what made this doctrine revolutionary was that it relied on the development of new conventional technologies to create what the Soviets called the reconnaissance-strike

[50] Barry R. Posen, *The Sources of Military Doctrine: France, Britain and Germany Between the World Wars* (Ithaca: Cornell University Press, 1984), p. 13. Kagan, *Finding the Target*, p. 52.

complex. Of particular importance was the development of VISTA (very intelligent surveillance and target acquisition) technologies. These systems were able to see into the operational depth of the enemy's positions. Improvements in data processing... allowed information to be provided almost instantaneously, and from this it would be possible to create a real-time picture of enemy activity. The enemy's command and control, transport infrastructure, logistic facilities and force concentrations could then be attacked in long-range precision strikes.[51]

The doctrine of AirLand Battle was a response to a pressing military/strategic challenge confronting the United States at a particular moment in history. But even though AirLand Battle was "tailored... to a specific enemy and a specific theater of war," Knox and Murray deem it "a genuine revolution; the concept of air-land battle provided an entirely new doctrinal framework."[52] The Tofflers characterize AirLand Battle as a "breakthrough to a new concept of warfare."[53] For this reason, RMA theorists saw AirLand Battle as more than a doctrinal response to a specific threat. The new framework also provided one of the earliest visions of how new technologies might change the conduct of war. All the essential elements emphasized by RMA theorists were present: speed, communications, improved information and intelligence, real-time knowledge of large battle spaces, integrating the elements of military power, precision targeting, and stand-off engagement. Although the Cold War ended without any need to put these ideas into practice against the intended target, they would continue to shape American thinking about how to apply military force against different and unexpected enemies.

While the authors of AirLand Battle were emphasizing the *"synergistic marshalling* of the [NATO] alliance's air and ground assets," other military theorists were moving in a different direction, focusing almost exclusively on the air component.[54] In stressing the integration of aerial and ground forces, the advocates of AirLand Battle had waded into one of the most contentious doctrinal debates of the twentieth century: the relationship between air and land power. Phrased more pointedly, the issue was whether airpower should be seen primarily in terms of the support it offers for ground operations or its independent contribution. Enthusiastic "prophets of the air" have always clung to a belief that airpower had the potential to be decisive in war, that maybe airpower alone could actually win wars. Given technological trends, it should come as no surprise that

[51] Warren Chin, "Technology, Industry and War, 1945–1991," in Geoffrey Jensen and Andrew Wiest, eds., *War in the Age of Technology* (New York: NYU Press, 2001), pp. 55–6.
[52] MacGregor Knox and Williamson Murray, "The Future Behind Us," in MacGregor Knox and Williamson Murray, eds., *The Dynamics of Military Revolution, 1300–2050* (Cambridge: Cambridge University Press, 2001), p. 189.
[53] Alvin and Heidi Toffler, *War and Anti-War*, p. 52.
[54] Lambeth, *The Transformation of American Air Power*, p. 82.

such ideas flourished again in somewhat new form during the 1980s. Even though the military benefits of advances in sensor, communication, guidance, and stealth technologies would be felt across the board, most realized their impact would be most profound in the realm of air power. As Charles Dunlap notes, "though technology [will] eventually transform land warfare, the pace is not nearly as rapid as it is with most aviation systems."[55] If there was an RMA in the offing, it was likely to be led by the Air Force. These technologies would not only change how air power is applied; there was the potential to fundamentally alter to role of air power and increase its relative importance and contribution. This realization led to what Frederick Kagan characterizes as *"revolution* in airpower theory."[56] Kagan is not alone in viewing the development of air doctrine in such dramatic terms: George and Meredith Friedman are of a similar opinion, arguing that "between the end of the Vietnam War and Desert Storm, a *revolution* in the theory of aerial warfare took place."[57]

Two theorists stand out in most discussions of this revolution in air power theory, U.S. Air Force Colonels John R. Boyd and John A. Warden. Warden focused explicitly on air doctrine while Boyd's contributions were more general and abstract. Boyd was interested in the nature of decision making. He noted that all individuals and organizations make decisions through a process that includes observation, orientation, decision, and action, which was christened the "OODA loop." In military terms, Boyd argued that there were advantages to moving through the decision cycle more rapidly than an opponent. If you move through the cycle more quickly, your opponent will be forced to make decisions based on old information. He will be constantly overtaken by events. The key is "to get inside the mind and the decision cycle of the adversary. This means the adversary is dealing with outdated and irrelevant information and thus becomes confused and disoriented and can't function."[58] If all goes according to plan, intellectual and decisional paralysis results from creating "a highly fluid and menacing environment to which the enemy cannot adapt."[59] Boyd's ideas may be intriguing and influential, but they probably do not constitute a military doctrine in the sense that most understand the concept. What Boyd offered was an extremely general framework for thinking about military action. Although Kagan may

[55] Charles Dunlap, "Developing Joint Counterinsurgency Doctrine," *Joint Force Quarterly* (2nd Quarter, 2008), p. 91.
[56] Kagan, *Finding the Target*, p. 103.
[57] Friedman, *The Future of War*, p. 255, emphasis added.
[58] Robert Coram, *Boyd: The Fighter Pilot Who Changed the Art of War* (New York: Back Bay Books, 2002), p. 335.
[59] David S. Fadok, *John Boyd and John Warden: Air Power's Quest for Strategic Paralysis.* (Maxwell Air Force Base, AL: Air University Press, February 1995), p. 37.

be right that Boyd's "ideas breathed new intellectual life into the way American officers, civilian leaders, and military analysts thought about war," he concedes that "the theoretical nature of [Boyd's] own writings limited their direct impact on U.S. strategy and planning."[60]

In terms of actual war-fighting doctrine, John Warden has been more influential. Like Boyd, Warden was attracted to the idea of achieving victory in war by paralyzing the enemy, but his approach was different. Boyd's notion of speeding up one's decision cycle in order to "get inside" the enemy's decision cycle was intended to induce a *psychological* paralysis. The enemy would still be able to think. He would just be hopelessly confused and disoriented. Warden, on the other hand, recommended direct attacks against targets that would actually degrade or eliminate the enemy's ability to think and communicate. Fadok points out that Warden's paralysis was *physical* rather than psychological. Whereas Boyd wanted to get inside the enemy's head, Warden preferred to chop it off. Although their objective of making the enemy incapable of coherent action at the strategic, operational, and/or tactical levels may have been the same, the means were very different. Warden was also had a fairly clear view of how to achieve this paralysis.

Warden is best known as one of the architects of Operation Instant Thunder in Desert Storm and author of the hugely influential book *The Air Campaign* (1988), which he described as "a philosophical and theoretical framework for conceptualizing, planning and executing an air campaign."[61] There are several critical elements of Warden's framework. First, he visualized the enemy in terms of five concentric circles. From the center outward these were (1) leadership, (2) economic/industrial production facilities, (3) infrastructure (roads and bridges), (4) population, and (5) fielded military forces. Second, in setting targeting priorities one should focus on the enemy's "center of gravity," which Warden defined as "that point where the enemy is most vulnerable and the point where an attack will have the best chance of being decisive." Third, the most important center of gravity is, not surprisingly, the innermost of the five circles – leadership, command, and control targets. As Warden explains, "command is the sine qua non of military operations. Without command, a military organization is nothing but rabble, a chicken with its head cut off."[62] Without a head and brain an organism ceases to function. This metaphorical equation of leadership targets with the head of a body is commonplace in such theorizing. This makes the targeting priority in war

---

[60] Kagan, *Finding the Target*, p. 112.
[61] John A. Warden, *The Air Campaign* (New York: toExel Press, 2000), originally published in 1988.
[62] Ibid., pp. 7 and 44.

clear: if one is able to attack leadership targets and paralyze the enemy as a result, this is where one's efforts should be focused. And, of course, modern air power with its guided munitions had an unprecedented ability to attack these targets. But just as important are the targets Warden did not consider critical: those in the outermost circle, the enemy's fielded forces. To use the metaphor of the enemy as a body, why bother trying to cut off your opponent's limbs if you can go right for the head and spinal cord? The absence of a brain and nervous system renders the limbs useless.

Although Kagan and others talk about a revolution in air power theory, not everyone was as impressed by Warden's revolutionary credentials. John Sherwood dissents, claiming that Warden "mainly repackaged certain useful theories" advanced decades "earlier [by] prophets of airpower, namely Gullio Douhet and Billy Mitchell."[63] Budiansky agrees with Sherwood, characterizing Warden's theory as "an astonishing throwback. With only tiny variations, it might have been written by the Air Corps Tactical School in 1935." These minor variations were largely semantic in that "Warden spoke of 'centers of gravity' rather than 'vital centers.'" In fact, Budiansky goes so far as to deem Warden's theory "*identical* to all the classic theories of strategic bombardment that had come before."[64] Such judgments seem a little harsh. It is difficult to believe that anyone could mistake Warden's *The Air Campaign* and Douhet's classic *Command of the Air* as the work of the same strategist: the former is not a mere restatement of the latter. Certainly there are important similarities. Passages about the critical importance of establishing air superiority could be lifted from either work. There are certain themes that run through the ideas of just about every air power strategist. But Douhet's suggestion, for example, that chemical and incendiary bombs be used against civilian targets to destroy morale has no parallel in Warden's theory.

How is it possible for some to portray Warden's ideas as revolutionary while others dismiss them as completely unoriginal? Part of the problem is an unrealistic standard. If one insists that doctrines lack any historical lineage in order to be considered truly revolutionary, the search for anything meeting that high bar will probably be in vain. It is extremely rare for any military doctrine to be different in every respect from what came before. One can almost always identify some intellectual debt to previous theorists. Are there similarities between Warden's theory and the ideas of earlier air power theorists? Certainly. Is his theory identical to what came before? Hardly. Although it is true that Warden's major

---

[63] John Darrell Sherwood, "Review of *John Warden and the Renaissance of American Airpower* by John Andreas Olsen," *Joint Force Quarterly* (April 2008), p. 146.
[64] Budiansky, *Air Power*, p. 141, emphasis added.

contribution might not be fundamentally new concepts, he did "repackage" many existing ideas in an innovative way and link them to new technologies. That is, Warden may have recognized that technology had finally caught up to, and permitted the realization of, previously chimerical air power doctrines. The ability to target and attack effectively the most important center of gravity – that is, the central leadership and its communication links – simply did not exist in Douhet's era. What was once mere fantasy was becoming realistic military doctrine.

Conclusion

Few doubt the magnitude of the American military's transformation in the decade and a half after the defeat in Vietnam. In the span of only fifteen years the American military came to terms with that defeat, adjusted to the creation of the AVF, reformed its military training regimens, developed and deployed an impressive array of new technologies and weapon systems, rethought some basic notions of how to apply force and fight wars, and responded to the Soviet military/strategic challenge. As result of the "revolutions" in training, technology, and doctrine that were part of this transformation "American and NATO service chiefs in the 1980s could confront with greater confidence a Warsaw Pact threat – one that a mere decade before had their predecessors privately fearing that NATO could not survive."[65] Whether this newfound confidence was warranted will always remain an unanswered question, thanks to the largely unexpected and sudden end of the Cold War and collapse of the Soviet Union between 1989 and 1991. We will never know whether better training, advanced technology, and new doctrine would have offset Soviet conventional advantages and led NATO to victory. The course and outcome of war between NATO and the Warsaw Pact will, fortunately, remain one of military history's great "what if's," something played out only in video war games.

For some, however, there was a lot more at stake in this transformation than America's military position vis-à-vis its Cold War rival. Although driven primarily by the need to compensate for Soviet conventional superiority, the exploitation of information technologies and the development of new war-fighting doctrines promised a transformation not merely of the American military but warfare itself. There was the possibility of epochal change in what is possible in warfare that would transcend the United States' particular and momentary strategic/military challenges. America's military transformation was synonymous with an emerging RMA. But RMAs do not take place on paper. Only the audit of war can

---

[65] Hallion, *Storm Over Iraq*, p. 273.

confirm predictions of changes in the character of warfare. Without the experience of war we have nothing other than speculation. The peaceful end of the Cold War denied such a test against a peer military competitor. When might this test of American military power and predictions of an RMA present itself? It would come sooner than anyone expected.

3   THE FIRST IRAQ WAR, 1991 –
A REVOLUTION DAWNS?

The Road to War

Although there had been indications toward the end of July of suspicious Iraqi troop movements, the August 2, 1990, invasion of Kuwait came as a surprise to almost everyone. The invasion was swift as the Kuwaiti military was able to offer only token resistance. Kuwaitis able to flee the country did so, leaving their less fortunate compatriots to suffer Iraq's brutal occupation. Saddam no doubt hoped the speed of conquest would present the world with a fait accompli. No one in the region possessed the military power to evict Iraq by force, and there was little reason for him to think that more distant powers would intervene on Kuwait's behalf. He must have expected that the world would eventually come to terms, however grudgingly, with Kuwait's incorporation into Iraq. Within a week of the invasion the conquest was complete, and Kuwait was declared part of a new nineteenth province of Iraq. Kuwait had ceased to exist as an independent state before anyone had a chance to react.

In that first week, however, Kuwait's fate was not the most immediate concern. There was little that could be done at the moment for Kuwait. The more pressing issue was whether the conquest of Kuwait was an end in itself or merely the prelude to an attack on the bigger prize of Saudi Arabia. Although the Saudi military might put up more of a fight, most bets would have been on Iraq in that matchup. The prospect of Saddam Hussein in control of the combined oil resources of Iraq, Kuwait, and Saudi Arabia – half the world's total reserves – was enough to make anyone shudder. The seriousness of the threat could be seen in the eagerness with which the Saudis accepted the American offer of military assistance. General Norman Schwarzkopf recalls his "state of complete shock" when Saudi King Fahd accepted without a moment's hesitation Secretary of Defense Cheney's offer to move American forces into the kingdom. Allowing western (i.e., largely Christian) forces onto sacred Saudi territory was not something done lightly. Once the Saudis agreed, it did not take long for American troops to arrive: planes were in the air almost immediately, and the first forces were on the ground by August 9. Over the next few months, well over half a million American troops followed. This initial deployment to Saudi Arabia, dubbed Operation Desert Shield, was relatively uncontroversial. Given Saudi Arabia's economic and strategic importance, it was not difficult to achieve a consensus both within the United States and internationally on the need to prevent further Iraqi expansion. Agreement on what to do about Kuwait was another matter.

Because only the United States had the military capability to reverse the Iraqi conquest of Kuwait, President George H.W. Bush's opinion mattered most. It did not take long for Bush to reveal where he stood. In comments to reporters on the White House lawn three days after the invasion, Bush spoke bluntly and unequivocally: "This will not stand. This will not stand, this aggression against Kuwait." His comments surprised many, including the Chairman of the Joint Chiefs of Staff, General Colin Powell, who learned of the President's position on television along with the rest of the nation. "That was, for me anyway," Powell recalled, "the first direct expression from the President that he had crossed the line and there's no question he will do what is necessary to get the Iraqis out of Kuwait."[1] Although Bush said nothing at that press conference about how and when this might be accomplished, Powell realized that the option of military force had been placed on the table.

President Bush was not alone in his desire to see Kuwait liberated. No one outside of Iraq looked favorably upon the conquest of Kuwait. Condemnations of the invasion and demands for an Iraqi withdrawal came from all quarters. Within days of the invasion, both the United Nations Security Council and the Arab League passed resolutions calling for an immediate Iraqi withdrawal, though the latter warned initially against outside military intervention. Agreement on the desired end, however, did not extend to the means. Issuing demands for an Iraqi withdrawal was easy. The same could not be said for finding a way to get Iraq out.

Two options dominated the debate over how to remove Iraq from Kuwait: economic sanctions and military force. Agreement on sanctions was reached easily. The Security Council acted with almost record speed, passing a resolution imposing economic sanctions against Iraq on August 6. The debate, however, was not about *whether* to impose sanctions, but rather the *sufficiency* of sanctions alone to force an Iraqi withdrawal. Skeptics of a sanctions-only approach pointed to the spotty historical record of economic sanctions and wondered how and why they would compel Iraq to give up what it had just acquired through war. The pain

---

[1] Colin Powell interview, *PBS Frontline: The Gulf War* (1996). Accessed at: www.pbs.org/wgbh/pages/frontline/gulf/oral/powell/1.html.

of sanctions would have to be quite severe to induce a humiliating exit from Kuwait. Sanctions could also take a long time, perhaps years, and there was no guarantee of success. The failure of sanctions after a year or two could be disastrous. With the passage of time outrage over the invasion would subside and the sense of urgency that drove action in the fall of 1990 would wane. The world just might, as Saddam surely hoped, grow accustomed to Kuwait as Iraq's nineteenth province. And while the world waited for sanctions to work, a sizable American force would have to remain in Saudi Arabia to deter further Iraqi expansion. Despite these problems and uncertainties, many viewed economic sanctions as preferable to the alternative, military force.

Support for sanctions rested partly on fears about military action. Sanctions provided the possibility of ostensibly meaningful action without the risks of war. Expelling Iraq from Kuwait by force would not be easy. On paper, Iraq was a formidable military foe. With almost a million men in uniform, 5,700 tanks, 3,700 artillery pieces, and 950 combat aircraft, "by the summer of 1990, Iraq possessed the world's fourth largest army (the U.S. was third), and the sixth largest air force."[2] With a few months to dig in and establish defensive positions along the border with Saudi Arabia "it was widely expected that Iraqi forces would only be expelled from Kuwait following a ferocious land battle."[3] The cost was expected to be very high. Edward C. Mann notes, "according to the best statistical simulation models, slugging it out with Hussein's army would produce 17,000 to 30,000 U.S. casualties."[4] The specter of chemical weapons, which Saddam had used during the Iran–Iraq War, loomed large. There was no telling to what lengths Saddam might go to avoid defeat in Kuwait. And in addition to the economic and human costs of war, there were the unpredictable consequences of a major military conflict in the heart of the world's most politically volatile region.

Throughout the fall of 1990 the debate about sanctions versus military force continued as feverish rounds of diplomacy and a series of United Nations resolutions ratcheted up the pressure on Iraq. There were, however, no indications that Iraq had any intention of leaving Kuwait. The Bush administration concluded early on that sanctions alone would not succeed and military force would be needed. President Bush tried but failed to build a consensus in favor of using force. Opinion in the United States and around the world remained divided. Although not achieving consensus, Bush and his Secretary of State James Baker successfully

[2] Richard Hallion, *Storm Over Iraq*, p. 128. Others rated the Iraqi army the third largest in the world.
[3] Lawrence Freedman and Efraim Karsh, "How Kuwait Was Won: Strategy in the Gulf War," *International Security* Vol. 16, No. 2 (Fall 1991), p. 5.
[4] Edward C. Mann, *Thunder and Lightening: Desert Storm and the Airpower Debates* (Mawell AFB: Air University Press, 1995), p. 19.

built sufficient political support for the use of force. The critical step on the road to war was the Security Council's passage of Resolution 678 on November 29. The resolution set a January 15, 1991, deadline for Iraq's withdrawal and authorized "all necessary means" to expel Iraq after that date. "All necessary means," of course, is the polite diplomatic euphemism for military force. A final series of negotiations between James Baker and Tariq Aziz, Iraq's Deputy Prime Minister, led nowhere, and Iraq's intransigence only strengthened the hand of those who favored war. As 1990 turned to 1991 it became clear that war was inevitable. On January 12, the United States Senate passed a resolution authorizing the use of force by a vote of 52–47, the smallest margin for such a resolution since the War of 1812. The U.N. deadline for withdrawal passed January 15, 1991, with Iraqi troops still in place. On January 17, the U.S.-led assault on Iraq began and Operation Desert Shield became Operation Desert Storm.

The War Plan

As war with Iraq approached, the United States faced the very real possibility of substantial military casualties for the first time since the Vietnam War. The prospect of thousands of young Americans returning from the Persian Gulf in body bags could not have been welcome. Partly for this reason, many in the military viewed the rush to war as hasty. Even Colin Powell preferred giving sanctions more time. But not everyone was convinced that substantial American casualties were inevitable. Perhaps the war simulations and resulting expectations of high casualties were based on outdated notions of how to wage war. Maybe the technologies and weapons that would have permitted outnumbered NATO forces to prevail over the Soviet Union would also enable the United States to defeat Iraq with relatively few casualties. A new way of fighting might leave those body bags unused.

For those wanting to fight a new kind of war, the key to minimizing American casualties was delaying or avoiding altogether the phase of the war expected to be the bloodiest: the ground campaign. Six months had passed since the Iraqi invasion of Kuwait. This was fortunate because it gave the United States time to move more than 500,000 troops and their supplies thousands of miles to the Persian Gulf. Unfortunately for the United States, Iraq also had that time to prepare for the attack the entire world knew was coming. Although the details of the attack might be a surprise, the attack itself would not. The U.N. withdrawal deadline even provided a pretty good idea of the attack's timing. The fear was that invading coalition forces would be drawn into a protracted and costly ground campaign as they encountered a well-prepared and entrenched Iraqi army whose only hope of winning was to erode the coalition's political will by inflicting maximum casualties. Kenneth Pollack explains, the Iraqi plan for countering an attempt to liberate Kuwait "consisted not so much of defeating Coalition forced but merely gaining a bloody stalemate that would force the Coalition to negotiations."[5] Recent history provided more than adequate grounds for concern: "in eight years of war with the Iranians," the Iraqis "learned how to bleed an attacker on cleverly designed defensive positions."[6] The United States did not want to suffer the same fate.

The dilemma confronting military planners was how to remove several hundred thousand Iraqi troops from Kuwait without a costly and grueling ground war.[7] Theorists such as John Warden thought they had an answer – fight the war largely or exclusively from the air. For Warden, the war represented an opportunity to demonstrate how the previous decade's technological advances had revolutionized air power. The combination of increased information, stealth, and guided munitions would allow the United States to attack Iraq in ways that would have been impossible just a decade before. The potential contribution of air power was greater than ever. There was nothing controversial per se about a greater reliance on air power: if one wants to minimize the costs of a ground campaign, air power is the obvious solution. But Warden went further. It was not just a matter of using air power to delay and make the eventual ground campaign easier. Warden and a handful of air power enthusiasts thought it might be possible to design and wage an air campaign that would completely obviate the need for a ground campaign. He hoped this might be the first war ever to be won with air power alone. The almost century-old dream of victory from the air was at hand.

As the Air Staff's Deputy Director of Plans for War fighting Concepts, Warden was presented with "an opportunity offered to not one military theorist in a thousand – he had the chance to put his ideas into almost immediate practice after Saddam Hussein invaded Kuwait."[8] Upon returning to Washington from vacation on August 6, Warden and his staff were charged with devising a strategic bombing campaign against Iraq in the event of war. In doing so they were faithful to Warden's vision of creating strategic paralysis by attacking the opponent's most important centers of gravity – that is, the central political/military leadership, its command, control and intelligence assets, and a handful of economic/infrastructure

5 Kenneth M. Pollack, *Arabs at War: Military Effectiveness, 1948–1991* (Lincoln, NE: University of Nebraska Press, 2002), p. 237.
6 Mann, *Thunder and Lightening: Desert Storm and the Airpower Debates*, p. 20.
7 Although estimates at the time indicated that Iraq had more than 500,000 troops in Kuwait, subsequent evidence suggests the number was closer to 340,000 when the war began. See Freedman and Karsh, *The Gulf Conflict, 1991*, p. 390; and Stephen Biddle "Victory Misunderstood: What the Gulf War Tells Us About the Future of International Conflict," *International Security* Vol. 21, No. 2 (Fall 1996), p. 136.
8 Kagan, *Finding the Target*, p. 120.

targets critical to Iraq's war-fighting capabilities. The emphasis would be on the innermost rings of Warden's five-ring schematic of the enemy. This became known as "inside-out warfare" because rather than fighting through the outer rings in sequence, one instead starts at the center and engages the outer rings later if at all. Precision weapons and stealth would allow simultaneous attacks on dozens of targets in Baghdad and elsewhere, creating a systemic breakdown and overwhelming the Iraqis in short order. Moreover, Warden's plan anticipated avoiding the large-scale collateral damage and civilian casualties typically associated with strategic bombing, thus denying Saddam images of death and devastation that might outrage public opinion and thereby increase opposition to the war. The plan was deemed "Instant Thunder," a not-so veiled reference to the much-maligned "Rolling Thunder" bombing campaign in Vietnam that relied on gradual escalation to coerce the North Vietnamese. The air campaign against Iraq would be anything but gradual. Instant Thunder entailed a massive but controlled aerial assault without historical parallel.

Even the casual observer, however, would notice something missing in Instant Thunder – it completely ignored Iraqi troops occupying Kuwait or dug in along the Saudi border. If liberating Kuwait was the fundamental goal, these troops would eventually have to leave. But how would attacking the inner rings of Iraqi power lead to the removal of Iraqi forces from Kuwait? This is where Warden made a few questionable assumptions. Mann explains that "Warden and many of the people working with him thought that once they achieved their military objectives (i.e., incapacitation of the key strategic target sets), the Iraqi forces in Kuwait would realize the futility of their situation and return home. Surely, Iraqi civilians or, more likely, the conscript forces – stranded in Kuwait by their now discredited regime – would overthrow Hussein."[9] The assumption that Instant Thunder alone would lead to the withdrawal of Iraqi forces without any need for the coalition to expel them by force struck many as the latest example of wishful thinking on the part of air power visionaries and dreamers.

On August 10, Warden presented Instant Thunder to General Norman Schwarzkopf. He proposed a six-day air campaign to shatter the Iraqi system, cut-off the leadership from its people and armed forces, and create an impression of an ineffective regime destined for defeat. After disabling Iraq's air defenses and air force, the coalition would proceed to systematically destroy the regime and its capacity for coherent action by attacking eighty-four carefully chosen targets: "about a thousand sorties would be flown each day, bombing presidential palaces, telephone exchanges, government ministries, internal security organs such as secret

---

[9] Mann, *Thunder and Lightening*, p. 40.

police headquarters, and electrical power, oil, bridges and railways."[10] Schwarzkopf, who encouraged creative thinking, liked what he heard. Although Budiansky describes him as "dazzled by the prospect of being able to win a war without risking any of his ground forces," Schwarzkopf maintains that he "never felt it was a complete option. I always felt that it would take ground forces on the ground to, in fact, eject the ground forces that were over there."[11] Instant Thunder, however, did have the benefit of giving Schwarzkopf a plausible military option if he needed one in the near term. It answered the question of how the United States might respond if Iraq attacked Saudi Arabia before the bulk of American forces had reached the Gulf.[12]

The next day Warden gave the same briefing to Colin Powell. Although skeptical of "flyboy promises," Powell listened intently. When Warden finished Powell asked the sixty-four thousand dollar question: "OK, it's day six.... now what?" Warden fell back on his assumption that the Iraqi regime would be so paralyzed, isolated, and discredited that its forces would have to leave Kuwait. But even after granting the possibility that Instant Thunder might induce an Iraqi withdrawal, Powell threw another wrench in the equation, telling Warden that he did not "want them to go home – I want to leave smoking tanks as kilometer fence posts all the way to Iraq."[13] Obviously, this could not be achieved without direct attacks on Iraqi forces. Powell's reservations reflected two widely shared concerns about Instant Thunder: first, there was no guarantee that strategic bombing would force an Iraqi withdrawal even if it achieved its operational objectives; and second, it could leave too much of Iraq's military power intact. Warden may have convinced Powell and Schwarzkopf of the value of an aggressive strategic air campaign, but he was less successful in persuading them that only six days of aerial attacks on Iraq would liberate Kuwait and achieve the United States' larger strategic and political goals. Powell and Schwarzkopf were certainly not willing to accept an entire war plan on the assumption that Iraqi forces in Kuwait would be withdrawn or simply walk home of their own volition. The United States needed to be prepared to expel the Iraqis by force.

Warden flew to Saudi Arabia in late August to brief Lt. Gen. Charles Horner of U.S. Central Command on his plan. Their meeting did not go well. On a personal level, Horner supposedly resented the interference by Warden and other Washington-types in planning the war. More

[10] Budiansky, *Air Power*, pp. 414–15.
[11] Norman Schwarzkopf interview, *PBS Frontline: The Gulf War* (1996). Accessed at: www.pbs.org/wgbh/pages/frontline/gulf/oral/schwarzkopf/1.html.
[12] On Instant Thunder, see also Michael R. Gordon and Bernard Trainor, *The Generals' War: The Inside Story of the Conflict in the Gulf* (Boston: Little, Brown and Company, 1995), pp. 81–90.
[13] Pape, *Bombing to Win*, p. 224.

substantively, Horner disagreed with Warden's exclusion of Iraqi forces, particularly the elite Republican Guard, from the targeting list. Warden was sent back to Washington after his meeting with Horner. While he may not have realized it at the time, Warden's role in planning the war had come to an abrupt end. Several years after the war, Horner commented on his disagreement with Warden in an interview with the *Washington Post*: "I disagree that there were tensions between bombing the Iraqi Army and Baghdad. That thought might be gained from listening to Col. [John] Warden, who wanted not to bomb the Iraqi Army. He didn't think it necessary and that is why he did not get the job as head planner."[14] Instead, Horner brought in Brig. Gen. Buster C. Glosson to plan the air war. Warden's theory that victory could be achieved with aerial attacks on strategic targets alone was not going to be put to the test in its purest form.[15]

Despite this apparent hostility to his plan, Warden's ideas were not completely abandoned. Horner's criticism of Instant Thunder focused on Warden's conviction that strategic bombing alone would suffice. Under Glosson's and Schwarzkopf's direction, Instant Thunder was maintained but expanded and subsumed within a broader air and ground campaign. Whereas Warden thought that hitting 84 critical targets would be enough to paralyze the Iraqi regime, Glosson expanded the list to more than 300 targets by the time the war began. More importantly, the eventual plan incorporated attacks on Iraqi forces in Kuwait with an eye toward "preparing the battlefield." Talk of a battlefield, of course, implicitly conceded that there might be coalition forces battling on the ground. Although some still held out hope that the air war might bring about the regime's collapse and a withdrawal from Kuwait, most viewed it in terms of making the ground war easier and less costly. The resulting plan, according to Freedman and Karsh, "was something of a compromise between the USAF's inclination to concentrate on the sources of Saddam's power and the Army's desire to see his ground forces cut down to size before it launched its offensive."[16] Despite the revisions, the air war plan built on the foundation of Warden's Instant Thunder, something he was more than willing to remind people of after the war. Noting that "success has a thousand fathers," Rick Atkinson observes that "paternity claims in the Persian Gulf War would mount in direct proportion to allied achievements. . . . [but] no claim was stronger than Warden's."[17]

---

[14] "Q&A With Lt. Gen. Charles Horner," *The Washington Post*, 1998. Accessed at: www.washingtonpost.com/wp-srv/inatl/longterm/fogofwar/hornertext.htm.
[15] On Warden's meeting with Horner, see also Gordon and Trainor, *The Generals' War*, pp. 91–4.
[16] Lawrence Freedman and Efraim Karsh, *The Gulf Conflict, 1990–1991*, p. 317.
[17] Rick Atkinson, *Crusade: The Untold Story of the Persian Gulf War* (Boston: Houghton-Mifflin, 1993), p. 56.

By the end of August this compromise came together as a four-phase war plan incorporating a strategic air campaign, attacks on Iraqi fielded forces, and a ground invasion.[18] Phase I was essentially the expanded version of Instant Thunder focused on establishing air superiority over Iraq and attacking leadership, command and control capabilities, and critical infrastructure targets. If Warden's views had prevailed, the war would have stopped with phase I. In phase II, attention would shift to the Kuwaiti theater of operations (KTO) with attacks on Iraqi theater air defenses. With coalition air superiority established over Kuwait, phase III would then proceed to prepare the battlefield for invasion with massive, day and night bombardment of Iraqi forces. For this phase "General Schwarzkopf's declared goal was to reduce the effective potential of Iraqi ground forces in the KTO by 50 percent."[19] With Iraqi capabilities sufficiently degraded, phase IV, the ground campaign, could finally commence.

This was an unprecedented war plan, particularly as it related to the use of air power. Phase I was the "strategic" component of the campaign that, despite some changes in targeting, "remained faithful to Instant Thunder's chief tenets."[20] The objective was to attack, isolate, and paralyze the Iraqi regime. Using the ubiquitous body metaphor, the goal was to "decapitate" the enemy. Robert Pape notes that this represented "the first major use of strategic bombing to decapitate an opponent's leadership. . . . the first systematic decapitation campaign in air history."[21] On some levels, the attacks on Iraqi forces were less novel. This was certainly not the first time an opponent's ground troops were bombed from the air. The magnitude of the attack, however, would far exceed anything attempted before. According to the *Gulf War Air Power Survey*, the goal of reducing Iraqi effectiveness by fifty percent "called on air power to destroy ground forces to a degree not heretofore planned for any air force."[22] Thus, in Desert Storm, the United States would rely on its air forces to accomplish military objectives never attempted, much less achieved, in the history of aerial warfare.

Even if all the objectives were met, the plan assumed a need for a ground invasion. Although we now know the ground war would last only 100 hours, the war planners did not anticipate such a rapid rout. They expected the air campaign to last about three weeks followed by a two-week ground war. Given coalition advantages, few doubted the eventual outcome. Coalition forces would outnumber Iraqi forces, would

---

[18] Two discussions of the plan's phases are Robert Pape, *Bombing to Win*, p. 220; and Alastair Finlan, *The Gulf War, 1991*, p. 34.
[19] Lambeth, *The Transformation of American Air Power*, p. 118.
[20] Pape, *Bombing to Win*, p. 228.
[21] Ibid., p. 211.
[22] Lambeth, *The Transformation of American Air Power*, p. 118.

be better equipped, enjoy information superiority, and fight under the cover of air forces that controlled the skies. Furthermore, they would be confronting Iraqi forces that had been subjected to the most punishing aerial bombardment in the history of warfare. But coalition advantages on the ground were not as great as they were in the air, and several hundred thousand Iraqi troops could still exact a heavy price.

How would the coalition force out the Iraqis while minimizing its casualties? There were three options for invading Kuwait: an amphibious landing from the Persian Gulf into eastern Kuwait, a frontal assault across the Saudi border into Iraqi defensive positions in southern Kuwait, or a sweeping flanking maneuver in the west through Iraq itself into Kuwait. This was a lot of territory to cover, and even several hundred thousand Iraqi troops would be spread relatively thin if positioned along all the lines of possible attack. Most knowledgeable observers expected the coalition to attack at some point along the Saudi-Kuwaiti border. John Mearsheimer, one of the only observers to predict a quick war with few casualties, speculated that "the U.S. will likely start the ground offensive by concentrating armor and airpower along a 20-mile portion of the Saudi-Kuwaiti border. It should be able to penetrate Iraq's defense line in no more than half a day." Once through, "U.S. armored spearheads will drive into Kuwait. They will avoid direct engagements with entrenched Iraqi operational reserves.... and instead concentrate on cutting Iraqi lines of communication. U.S. air and ground superiority will make it difficult for the Iraqis to confront America's armored spearheads in free wheeling tank battles."[23] This is probably what the Iraqis expected as well, and the coalition was happy for them to think so. Indeed, there were elaborate efforts to deceive the Iraqis into expecting, and preparing for, such a frontal assault combined with an amphibious attack. But it was not to be.[24]

Two major points of attack were incorporated into the final war plan (see Map 3.1). Two Marine divisions would attack into the "heel" of Kuwait, breaching Iraqi defensive lines before heading north to Kuwait City, as Arab forces invaded a little to the west and further to the east near the coast. This is the type of attack most expected. In the other major thrust, Army divisions would cross the Saudi border far to the west into Iraq itself, heading north before turning east toward Kuwait. Dubbed the "Hail Mary plan," Schwarzkopf developed this "innovative flanking attack" that was "far removed from the hey-diddle-diddle-straight-up-the-middle plan proffered in October."[25] This move far to the west of Kuwait was designed to exploit American advantages in mobility, air

[23] Mearsheimer, "Will Iraq Fold Its Tent: Victory in Less than a Week," *The New York Times* (February 8, 1991), p. A31.
[24] On the development of the ground plan and the western flank attack, see Gordon and Trainor, *The Generals' War*, pp. 122–58.
[25] Atkinson, *Crusade*, p. 247.

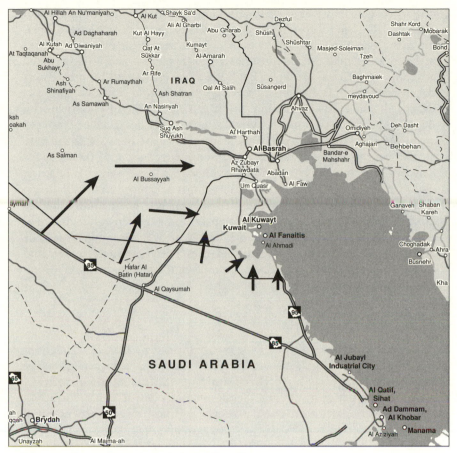

Map 3.1. Desert Storm (1991) ground invasion.

power, and information. The goals were to restore an element of tactical surprise, avoid Iraq's more elaborate fixed defenses, cut Iraqi lines
of communication, and trap Iraqi forces in Kuwait for destruction by
enveloping them from the rear.

The War

The Gulf War began in the early morning hours of January 17, 1991,
just two days after the passing of the U.N. deadline, with four official
objectives: (1) removal of Iraqi forces from Kuwait, (2) restoration of
Kuwait's sovereignty, (3) establishment of regional security and stability, and (4) protection of American lives. Four Apache helicopters fired
the first shots, attacking and destroying two critical early warning radar
installations in southern Iraq with laser-guided missiles. As the Apache
crews celebrated their successful mission, F-117 stealth fighters and

dozens of Tomahawk cruise missiles launched from ships in the Persian Gulf and Red Sea raced toward downtown Baghdad. Tomahawks, costing more than a million dollars each, were designed for precision strikes in heavily defended areas considered too dangerous for most manned aircraft. Since "after Moscow, Baghdad was surrounded by the densest concentration of air defenses of any city in the world," the Tomahawks were well suited to the mission.[26] On this first night of Desert Storm, Baghdad became "the most heavily defended city ever attacked from the air."[27] With its ability to avoid radar detection, the F-117 was the only aircraft sent to Baghdad during these first hours. Not until the city's air defenses were out of commission would other aircraft be sent. The first night's assault was overwhelming, encompassing more than 700 coalition aircraft flying more than 800 sorties, making "the opening round of Desert Storm the largest single air offensive to have been conducted anywhere in the world since the end of World War II."[28] And given the scale of the attack and extent of Iraqi air defenses, everyone was surprised and relieved when, despite predictions of ten percent losses, only one coalition aircraft failed to return safely that night.

The Strategic Air Campaign

The first attacks focused on a wide range of strategic targets throughout Iraq and Kuwait largely consistent with Warden's target categories in Instant Thunder: Iraqi air defenses and airfields, the national electrical grid, leadership targets, and military command, control, communication, and intelligence facilities. The destruction of these targets was essential for the coalition to achieve its early goals of air superiority, information dominance, and regime isolation. The most important of these initial objectives was air superiority because "prompt control of the air was the sine qua non of everything that followed."[29]

To achieve air superiority, the coalition needed to destroy or neutralize Iraqi air defenses and the Iraqi Air Force (IAF). Both appeared to be difficult tasks. In addition to the air defenses surrounding Baghdad, Iraq maintained a "formidable air-defence network" throughout large parts of the country constructed during its war with Iran when it was able "to acquire state-of-the-art passive and active air defenses."[30] Stealth aircraft and guided munitions, however, made quick work of Iraqi network. With more than 100 sorties directed at Iraq's air defenses, "the heart of the Iraqi IADS [integrated air defense system] was taken out in

---

[26] Lambeth, *The Transformation of American Air Power*, p. 110.
[27] Boot, *War Made New*, p. 320.
[28] Lambeth, *The Transformation of American Air Power*, p. 116.
[29] Ibid., p. 269.
[30] Finlan, *The Gulf War, 1991*, p. 333.

the first hour ... [and] the entire system was rendered nonoperational in 36 hours."[31] The Iraqis were soon reduced to firing into the sky randomly in hopes of hitting something by chance. The *Gulf War Air Power Survey* presents a vivid description of the initial attack: "on the first night of the air war, an elaborately choreographed combination of stealth aircraft, specialized electronic warfare aircraft, decoys, cruise missiles, and attack aircraft delivered a sudden, paralyzing blow to the integrated air defense system from which the Iraqis never recovered."[32] Unfortunately for the Iraqis, their air defense network, which may have been adequate for smaller attacks by Israel or Iran, was completely overwhelmed by the coalition's massive onslaught.[33] As a result, "Iraq's radar network was neutralized to the point that during the last four weeks of Desert Storm only about 15 percent of the 480 radar SAMs [surface-to-air missiles] appear to have been guided." This rapid neutralization of Iraqi air defenses helps explain why throughout the war "the coalition lost just thirty-eight aircraft, or about one for every eighteen hundred sorties, the lowest rate for sustained combat in aviation history."[34]

Iraq's air force was neutralized just as easily, partly because "the Iraqis probably never intended to contest air superiority even over Iraq at risk of losing their modern fixed-wing aircraft."[35] There is some debate about the precise size and composition of the IAF on the eve of Desert Storm, largely because Iraq's loses in the Iran–Iraq War are unclear. Most estimate that Iraq possessed between 500 and 700 combat aircraft, including some advanced Soviet MIG and French Mirage fighters. The coalition neutralized the IAF indirectly by attacking radar and other installations required to manage combat aircraft as well as directly with attacks on airfields and bunkers. Very few Iraqi planes took to the skies to meet the coalition attack, and those that did were quickly detected by American AWACS and targeted by the coalition. Air engagements were few and far between, and "the Iraqi Air Force barely managed to achieve one aerial combat kill against an armada of aircraft that attacked the country night after night."[36] Only 34 Iraqi aircraft were shot down whereas about 100 were destroyed on the ground and 100 others escaped to Iran. The lack of aerial combat was even something of a "disappointment as the coalition's air-to-air pilots ... found themselves deprived ... of an opportunity to validate in combat what they had learned during

[31] Lambeth, *The Transformation of American Air Power*, p. 113.
[32] Keaney and Cohen, *Gulf War Air Power Survey*, p. 284.
[33] Gordon and Trainor, *The Generals' War*, p. 108; Pollack, *Arabs at War*, p. 241.
[34] Pape, *Bombing to Win*, p. 228.
[35] Thomas A. Keaney, "Surveying Gulf War Airpower," *Joint Force Quarterly* No. 2 (Autumn 1993), p. 27.
[36] Freedman and Karsh, "How Kuwait Was Won: Strategy in the Gulf War," p. 39.

the 15 years of Red Flag."[37] If a war requires more than one participant, this was not really an air war at all but rather the unilateral application of air power against a virtually helpless or clueless opponent. As a result, it did not take long for the coalition to accomplish its most important military objective. Although the coalition would not formally declare air supremacy until January 27, for "all intents and purposes, allied control of the air over Iraq was achieved in the opening moments of Desert Storm."[38]

Air superiority was critical not only because it allowed the coalition to attack at will but also because it guaranteed allied information dominance. While coalition fighters and bombers would have free rein over Iraq and Kuwait, so too would "the most powerful information weapons of all – AWACS and J-STARS."[39] The ability of aerial reconnaissance assets to roam uncontested over the battle space ensured that the coalition would have unprecedented information regarding the location and movement of friendly and hostile forces while the absence of any aerial reconnaissance assets would deny Iraqi leaders similar information. The information imbalance would be tremendous. Mann explains that "Saddam's forces had nothing to rival the coalition's [information] collection capability... [and] the gap in information collection – huge at the outset of hostilities – grew rapidly over time."[40] When this lack of information was coupled with attacks on critical communications assets such as the electrical grid, telephone exchanges, microwave relay towers, fiber optic cable nodes, bridges that carried communications cables, and radio and television facilities, the regime would be paralyzed. The Iraqi leadership would have no idea what was going on and it would be unable to engage in coherent strategic action. It would be blind, deaf, and dumb. This was the essence of a "decapitation" strategy. At least that was the plan. The reality was slightly different.

Although there is no question that strategic bombing was able to establish coalition air superiority, did it also succeed in decapitating the enemy? Postwar evaluation of the air campaign has focused on this question, which is understandable given the extravagant pre- and postwar claims of air power enthusiasts. The hope of some that strategic bombing would eliminate the regime through Saddam's death or a coup was obviously not to be. Robert Pape is blunt: "Instant Thunder failed to kill, overthrow, or isolate Saddam or his regime. It posed no significant threat to Iraq's senior political and military leadership at all. None of Iraq's top

---

[37] Lambeth, *The Transformation of American Air Power*, p. 115.
[38] Ibid., p. 116.
[39] Toffler and Toffler, *War and Anti-War*, p. 70.
[40] Edward Mann, "Desert Storm: The First Information War?" *Airpower Journal* Vol. 8, No. 4 (Winter 1994). Accessed at: www.airpower.maxwell.af.mil/airchronicles/apj/apj94/win94/man1.html.

political or military leadership was killed during Desert Storm."[41] In the end, "the Iraqi regime's control over its people proved remarkably resilient" and Saddam would remain in charge long after President Bush was voted out of office the following year.[42] In fairness, however, Warden might have expected the strategic campaign to doom Saddam's regime, but this was never an official objective of the war, even if it was an unspoken desire.

The results of the air campaign are somewhat less clear regarding the more modest objective of inducing paralysis by overwhelming the regime, eliminating its sources of information and severing its lines of communication, leaving the leadership in power but unable to lead in any meaningful sense. Everyone concedes that the strategic campaign did great damage to Iraq's intelligence and communication assets. Hallion reflects the prevailing view that "Iraq's command, control, communications, and intelligence [capabilities]... were *in a shambles*" within hours after the air attacks began.[43] Even Biddle, whose overall assessment of the air campaign tends to be less glowing than Hallion, agrees that the initial attacks "quickly *crippled*... key elements of the Iraqi command and control network."[44] But others question the extent of the damage. Pape, for example, offers a slightly different analysis. Although conceding that "the air war *degraded* communication between Baghdad and the KTO *significantly*," it was *"not enough to cripple* Saddam's ability to direct theater-wide operations."[45] The strategic bombing campaign may have disabled or "crippled" the regime, perhaps even to an unprecedented extent, but it did not kill or paralyze it. Nonetheless, the *Gulf War Air Power Survey* cautions that "coalition attacks... need not, however, be judged against this ambitious goal. In retrospect, it may be fairer to ask how *much* disruption and dislocation these attacks imposed on the functioning of the Iraqi government and its telecommunications." Although available evidence is insufficient to reach any definitive judgment, "common sense would argue that strikes against these two target categories [i.e., leadership and command/control] must have imposed *some*, if not *considerable*, disruption and dislocation on the Iraqis involved."[46]

Preparing the Battlefield

The original war plan called for the air campaign to progress in phases, with attacks on strategic targets preceding attacks on Iraqi forces in

---

[41] Pape, *Bombing to Win*, p. 230.
[42] House, *Combined Arms Warfare in the Twentieth Century*, p. 271.
[43] Hallion, *Storm Over Iraq*, p. 117, emphasis added.
[44] Stephen Biddle, "Victory Misunderstood," p. 144, emphasis added.
[45] Pape, *Bombing to Win*, p. 239, emphasis added.
[46] Keaney and Cohen, *Gulf War Air Power Survey*, p. 99.

Kuwait. In reality, the full range of strategic and theater targets were attacked beginning day one. The rapid achievement of air superiority and the magnitude of coalition air forces deployed to the Gulf eliminated the need for a phased campaign. Since the coalition could attack everything at once, there was no reason not to. Preparation of the battlefield began that first night with attacks on Republican Guard units in Kuwait that would continue for weeks.

By week two, the theater campaign was in full swing, focusing on preparatory bombardment of Iraqi ground forces and the destruction of bridges and roads that could be used as reinforcement and resupply routes into and within Kuwait. Although some attacks against smaller discrete targets (e.g., bridges) were carried out with guided munitions, the coalition relied heavily on old-fashioned unguided munitions for its attacks on Iraqi forces. Rather than employing advanced (and often very expensive) laser- or satellite-guided bombs against Iraqi troop concentrations, they were usually attacked by B-52s dropping large quantities of "dumb" bombs. Many Americans might be surprised to learn that these attacks were more typical than the precision strikes they saw on their television screens. Overall, guided munitions constituted less than 10 percent of the ordnance used in the war, though they probably accounted for almost 100 percent of the war's video images. This reliance on unguided bombs resulted in part from the United States' limited stockpile of guided weapons in 1991. Most combat aircraft were also not yet equipped to deliver laser- or satellite-guided munitions. But in many cases there was simply no need to use them. After all, in the middle of the Kuwaiti desert, the coalition was not worried about collateral damage and civilian casualties because there was no collateral or civilians around. When the coalition bombed targets in the desert, it wanted to destroy everything in the area. In some settings, indiscriminate bombing is preferable even if precision weapons are available. These massive attacks on Iraqi forces were intended not only to degrade their effectiveness by destroying equipment and killing soldiers but also, and perhaps most importantly, by eroding morale. Bombing day and night, the coalition hoped that Iraqi troops would realize the hopelessness and futility of their situation.

Guided weapons did prove extremely useful for some aspects of battlefield preparation, most famously so-called tank plinking. To meet Schwarzkopf's goal of reducing Iraqi effectiveness by fifty percent, coalition aircraft needed to eliminate as much Iraqi armor and artillery as possible, but early efforts fell short. In late January, however, certain air force officers realized that at night Iraqi tanks retained much of the heat absorbed during the day, making them stand out in the cold desert to thermal sensors, even if the tanks were buried in sand to prevent visual detection. Once located, the tanks were susceptible to attacks using 500-lb laser-guided bombs delivered from F-111s or A-10 "Warthogs." An initial experiment in early February was extremely encouraging.[47] Although he wondered "why didn't we think of this weeks ago," General Calvin Waller was "elated" with the success of tank plinking because "now finally we are providing the ground commanders with something that they sorely needed to reduce the number of tanks that they're going to be faced with or reduce the number of artillery pieces that will be bringing fire upon them."[48] After the war, an Iraqi POW spoke about the success of tank plinking: "during the Iran War," he explained, "my tank was my friend because I could sleep in it and know I was safe . . . during this war. . . . none of my troops would get near a tank at night because they just kept blowing up."[49]

Although both strategic and theater targets were hit just about every day, the mix shifted to the latter as the air campaign progressed. The prioritization of targets was a constant source of tension. General Frederick Franks recalls that there were "some intense discussions" about targeting priorities.[50] General Waller was less understated: "we had enormous problems trying to shape the battlefield . . . telling and showing and pleading and cajoling and threatening Buster [Glosson] and his other band of merry men to make sure that we were giving the ground commanders what they needed and wanted."[51] After weeks of bombing and thousands of sorties, some wondered what strategic targets could possibly remain in Iraq: how many times did the coalition need to attack the Baath Party Headquarters? Army officers in particular "were frustrated with what they judged to be the U.S Air Force's preoccupation with precision weapons attacks and the 'decapitation' of the Iraqi leadership . . . [which] created the impression that the allies were more concerned with pounding Baghdad than getting on with the ground campaign."[52] Despite such complaints, the attacks on Iraqi forces were devastating. Citino explains that for nearly four weeks "the Iraqi forces in the Kuwaiti Theater of Operations (KTO) sat and were bombarded, taking a fierce pounding day and night. The B-52s hit them with area bombing, while Coalition fighter-bombers took them out vehicle by vehicle and gun by gun."[53] Lt. Col. David Deptula offered a clever turn of the familiar phrase: "we are not *preparing* battlefield, we are *destroying* it."[54] By the end of the war "the vast weight of the Coalition air effort in the war flew either

[47] Budiansky, *Air Power*, p. 424.
[48] Calvin Waller interview, *PBS Frontline: The Gulf War* (1996). Accessed at: www.pbs .org/wgbh/pages/frontline/gulf/oral/waller/1.html.
[49] Hallion, *Storm Over Iraq*, pp. 201–2.
[50] Frederick Franks interview, *PBS Frontline: The Gulf War* (1996). Accessed at: www.pbs .org/wgbh/pages/frontline/gulf/oral/franks/1.html.
[51] Calvin Waller interview, *PBS Frontline: The Gulf War*.
[52] Freedman and Karsh, *The Gulf Conflict, 1990–1991*, p. 328.
[53] Citino, *Blitzkrieg to Desert Storm*, p. 284.
[54] Hallion, *Storm Over Iraq*, p. 209.

directly against Iraqi ground forces in the Kuwait theater or against the supply lines to those forces."[55] General Glosson, refuting charges of insufficient attacks on Iraqi forces, points to the ease of the ground war in terms unlikely to make him many friends in the Army: "the bottom line is . . . how effective was the force confronting the ground forces when they started the war. I mean, if it had been any easier we should have sent a police force over there. I mean, it took only three days."[56]

A critical turning point came on February 13 when two stealth fighters attacked a bomb shelter in the Al Firdos section of Baghdad with two 2,000-lb laser-guided bombs. Intelligence reports identified the bunker as a command center and shelter for high-ranking government officials. When the smoke cleared, however, about 400 civilians, including women and children, were dead and many others wounded.[57] The images of Iraqi civilians killed by American bombs provided exactly the sort of public relations coup Saddam had hoped for all along but thus far been denied. Even before Al Firdos, Schwarzkopf admits, "we'd arrived at a time when we were retargeting targets that had already been hit several times within Baghdad, or we were targeting new command and control facilities that came up." By the middle of February "we'd gotten just about all we c[ould] out of the strategic bombing campaign down in Baghdad."[58] In the wake of Al Firdos, new orders were issued requiring approval at the highest levels for any further attacks in Baghdad. Consequently, "only five targets in Baghdad were hit during the remainder of the war."[59] Attention turned to final preparations for the ground invasion.

After five weeks of intense bombing of strategic and theater targets, Iraqi forces remained in Kuwait and showed no sign of budging. But there was no obvious military imperative for the ground war to start. Bombing could continue as needed, and Iraq's military position was certainly not going to improve. But the ground war could not be delayed indefinitely as hundreds of thousands of coalition forces waited in the desert. General Waller reflected the prevailing view: "We had 41 days of bombing, so how many more days do you need to bring them to their knees?. . . . ultimately, if you want to gain Kuwait back . . . you've got to go on the ground and take it back."[60] Even General Glosson, who opposed the post-Al Firdos easing of attacks in Baghdad, conceded that "when General Schwarzkopf decided to start the land war I thought that we had reached a point where it was in the best interests of the coalition and the nation to start the

---

[55] Keaney and Cohen, *Gulf War Air Power Survey*, p. 124.
[56] Buster Glosson interview, *PBS Frontline: The Gulf War* (1996). Accessed at: www.pbs .org/wgbh/pages/frontline/gulf/oral/glosson/1.html.
[57] Gordon and Trainor, *The Generals' War*, pp. 324–6.
[58] Schwarzkopf interview, *PBS Frontline: The Gulf War*.
[59] Pape, *Bombing to Win*, p. 230.
[60] Waller interview, *PBS Frontline: The Gulf War*.

land war."[61] Freedman and Karsh highlight the political, as opposed to military, imperative at work: "the only real factor that began to create pressure to get the land campaign underway was unease in the West over the judgment, implicit in the massive air campaign, that any number of Iraqi deaths was worth the reduction of risk to coalition forces."[62]

As the ground war loomed, what did the battlefield look like? How well had weeks of aerial bombardment "prepared" the battlefield for coalition forces? Although Glosson was no doubt engaging in a little exaggeration in suggesting that a random police force could have evicted the Iraqis after their aerial pounding, the theater (or tactical) air campaign certainly did exact a heavy toll, though there remains disagreement about its accomplishments. To evaluate the theater air campaign, one needs to focus on its logistical, material, and psychological objectives. Logistically, interdiction sought to prevent the reinforcement, resupply, and withdrawal of Iraqi forces in Kuwait. Materially, tank plinking and other attacks attempted to destroy as much Iraqi armor and artillery as possible. Psychologically, constant bombardment aimed to undermine Iraqi morale and the will to fight.

Interdiction is one of those tasks for which guided munitions are invaluable because it requires hitting relatively small targets from a distance such as bridges and railroads. Critical targets in Iraq were hit multiple times and were retargeted if repaired (e.g., pontoon bridges constructed to replace more permanent structures). There is little debate that these attacks proved extremely successful. By the time the ground war started "supply lines between Baghdad and the front were effectively severed: only four out of fifty-four railroad and highway bridges were undamaged and forty were inoperable."[63] Hallion goes so far as to claim that "the strategic air campaign achieved clear-cut interdiction of Iraqi transport into the Kuwaiti theater of operations. This was the first clearcut case of air interdiction in military aviation history."[64] These attacks undoubtedly reduced the flow of supplies into Kuwait. But there is less agreement on the effects. Even if the flow of reinforcements and supplies had been reduced to a trickle, this might not be a problem if the Iraqis already had enough manpower and supplies in place. The Iraqis, after all, had five months to move soldiers, fuel, ammunition, food, and water into Kuwait. At the end of the war, most Iraqi units still had sufficient supplies of ammunition and fuel to sustain them in battle for some time had they been inclined to fight. Iraqi resistance did not collapse for lack of supplies, though there were some serious shortages of food, water, and

[61] Glosson interview, *PBS Frontline: The Gulf War*.
[62] Freedman and Karsh, "How Kuwait Was Won," p. 31.
[63] Freedman and Karsh, *The Gulf Conflict, 1990–1991*, p. 389.
[64] Hallion, *Storm Over Iraq*, p. 193.

basic medical supplies, especially for frontline units, who were "generally in wretched health and malnourished"[65] when the coalition moved in. This was certainly no recipe for good morale or combat effectiveness. Providing some ammunition for air power enthusiasts, Pollack reports that "many Iraqi generals captured during the war opined that if the air campaign had been allowed to continue for two or three weeks, the Iraqi army would have been forced to withdraw from Kuwait as a result of logistical strangulation."[66]

The success of coalition efforts to destroy Iraqi armor and artillery by aerial attacks remains one of the most controversial issues in postwar assessments. The previously discussed tank plinking is a case in point. The technique succeeded in destroying a large number of tanks, as evidenced by postwar images of charred and mangled Iraqi tanks. But was this really a "wholesale slaughter of armored vehicles?"[67] Biddle notes that "while some units suffered nearly 100 percent tank losses, others were virtually untouched. Overall, Iraqi tank attrition averaged 48 percent, armored troop carrier losses were about 30 percent, and artillery losses were just under 60 percent."[68] These are high attrition rates, though Biddle seems more impressed by what survived than how much was destroyed. The problem is that Biddle's analysis depends on estimates of what the Iraqis had when the war began. Intelligence reports indicated slightly more than 4,000 Iraqi tanks at the start of the war, and Biddle reports that 2,000 remained at the end – hence the approximately fifty percent attrition rate. But Keaney, co-author of the *Gulf War Air Power Survey*, suggests that prewar estimates likely exaggerated Iraqi armor and artillery levels.[69] Even during the war, there were intense disagreements in battle damage assessment (BDA). Atkinson relates that in early February the military claimed 1,400 Iraqi tank kills, while the CIA verified only 358.[70] But even if the coalition had wanted to destroy every tank before the ground invasion, in 1991 "there were not enough smart munitions in the world to destroy the entire Iraqi armored force from the sky."[71]

One aspect of the theater air campaign about which there appears to be a universal agreement is its psychological impact in Iraqi forces. In the context of BDA debates, for example, Keaney argues that it is a mistake to dwell on quantitative indicators of material attrition because "the loss of equipment . . . was not decisive in any direct way." The bombing aimed at destroying Iraqi armor and artillery affected Iraqi soldiers whether

[65] Pape, *Bombing to Win*, p. 248.
[66] Pollack, *Arabs at War*, p. 246.
[67] Atkinson, *Crusade*, p. 264.
[68] Biddle, "Victory Misunderstood," p. 149.
[69] Keaney, "Surveying Gulf War Airpower," p. 35.
[70] Atkinson, *Crusade*, p. 265.
[71] House, *Combined Arms Warfare in the Twentieth Century*, p. 271.

or not it destroyed their equipment. The intensity of bombing and the ability to strike at any moment led Iraqi forces to lose "confidence that their equipment was going to do them any good" even if it survived.[72] Similarly, when Lambeth discusses tank plinking and round-the-clock bombardment of Iraqi forces, he argues that "the effect on enemy behavior was to heighten the individual soldier's sense of futility."[73] There is virtually no dissent from the conclusion that the theater air campaign had a devastating impact on Iraqi will and morale that went well beyond any quantitative measure of combat effectiveness. This would be evident as soon as the ground war began.

The Ground Campaign

The Iraqis prepared for a coalition attack across the Saudi–Kuwaiti border by constructing two elaborate defensive belts including minefields, barbed wire, ditches, and oil-filled trenches that became known as the "Saddam Line." The worst-case scenario was that coalition forces would have difficulty in breaching these defenses, perhaps getting trapped between the lines and attacked with chemical weapons. Even if they broke through, casualties in such a frontal assault could be high. Partly for this reason the main attack would take place elsewhere. During the air campaign, the coalition repositioned about 270,000 American, British, and French troops up to 250 miles westward into the desert along the Saudi–Iraqi border. Remarkably, the Iraqis apparently had no idea that a quarter of a million troops were being moved into position for an attack into Iraq itself: "coalition air power denied such information to the Iraqis, making it possible to convince them to defend against a bogus deployment of coalition forces while the actual deployment proceeded to flank, envelop, and engage them before they knew what was happening."[74] Coalition forces in the west would thus avoid "a frontal assault on the main Iraqi positions in Kuwait ... exploiting their speed, both mechanized and air-mobile, driving deep into the flank of the Iraqi positions, catching the defenders unprepared and literally facing the wrong way."[75] Avoiding the most extensive Iraqi defenses, the XVIII and VII Corps in the west were to move rapidly north, penetrating deep into Iraq before turning east to cut off Iraqi lines of communication, trap and isolate Iraqi forces in Kuwait, and destroy Iraqi forces encountered along the way, particularly the elite Republican Guard. This main attack to the west was supported

---

[72] Keaney, "Surveying Gulf War Airpower," p. 35.
[73] Lambeth, *The Transformation of American Air Power*, p. 125.
[74] Mann, *Thunder and Lightening*, p. 22. Pollack also explains that the Iraqis, lacking an appreciation of technologies such as GPS navigation, could not imagine how such an attack would be possible; see Pollack, *Arabs at War*, p. 239.
[75] Citino, *Blitzkreig to Desert Storm*, p. 287.

by two Marine assaults into the "heel" of Kuwait close to the Persian Gulf, where two defensive belts would have to be breached before heading north to Kuwait City. The supporting Marine attacks directly into Kuwait were designed to attract Iraqi forces and fix them in place as the flanking movement out west progressed.

Coalition ground forces finally attacked in the early morning hours of February 24. Schwarzkopf's Hail Mary out west, which Citino describes as "the most audacious decision in U.S. military history," worked exactly as planned, if not better.[76] Movement was rapid as troops involved in the sweep advanced 50 miles into Iraq on the first day and another 120 miles the next. This was possible in part because technology allowed coalition forces to move and fight both day and night: "Night-vision devices like low-altitude navigation infrared for night (LANTIRN), forward looking infrared (FLIR) pods on aircraft, thermal sights like thermal and optical gun sights (TOGS) and night-vision goggles for soldiers enabled the coalition to fight around the clock."[77] Many of the coalition's most intense engagements with Iraqi forces occurred at night, maximizing its technological advantages. Although not all the system's satellites were in place, GPS receivers in particular were critical in allowing coalition forces to navigate the desert terrain with few natural landmarks even in complete darkness. This western sweep clearly "dislocated Iraqi plans. . . . Iraqi command, control and communications systems had difficulty reacting in a timely manner to this threat to its right flank."[78] Reflecting their tremendous informational deficit, Iraqi leaders "apparently did not know of the shift until their Republican Guard formations were getting acquainted with VII Corps."[79]

Although Kagan is correct to remind us that "the ground advance into Iraq [and Kuwait] was not an unopposed movement consisting mainly of Iraqis demoralized by air strikes surrendering to advancing forces," it was soon clear to all that Iraqi forces were wildly overmatched on every level.[80] And although there certainly was a handful of intense battles and Iraqi counterattacks, "it was apparent after the first day that the land war would in effect be a walkover."[81] Iraqi frontline forces, consisting overwhelmingly of poorly trained and unmotivated conscripts and reservists, offered little resistance. As coalition forces approached their positions the Iraqis often surrendered in large numbers. Their morale, probably not very great from the start, suffered during "the most punishing air

---

[76] Ibid., p. 290.
[77] Finlan, *The Gulf War, 1991*, p. 86.
[78] House, *Combined Arms Warfare in the Twentieth Century*, p. 273.
[79] Citino, *Blitzkrieng to Desert Storm*, p. 290.
[80] Kagan, *Finding the Target*, p. 169.
[81] Freedman and Karsh, *The Gulf Conflict, 1990–1991*, p. 397.

assault in military history."[82] "Unable to attack or retreat in the face of Coalition air power," Iraqi troops "could only hunker down and continue to suffer mounting punishment, both physical and psychological, from the air."[83] One result was "massive desertions in the frontline infantry divisions . . . postwar studies suggest that about 100,000 desertions occurred across the theater." By the conclusion of the land war, coalition forces had to deal with the unexpected problem of thousands of POWs who preferred surrender to fighting. Interviews testified to the impact of bombing and the lack of basic supplies such as food and water, especially for frontline units. One prisoner indicated that thirty minutes of coalition bombing was worse than what he experienced in eight years of war with Iran.[84] Area bombing by B-52s "made the ground shake like a form of man-made earthquake" and as a result "the impact of these strikes on the morale of the average soldier on the ground was immense."[85]

On February 26, the Iraqi leadership finally grasped the gravity of the situation. The swift movement of coalition forces from the west risked trapping their forces in Kuwait. The order to withdraw was issued. JSTARS surveillance indicated a massive Iraqi exodus from Kuwait City along Highway 80 toward Basra in southern Iraq. Still pursuing the goal of reducing Iraqi military strength as part of preserving regional peace and security, coalition aircraft attacked the retreating column the night of February 26–27, leaving a trail of destruction miles long. Although we know about 1,500 vehicles were destroyed along what became known as the "highway of death," the number of soldiers and civilians killed remains a matter of controversy. Pictures of the devastation are now iconic images of the war because they seem to capture the lopsided nature of its outcome. But the attack made it appear as though the war had turned into little more than a high-tech turkey shoot, or, as one reporter described it, "a grim symphony of destruction."[86] The ease and magnitude of the destruction made many uneasy. Colin Powell explains that he "started to see some scenes that were unpleasant . . . [such as] at the so-called 'highway of death' where people were just being slaughtered as our planes went up and down."[87] Such concerns were among the reasons why President Bush decided to bring the war to end with a cease-fire effective at 8:00 A.M. on February 28, exactly 100 hours from the moment coalition forces initiated the ground attack.

---

[82] Citino, *Blitzkreig to Desert Storm*, p. 282.
[83] Keaney and Cohen, *Gulf War Air Power Survey*, p. 303.
[84] Budiansky, *Air Power*, p. 425.
[85] Finlan, *The Gulf War, 1991*, p. 35.
[86] Lambeth, *The Transformation of American Air Power*, p. 126.
[87] Colin Powell interview, *PBS Frontline: The Gulf War*.

Evaluating the First Iraq War

Debates about the effectiveness of the strategic and tactical air campaigns suggest that Lambeth was at best premature in assuring us that "the basic facts of Desert Storm are no longer in dispute."[88] That these "facts" will ever be established to everyone's satisfaction seems unlikely. After all, more than half a century later arguments persist about the achievements of the Combined Bomber Offensive against Germany in World War II. As important as these details of military effectiveness are, however, they are overshadowed by the larger debate about the meaning and significance of the Gulf War. The critical question is whether the Gulf War marked a turning point in the history of warfare, a new RMA. Many participants and observers clearly thought it did. General Horner, for example, asked to evaluate the Desert Storm air campaign in a broader historical context, judged that "in some ways the Gulf War is a watershed in the history of warfare, it is a revolution."[89] Richard Hallion agrees: "the Persian Gulf War will be studied by generations of military students, for it confirmed a major transformation in the nature of warfare."[90] Though obviously a tremendous military success for the United States, what was it about the war that led many to declare it proof of a new military revolution? Even before observers analyzed the conduct of the war carefully, the outcome alone raised suspicions that a military transformation might be underway. Rogers notes that RMAs can "often be recognized by the ease with which 'participating' armed forces can defeat 'nonparticipating' ones. An often-cited example is the blitzkrieg style of warfare developed by the Germans in the interwar period and unleashed against Poland and France in 1939–1940."[91] Shapiro echoes Rogers: "one harbinger of a military revolution is an *unexpected* or *extremely lopsided* victory."[92] At first glance, Desert Storm appears to fulfill the criteria.

What Kind of Victory?

Few outside of Baghdad could have been surprised by the coalition's victory. Given its advantages in both tangible and intangible elements of military power, the eventual outcome was overdetermined: "the United States . . . so overmatched its opponent in Baghdad that loss was inconceivable."[93] The most remarkable aspect of the war was not the outcome

---

[88] Lambeth, *The Transformation of American Air Power*, p. 104.
[89] Charles Horner interview, *PBS Frontline: The Gulf War.*
[90] Hallion, *Storm Over Iraq*, p. 1.
[91] Rogers, "'Military Revolutions' and 'Revolutions in Military Affairs,'" p. 23.
[92] Jeremy Shapiro, "Information and War: Is It a Revolution," p. 130, emphasis added.
[93] Stephen Cimbala, "Transformation in Concept and Policy," *Joint Force Quarterly* No. 38 (July 2005), p. 30.

per se but its lopsidedness. The 197 coalition battle deaths will surely become one of the more amazing and often cited statistics in military history, on par with the miniscule casualties colonial armies of the nineteenth century often suffered when they fought native forces lacking guns and machine guns. The coalition's casualty rate was historically unprecedented – "less than one-tenth of the Israelis' in either the Six-Day War or the Bekka Valley campaign in 1982, less than one-twentieth of the Germans' in their blitzkriegs against Poland and France in 1939–40, and one-one-thousandth of the U.S. Marines' in the invasion of Tarwara in 1943."[94] Indeed, losses were "so low that American males were safer in the war zone than in peacetime conditions in the United States."[95]

Although Shapiro cites unexpected *or* lopsided victory as signifying a possible military revolution, it is probably more useful to think in terms of unexpected *and* lopsided victories. A lopsided defeat of Grenada, for example, would not indicate a military revolution because the disparity of power was so great that the outcome could be explained on that basis alone. Similarly, the success of Germany's blitzkrieg against France was more telling than against Poland because the former was a substantial military power that should have been able to resist. The overwhelming defeat of Poland was expected; the rout of France was not. Thus, we should view *unexpectedly lopsided victories* as possible harbingers of military revolutions. Was the coalition's victory in the Gulf War unexpectedly lopsided? There is disagreement.

While no one views Iraq in 1991 as a paragon of military excellence, there are varying assessments of Iraqi military prowess. For some, the war's lopsided outcome is remarkable because Iraq should not have been a pushover. According to Berkowitz, "Iraq had the third largest army in the world and had just killed 300,000 Iranians in eight years of the most gruesome warfare of the twentieth century."[96] Iraq possessed some of the most advanced (largely Soviet) weapons Saddam could buy with his country's substantial oil wealth. And as a result of eight years of war with Iran, Iraqi soldiers and officers were experienced and battle-hardened. Whatever its shortcomings in leadership, training, and professionalism, it was probably the most powerful military the United States faced since the end of World War II. It was more than capable of putting up a fight and inflicting a lot of damage. This is among the reasons why Citino thinks "Desert Storm was the most successful campaign in U.S. military history." He emphasizes the scale and magnitude of the military accomplishment: the United States "evict[ed] a huge mechanized army out

---

[94] Stephen Biddle, *Military Power*, p. 133.
[95] Grant T. Hammond, "Myths of the Gulf War: Some Lessons Not to Learn," *Airpower Journal* (Fall 1998), p. 6.
[96] Berkowitz, *The New Face of War*, p. 2.

of its heavily fortified positions and then destroyed it at almost nonexistent cost. Coalition forces destroyed more than thirty divisions, captured or destroyed nearly four thousand tanks, and took almost ninety thousand prisoners in less than four days of fighting. It ranks with the great annihilation battles of all time."[97] In this framing, the outcome is significant because it came against a genuinely formidable military power.[98]

Not everyone, however, sees Desert Storm in these terms. The *Gulf War Air Power Survey*, for example, casts the outcome in a somewhat different light, claiming that "at a distance of two years and after careful scrutiny of the evidence, some aspects of the war that seemed most dramatic at the time appear less so than they did in the immediate afterglow of one of the most lopsided campaigns in military history." The outcome is less surprising in retrospect because "despite the talk of Iraq possessing the fourth largest army in the world, the fact remains that in this war a *minor military power* found itself confronted by the full weight of the world's sole superpower."[99] The terminology here is telling: the lopsided defeat of the "world's third largest army" seems more impressive and unexpected than crushing a "minor military power." Daryl Press goes so far as to argue that "the Iraqis fielded a military that was *mediocre even by third world standards*."[100] John Mueller also questions the significance of Desert Storm, arguing that the war "was over before it began" because it was fought against "an enemy that ha[d] little in the way of effective defenses, strategy, tactics, planning, morale, or leadership."[101] And though cautioning that his assessment "is not a commentary on the outstanding performance of American soldiers," Adrian Lewis thinks "the Iraqi Army deserved considerable credit for it defeat. It was one of the worst led, worst fought forces in the history of warfare."[102] Thus, analysts do not agree on whether Desert Storm was an unexpectedly easy military triumph over a genuinely formidable foe or a readily explainable victory over an enemy that appeared mighty on paper but was a military Potemkin village in reality. Observers who see the war as the former are more likely to suspect that a military revolution is underway.

---

[97] Citino, *Blitzkrieg to Desert Storm*, p. 288.

[98] Adrian R. Lewis provides quite an inventory of prewar military analyses that portrayed the Iraqi military a well-equipped and battle-tested foe capable of a putting up a real fight in *The American Culture of War: The History of U.S. Military Force from World War II to Operation Iraqi Freedom* (New York: Routledge, 2007), pp. 321–5.

[99] Keaney and Cohen, *Gulf War Air Power Survey*, pp. 308–9, emphasis added.

[100] Daryl G. Press, "The Myth of Air Power in the Persian Gulf War and the Future of Warfare," *International Security* Vol. 26, No. 2 (Fall 2001), p. 7, emphasis added.

[101] John Mueller, "The Perfect Enemy: Assessing the Gulf War," *Security Studies* Vol. 5, No. 1 (Autumn 1995), pp. 79 and 111.

[102] Lewis, *The American Culture of War*, p. 340.

What Kind of "Revolution?"

Even if the outcome of the Gulf War was unexpectedly lopsided, this does not prove the existence of a revolution; it is merely a red flag suggesting that something important may be happening, an invitation to further analysis. In addition to the lopsided outcome, the appearance of a suite of new technologies and weapons lent initial credence to claims of a new RMA. Stealth fighters, laser- and satellite-guided munitions, JSTARS and AWACS, the global positioning satellites, and other systems appeared to make possible what once seemed like science fiction. Indeed, the outcome was often explained as a result of these technologies. Although many of the weapons appeared on a smaller scale or in embryonic form in earlier wars, their combined use on a large scale in Desert Storm suggested that some critical mass had been achieved or threshold surpassed. And even though almost everyone involved in the debate cautions that technological change alone does not make an RMA, the combination of easy victory and new weapons fueled speculation about a new RMA in the aftermath of Desert Storm. But in the end, even the combination of a lopsided outcome and new technologies is merely suggestive of an RMA.

The evidence of whether the Gulf War marked the beginning of an RMA is ultimately to be found in the war's conduct, not its outcome. Because RMAs involve changes in the character of warfare, the question is whether there was anything revolutionary about the manner in which the war was waged. More than a few observers thought there was, focusing on three potentially revolutionary aspects of the war: the dominance of air power, the reliance on precision targeting, and the dramatic improvement in information technologies and situational awareness. One of the first to weigh in was John Warden, the architect of the strategic air campaign. He deemed the conflict as the first "hyperwar" which "capitalize[d] on high technology, unprecedented accuracy, operational and strategic surprise through stealth, and the ability to bring all of the enemy's key operational and strategic nodes under near simultaneous attack." Warden emphasized how stealth and precision revolutionized air power in particular, allowing the coalition to suppress Iraqi air defenses in short order and establish air supremacy. From that point on, Iraq "had in fact become an occupied state – from the air." He had no doubt that "the world ha[d] just witnessed a new kind of warfare."[103]

Given the length of the air campaign compared to the ground war, it is understandable that observers and participants alike focused on changes in air power as one of the potentially revolutionary aspects of the war. General Horner, for example, pointed out that "it was the first time the

---

[103] Kagan, *Finding the Target*, p. 161.

air campaign was the dominant plan, all other plans were supporting that plan."[104] Desert Storm represented the first war in which the ground campaign appeared to support the air campaign rather than vice versa. Although there was disagreement on which portions of the air campaign deserved credit, claims that air power was "decisive" or "won" the war were commonplace. Air Force Chief of Staff General Merrill McPeak claimed air power "came of age as a *decisive* element in combined-arms warfare" during Desert Storm, which was "the first time in history that a fielded army had been defeated by air power."[105] Richard Hallion argues that while "few expected it to be the war's decisive force," it turns out that "air power won the Gulf War." This was "a victory that, in its swiftness, decisiveness, and scope, came from the wise and appropriate application of air power by courageous men and women, *assisted by* their comrades on the ground and at sea."[106] Finally, according to George and Meredith Friedman, "to argue that airpower was not decisive, it would be necessary to argue that, even without the successful six-week air campaign, the ground assault could have been concluded in a matter of days with almost no casualties," a position they characterize as a "fantasy."[107] Such observations reflect a belief that Desert Storm revealed a new formula for military victory, one in which the relative importance and contribution of air power increased substantially, even if it did not win the war on its own.

This increased reliance on air power was a consequence of technologies, most importantly guided munitions, which made it possible to attack new targets in new ways. The *Gulf War Air Power Survey* explains that "it would not have occurred to air planners during World War II, for example, to think that one might systematically attack an enemy's entire telephone system, even if one could, on extraordinary occasions, conduct isolated precision attacks against pieces of it."[108] For Budiansky, the ability "to strike at the heart of an enemy city with only minimal risk to civilians" constituted an "astonishing revolution in the nature of warfare."[109] Lambeth claims boldly that "laser-guided bombs (LGBs) largely swung the outcome of the 1991 Gulf war."[110] And Boot claims that "the most revolutionary weapons system of all in 1991 was a stealth attack aircraft equipped with two-thousand pound laser guided bombs."[111] A similar theme runs through such observations: the revolution in airpower was

---

[104] Charles Horner interview, *PBS Frontline: The Gulf War.*
[105] Lambeth, *The Transformation of American Air Power*, p. 4, emphasis added.
[106] Hallion, *Storm Over Iraq*, pp. 1 and 239, emphasis added. Needless to say, the idea that ground forces merely "assisted" in the defeat of Iraq was not universally shared.
[107] Friedman and Friedman, *The Future of War*, p. 254.
[108] Keaney and Cohen, *Gulf War Air Power Survey*, p. 300.
[109] Budiansky, *Air Power*, p. 429.
[110] Lambeth, *Transformation of American Air Power*, p. 160.
[111] Boot, *War Made New*, p. 328.

largely dependent on improvements in precision guidance technologies. If stealth aircraft had been armed with old-fashioned unguided bombs, not much about the use of air power would have changed. Attacking targets would still have required mass effort – that is, lots of planes dropping lots of bombs in the hope that some might land on their intended targets.

Guided munitions were revolutionary not only because they make certain categories of targets vulnerable for the first time, but also, somewhat less obviously, because they increase the *number* of targets that can be attacked. In the era of unguided munitions, it was generally necessary to plan an air campaign in terms of the number of sorties per target because any one sortie had only a small chance of success. With guided munitions dramatically increasing the likelihood of a single sortie's success, it becomes possible to plan in terms of the number of targets per sortie, thus reversing the historical equation and making possible "an economy of force never before seen in air war."[112] Watts explains that "the realization that LGBs provided the wherewithal for a single fighter-bomber to attack multiple aim points or targets on a single mission.... was a watershed for TAC [Tactical Air Command] and the Air Force."[113] This is the key to the concept of "parallel warfare" in which "hundreds of targets can be attacked in one day and reattacks can outpace repairs."[114] This was evident in the first hours of Desert Storm. The *Gulf War Air Power Survey* explains that "the concept of *what* to attack to disorganize and paralyze an enemy nation did not differ substantially from previous air campaigns." What changed was the *ability* to attack these targets. As a result, "the Coalition achieved successes against some of these target systems (especially strategic air defenses and electric power) extraordinarily quickly – what took a day or two to accomplish in this conflict might have taken months in others."[115] According to Kagan, "they called this sort of attack 'parallel war,' and *rightly believed* that it represented a fundamental transformation in warfare."[116]

The Iraqis did not anticipate, and were unable to cope with, the phenomenon of parallel war in which they were attacked relentlessly and simultaneously throughout Kuwait and Iraq. According to Pollack, "the Iraqis expected fighting would be characterized by brief, sharp clashes followed by long periods of regrouping and reorganization." And even though "Baghdad clearly recognized the Coalition would be able to rely on air power to greater extent than had Iran" in the 1980s, they

[112] Friedman and Friedman, *The Future of War*, p. 278.
[113] Watts, *Six Decades of Guided Munitions and Battle Networks*, p. 260.
[114] Mann, *Thunder and Lightening*, p.103.
[115] Keaney and Cohen, *Gulf War Air Power Survey*.
[116] Kagan, *Finding the Target*, p. 123, emphasis added. A similar argument can be found in Steven M. Schneider, *Parallel Warfare: A Strategy for the Future* (Fort Leavenworth, KS: U.S. Army Command and General Staff College, 1998).

"nevertheless expected that combat would be limited to the front lines and the rear areas would generally be as quiet as in the Iran-Iraq War."[117] But as Cohen and other RMA theorists have argued, the very concept of front and rear areas was becoming obsolete as technological advances in surveillance, stealth, and precision obviated the need for serial or sequential operations.[118]

It is possible to exaggerate the role of guided munitions in the Gulf War. The Tofflers make the useful observation that "the United States and its allies simultaneously fought two very different wars" against Iraq: "one war in Iraq was fought with Second Wave weapons designed to create mass destruction. Very little of that war was shown on the world's video screens; the other war was fought with Third Wave weapons designed for pinpoint accuracy, customized destruction and minimal 'collateral damage.' That war was shown."[119] As noted earlier, less than ten percent of munitions used in the Gulf War were guided. By this crude measure the Tofflers' "second wave" war was many times larger than the "third wave" war. It is also possible to overstate the precision and reliability of guided munitions, which did not hit their intended targets 100 percent of the time. A laser-guided bomb, for example, only hits its target if the laser designator remains on the target until impact. Even the Department of Defense admitted that laser-guided bombs from F-117s hit their targets only 80 percent of the time, not quite the "one target, one bomb" some claimed. Other studies suggested the rate was even lower, between 41 and 60 percent.[120] But even if the lower accuracy figures are correct, two or three bombs would virtually guarantee a target's destruction, a vast improvement over the three hundred required in Vietnam.[121] And although one should not rely too heavily on anecdotal evidence, journalists in Baghdad were consistently amazed at the accuracy of bombs dropped in the city. The *New Republic's* Michael Kelly, for example, recalls touring Baghdad the morning after the first attacks. The scene was uncanny, almost eerie. The Iraqi Ministry of Defense, he reported, was reduced to "burning rubble" while "the hospital next to it...was untouched, and so were the homes that surrounded it."[122]

As a result of the combination of stealth and precision, more than a few observers claimed that air power finally came of age in the Gulf War in the sense that technological advances allowed it to fulfill the vision of earlier

---

[117] Pollack, *Arabs at War*, p. 257.
[118] Steven Schneider (writing in 1998) claimed that "Desert Storm [was] the first and only test of parallel warfare on a total scale." See Schneider, *Parallel Warfare*, p. 28.
[119] Heidi and Alvin Toffler, *War and Anti-War*, p. 65.
[120] See *Operation Desert Storm: Evaluation of the Air Campaign* (Washington, DC: General Accounting Office, 1997), pp. 1 and 24–5. For the DoD "success" entailed hitting within ten feet of the aim point.
[121] Friedman and Friedman, *The Future of Warfare*, p. 269.
[122] In Hallion, *Storm Over Iraq*, p. 197.

theorists. This is only partly correct and depends on which theorist one is referring to. Contrary to visions of many early air power theorists, for example, "there were no serious proposals to attack the regime through direct assaults on the civilian population and its morale."[123] And rather than focusing on industrial and economic targets broadly, "the Desert Storm air campaign sought preeminently to disorganize the 'central nervous system' of the enemy."[124] In restricting the range of targets, George and Meredith Friedman argue that "Air Force planners reacted *against* the radical presumptions of earlier theorists – that air power was supposed to assault the industrial base or even social fabric" of the enemy. What the world saw in Desert Storm "was the coming together of an extremely conservative war-fighting doctrine and an extremely advanced war fighting technology."[125] New technologies allowed war planners to transcend, not fulfill, the vision of many earlier theorists.

While some viewed stealthy F-117s or guided munitions as embodying a new RMA based on air power or precision targeting, others pointed to systems such as JSTARS and AWACS as the leading edge of an RMA driven by radical improvements in surveillance and communications. This is reflected in claims that the Gulf War was the first "information war" in which the coalition's dramatic advantage in situational awareness allowed it to exploit its advantages in stealth and precision. From this perspective, the critical systems were the planes, UAVs, and satellites that located targets and disseminated information to commanders and pilots. Pointing to these systems, Finlan notes "GPS allowed unprecedented levels of accuracy concerning battlefield navigation ... [and] JSTARS offered previously unheard of real-time access to the overall strategic picture on the ground."[126] Mann presents a glowing picture of the results: "with observation platforms such as TR-1 and JSTARS linked directly (or through AWACS) to both command elements and fighting elements, coalition forces could spot, target, attack and destroy Iraqi armor and supply columns, literally in minutes."[127] Although he recognizes the importance of stealth and precision guidance, Eliot Cohen focuses on the centrality of information in the Gulf War: "the most profound change in military technology ... was the vast increase in usable and communicable information."[128]

Although it may be true that "the capacity of U.S. military forces to collect and disseminate information during the campaign was without

[123] Freedman and Karsh, "How Kuwait Was Won," p. 19.
[124] Keaney and Cohen, *The Gulf War Air Power Survey*, p. 291.
[125] Friedman and Friedman, *The Future of Warfare*, pp. 257 and 258.
[126] Finlan, *The Gulf War, 1991*, p. 87.
[127] Mann, "Desert Storm: The First Information War," p. 3.
[128] Eliot A. Cohen, "The Mystique of U.S. Air Power," *Foreign Affairs* Vol. 73, No. 1 (January/February 1994), p. 110.

historical precedent," it is easy to overstate the case.[129] The coalition's situational awareness did not, for example, prevent a regrettably large number of friendly fire incidents during the ground campaign that resulted in thirty-five American deaths, or twenty percent of all casualties.[130] Theater commanders also complained that it took too long to receive needed information through normal channels. Ground commanders often resorted to informal networks to acquire the intelligence they needed.[131] General Walt Boomer, who led the Marine assault into Kuwait, was not shy in expressing his frustration: "the intelligence stunk. I mean it was lousy. We didn't have all the pictures that we needed...Doesn't do you any good if you've got all these great pictures back in Washington, if I can't get them to the platoon commander. Then the hell with it."[132] The need to improve real-time access to information was one of the major lessons of the war.

Although discussions of the Gulf War's revolutionary nature tend to focus on the air campaign, advanced technologies also contributed to the ground campaign's success. Schwarzkopf's "Hail Mary" pass to the west, for example, was facilitated by satellite navigation (GPS) that allowed coalition forces to move through the desert day and night. The American M1A1 tank was equipped with battle sights and sensors that allowed it to attack Iraqi forces from a distance of 2,400 meters, or 600 meters before the Iraqis could even see them. Such technologies contributed to the extremely lopsided outcome of the few battles fought during the four-day campaign. The statistics are telling: the Iraqis did not destroy or penetrate a single M1 tank, and the coalition used only two percent of the 220,000 rounds of ammunition shipped to the Gulf.[133] There is no doubt that revolutionary technologies made coalition ground forces much more effective and lethal. But was there anything fundamentally new or revolutionary about the manner in which the ground campaign was waged?

Most of the debate centers on whether the campaign embodied the basic tenets of AirLand Battle developed in the 1980s to counter a Soviet invasion of Europe. Explaining that the doctrine "called for attacking the Red Army rear echelons, seizing the initiative, outmaneuvering the enemy, and using a variety of weapons simultaneously to produce a counteroffensive that would be 'rapid, unpredictable, violent, and disorienting to the

---

[129] William C. Martell, *Victory in War: Foundations of Modern Military Policy* (Cambridge: Cambridge University Press, 2006), p. 190.

[130] Sharon Crenson and Martha Mendoza, "Friendly Fire Worries Still Plague Military 12 years After Persian Gulf War," *AP News Service* (March 5, 2003). Accessed at: www.globalsecurity.org/org/news/2003/030305-friendly01.htm.

[131] Mann, *Thunder and Lightening*, p. 151.

[132] Walt Boomer interview, *PBS Frontline: The Gulf War* (1996).

[133] Mahnken, *Technology and the American Way of War Since 1945*, p. 133; Lambeth, *The Transformation of American Air Power*, p. 129.

enemy,'" Max Boot concludes that "this was in essence the strategy put to use in Desert Storm . . . AirLand Battle proved ideally suited to counter Soviet-style tank armies in the deserts of the Middle East."[134] Without specific reference to AirLand Battle but focusing on one of its key elements, Biddle notes that "Desert Storm supported its breakthrough effort with an extensive deep battle program. Iraqi command posts, communications systems, transportation arteries, logistical nodes and reserve troop concentrations were struck almost simultaneously across the theater." Although skeptical of exaggerated claims about its accomplishments, Biddle argues, "The Desert Storm deep battle program . . . represented the twentieth century's most extensive implementation of modern-system deep attack."[135] The Tofflers, Harry Summers, and Robert Paquin agree that Desert Storm implemented the tenets of AirLand Battle.[136] This is not a universally shared assessment.

Richard Hallion focuses on the revolutionary aspects of the air campaign, arguing that too many observers "mistakenly credit the appearance of *elements* of AirLand Battle for the decisive application of the *entire* doctrine." Because aerial attacks neutralized Iraqi forces in advance of the ground campaign "AirLand Battle . . . could not really occur."[137] Similarly, Citino finds it "difficult to see the hand of AirLand Battle in this conflict. Rather, it would be more accurate to say that it was an air-land battle." Here, Citino is questioning whether Desert Storm integrated and coordinated ground and aerial attacks as called for in AirLand Battle. Instead, he sees Desert Storm as consisting of distinct air and land battles rather than a synchronized "AirLand" battle: "it opened with a long, immense, and tremendously successful air campaign that destroyed the Iraqi command net, a large part of the Iraqi army in Kuwait, and the logistics and communications lines that linked the two." Only after the air campaign achieved its objectives, did the coalition initiate a "well designed land operation."[138] This is not how AirLand Battle envisaged a war with the Soviet Union. Indeed, one could argue that the very idea of a separate air campaign represents a rejection of AirLand Battle.

Assessing whether Desert Storm embodied AirLand Battle is difficult because the doctrine was originally conceived as a response to a Soviet invasion of Western Europe. In this scenario, there would have been no time for a separate air campaign. The military tasks undertaken as

---

[134] Max Boot, *War Made New*, p. 333.
[135] Steven Biddle, *Military Power*, p. 140.
[136] Toffler and Toffler, *War and Anti-War*, p. 86; Harry G. Summers Jr., *On Strategy II: A Critical Analysis of the Gulf War* (New York: Dell, 1992), pp. 157–9; and Robert J. Paquin, *Desert Storm: Doctrinal AirLand Battle or "The American Way of War"* (Fort Leavenworth, KS: United States Army Command and General Staff College, 1999).
[137] Hallion, *Storm Over Iraq*, p. 252.
[138] Citino, *Blitzkrieg to Desert Storm*, p. 289.

different phases in Desert Storm would have been simultaneous in such a scenario. Rear echelon forces and resupply routes, for example, would have been attacked while frontline troops were being engaged. In January 1991, however, Iraq did not invade Saudi Arabia. Iraqi forces remained in Kuwait. This allowed rear echelon forces and resupply routes to be attacked before frontline ground engagements. As a result, all of the elements of AirLand Battle may have been present in Desert Storm, but not in their envisaged sequence. Thus, whether Desert Storm was faithful to AirLand Battle depends on whether it requires a particular sequencing of its elements.

While some were debating the precise nature and extent of the military revolution revealed in 1991, others were questioning whether there was anything revolutionary about the war at all. Not surprisingly, Stephen Biddle is among those most unimpressed by its revolutionary credentials, emphasizing "the Gulf War's failure to provide evidence for a revolution in military affairs."[139] Challenging prevailing wisdom about the war, Biddle argues that RMA proponents drew the wrong lessons in interpreting it as a triumph of technology that allowed the United States and its allies to defeat the Iraqis at a radically low cost. He frames the debate about the Gulf War and the RMA in terms of competing explanations or theories for the war's result. The "orthodox" account "explains the war's one-sidedness in terms of the Coalition's strengths, especially its advanced technology, which is often held to have destroyed the Iraqis' equipment or broken their will to fight."[140] "The air technology explanation" in particular "implies that Iraqi resistance had been *eliminated* before the ground war began."[141] Biddle notes that this was obviously not so: about 2,000 Iraqi tanks survived and some Iraqi units actually put up a fight. Coalition forces did have to battle their way through Iraqi defenses by employing modern system tactics. On this, Biddle is absolutely correct, but it seems as though he is constructing and attacking a straw man. Contrary to his assertion, there is nothing in the air technology explanation implying that Iraqi resistance was *eliminated* by the air campaign. In terms of explaining the war's outcome, the claim is that almost six weeks of relentless aerial bombing greatly *diminished* Iraqi resistance, thus facilitating a quick low-casualty ground campaign. Biddle ultimately rejects the air technology explanation and claims of a new RMA because a few battles took place in which Coalition forces successfully employed modern system tactics while the Iraqis did not. But even Biddle's gripping account of those battles cannot change that fact that the most remarkable aspect of "Desert Storm's final 100 hours is not that some Iraqi ground

[139] Biddle, "Victory Misunderstood," p. 177, emphasis added.
[140] Ibid., p. 148.
[141] Biddle, *Military Power*, p. 149, emphasis added.

units survived to fight, but how *few* ground engagements occurred and the comparatively small scale of those that did."[142]

Having rejected the orthodox explanation, Biddle presents a "new theory" that "a synergistic interaction between a major skill imbalance and new technology caused the radical outcome of 1991."[143] He readily admits that "for the new theory as well as the old, advanced technology is *necessary* to explain a historically unprecedented low U.S. loss rate."[144] This new theory, however, involves an important concession: without the technologies associated with the RMA a victory at such low cost could not have been achieved. Biddle sees the war's outcome as a result of superior technology combined with Coalition skill and Iraqi ineptitude. It is impossible to argue with this commonsensical conclusion, and Biddle fails to cite anyone who does. Certainly those who advocated a greater reliance on advanced technologies would willingly grant that technological advantages per se are never going to win wars, and they did not win the Gulf War.[145] Technology always needs to be employed and exploited skillfully. Both are essential. This is part of the reason the adoption of new technologies in the 1970s and 1980s was accompanied by improvements in training. This explains why RMA militaries rely increasingly on highly trained professionals rather than short-term conscripts.

Biddle's argument about the lack of revolutionary change in the Gulf War ultimately rests on his understanding of the modern system. Even though "U.S. surveillance, precision guidance, and air defense suppression technologies gave American air power *radical new lethality*," the Gulf War was not won with aerial firepower alone.[146] The hopes of Warden and others for victory without ground combat did not materialize, and whether continued bombing might have forced an Iraqi withdrawal is sheer speculation. Coalition forces eventually engaged the Iraqis on the ground. Aerial attacks degraded Iraqi capabilities substantially; they did not completely eliminate the ability or willingness of some units to fight. When faced with Iraqi resistance, Coalition forces successfully employed modern system tactics and operations, resulting in favorable

[142] Thomas G. Mahnken and Barry D. Watts, "What the Gulf War Can (and Cannot) Tell Us about the Future of Warfare," *International Security* Vol. 22, No. 2 (Fall 1997), p. 159.

[143] Biddle, "Victory Misunderstood," p. 140. In *Military Power* (2004), Biddle presents his new explanation in terms of the combination of new technology and "superior force employment."

[144] Biddle, *Military Power*, p. 146, emphasis added.

[145] Responding to Biddle, Daryl G. Press argues that American advantages in skill and technology in the Gulf War were so great that either would have been sufficient to produce lopsided battle outcomes. He notes, however, that the absence of any engagements between American forces and equally skilled Iraqis precludes any definitive conclusions. See "Lessons from Ground Combat in the Gulf: The Impact of Training and Technology," *International Security* Vol. 22, No. 2 (Fall 1997), pp. 137–46.

[146] Biddle, *Military Power*, p. 135.

outcomes with minimal losses. Because an RMA must render the modern system obsolete, any war involving significant ground combat in which battle success depends on skillful force employment provides evidence of continuity rather than change.

Other analyses of the Gulf War reached a more equivocal conclusion, withholding judgment on whether the Gulf War was revolutionary. The exhaustive *Gulf War Air Power Survey* provides a more moderate and tentative evaluation. While recognizing that "the ingredients for a transformation of war may well have become visible in the Gulf War," it cautions that "it is probably too soon to conclude without reservation that we have entered a new era of warfare."[147] The *Survey*'s authors are hesitant to proclaim an RMA in part because "the majority of the military systems and operational concepts central to the Desert Storm air campaign ... had historical precedents." Guided munitions, for example, were used in Vietnam almost two decades earlier and, "with few exceptions, the planners of Desert Storm used the same target categories as in previous wars."[148] They are quick to note, however, that this does not disprove the existence of an RMA because "even if the technologies and concepts were not new, the ways in which Coalition forces used them were."[149] That guided munitions were used previously is not critical for judging whether the Gulf War was revolutionary. What matters is how they were used and what they achieved. In the Gulf War, greater numbers of more accurate guided munitions were deployed against a much wider range of targets in a shorter period of time. On some levels, this can be seen as a difference of degree, not kind. There comes a point, however, when differences of degree grow so large as to become differences in kind. The *Survey* hints that this may be the strongest basis for viewing the Gulf War as revolutionary: "in this war, air power crossed some operational thresholds that, if not as obvious as the initial use of a new weapon or operational concept, did suggest a transformation of war."[150] In other words, "quantitative changes in the conduct of war have a way of becoming qualitative transformations."[151] If the Gulf War did not yet mark a "qualitative transformation," things were certainly headed in that direction.

Conclusion

For nearly fifteen years the American military tried to recover from the debacle of Vietnam while trying to counter the Soviet Union's military challenge. New weapons, improved training, and innovative doctrine were developed so that NATO's numerically inferior forces might prevail

---

[147] Keaney and Cohen, *Gulf War Air Power Survey*, p. 309.
[148] Ibid., pp. 294–5.
[149] Ibid., p. 298.
[150] Ibid., p. 299.
[151] Ibid., pp. 298–9.

in the event of a Soviet invasion. For some, these military reforms were more than a specific response to a particular challenge – they were manifestations a new technology-driven RMA. Although no one expected American military power or claims of an RMA to be put to the test against Iraq, in retrospect this was not such a bad test. Citino explains that "although the American military never fought the battle for which it had prepared so long . . . it now got its chance to cross swords with a large, heavy mechanized force organized and trained more or less on the Soviet model."[152] In Iraq the United States confronted an opponent "that had been a constant friend and beneficiary of the Soviets, whose military machine was modeled on the Soviet style of command and tactical doctrine, and which was equipped overwhelmingly with the products of Soviet technology."[153] Although the war was fought in the Arabian Desert rather than on the plains of Europe, the United States had the good fortune to face an enemy that was essentially a smaller and less competent version of the Soviet military it had prepared for. In terms of military performance, the test was passed, though some question the exam's difficulty.

The Gulf War did more than demonstrate American military power. It also shaped debates about the direction of American defense policy and the future of warfare generally. Whatever one's opinion about the war's revolutionary nature, it is hard to disagree with Biddle's claim that it "changed the whole course of American military thought."[154] While a handful of analysts and strategists discussed the possibility of an RMA before the war, its lopsided outcome, the apparent success of guided munitions, the increased effectiveness of air power, and the importance of information technologies convinced many others that a fundamental change in warfare was indeed underway. What had been the speculation of a few was increasingly accepted as common wisdom. Department of Defense documents and vision statements came to assume the existence of an RMA in the aftermath of the Gulf War. But was this the right lesson?

The *Gulf War Air Power Survey* probably strikes the right tone of possibility balanced with caution. There undoubtedly were elements of the Gulf War supporting the case for an RMA. The large-scale use of guided weapons, for example, held out the promise of reversing the industrial age reliance on mass to compensate for inaccuracy. In air warfare this made it possible to strike large numbers of targets reliably in a short period of time with little collateral damage even in densely populated areas. Less than fifty years after conventional and nuclear weapons reduced Hamburg, Dresden, Tokyo, and Hiroshima to ruins from the air, this alone seems revolutionary. As a result, it is simply difficult to accept

---

[152] Citino, *Blitzkrieg to Desert Storm*, p. 275.
[153] Hallion, *Storm Over Iraq*, p. 81.
[154] Biddle, *Military Power*, p. 133.

alone seems revolutionary. As a result, it is simply difficult to accept the conclusion that the Gulf War failed to provide any evidence of an RMA. Did the Gulf War provide *compelling* and *conclusive* evidence of an RMA? Probably not. But it strains credulity to argue that there was no evidence of a possible RMA. Perhaps we have grown so accustomed to technological advances that what seems revolutionary one day is regarded as unremarkable the next.

Similarly, bold claims that the Gulf War unquestionably marked the dawn of a new age of warfare need to be tempered by the recognition that it is difficult to draw such sweeping conclusions from on a single conflict, particularly one that lasted only a few weeks. With a sample of one it is always easy to make unwarranted generalizations by mistaking unique events for emerging trends. Even many who suspected that the Gulf War might be a turning point worried that it was too anomalous to support any general conclusion. According to Lawrence Freedman, for example, "because the Gulf War was so one-sided, it provided an opportunity to display in a most flattering light the potential of modern military systems. It was as if Saddam had been asked to organize his forces in such a way as to offer coalition countries the opportunity to show off their forces to the best advantage."[155] This is not very unusual, however. As MacGregor Knox and Williamson Murray point out, "virtually every other revolution in military affairs has required a victim whose battlefield inadequacies have accentuated the disparity between old and new."[156] The Gulf War certainly did that. The question is whether the war would have seemed as revolutionary if the sides had been more evenly matched. Would the revolution in air power, for example, have been as striking against an enemy unwilling to concede air superiority from the outset? Would air power and guided munitions have been as effective in degrading Iraqi forces were it not for a desert terrain that afforded them few opportunities to hide? The *Gulf War Air Power Survey* concluded that a final verdict on the RMA would have to await future wars waged in a variety of settings against different opponents. And because an endless series of lopsided engagements against inferior adversaries could be equally inconclusive, it might require "a sterner test against a more capable adversary."[157] There were more tests to come, but given the post–Cold War disparity in military power in favor of the United States, capable adversaries were few and far between.

[155] Freedman, *The Revolution in Strategic Affairs*, p. 29.
[156] Knox and Murray, "The Future Behind Us," p. 188.
[157] Keaney and Cohen, *Gulf War Air Power Survey*, p. 298.

4 THE IRAQI INTERREGNUM, 1991–2000

The Calm After the Storm

It is hard to argue with success, and there is little doubt that Desert Storm was a success, at least in military terms. Certainly the war revealed deficiencies, and nothing is ever perfect. But on the whole, the war's result was taken as a vindication of American defense policy over the preceding fifteen years. Not everyone had been convinced that the United States was on the right track. Politicians and defense analysts associated with the "military reform movement" in the early 1980s, for example, viewed with suspicion the Defense Department's fascination or fixation with high-tech weapons they considered too expensive, complex, and unreliable. Better they thought to acquire a larger quantity of cheaper weapons that worked than some technological marvel prone to break-down that might be too expensive to risk losing in battle.[1] The Gulf War appeared to resolve this debate as key weapons systems performed better than even many of their supporters hoped. This positive evaluation of the road taken was easily transformed into a prospective judgment about the road ahead: American defense policy should continue along the same trajectory that brought it from Vietnam to Desert Storm. Not only is it difficult to argue with success; it is also best not to mess with it.

Reflecting an assessment similar to that of the *Gulf War Air Power Survey*, Michael Vickers argues that "when the Cold War ended and victory in the Persian Gulf endowed the United States with the mantel of the 'world's only superpower,' Americans found themselves in the possession of a force already exhibiting incipient RMA capabilities – stealth, precision-guided munitions (PGMs) and all weather-imaging satellites,

---

[1] The quintessential expression of this view can be found in James Fallows's bestselling *National Defense* (New York: Random House, 1981).

for example."[2] These capabilities were "incipient" in part because United States had just begun to adopt and exploit many of them. Commercial Global Positioning System (GPS) receivers, for example, had to be rushed to the Gulf for American troops because their equipment lacked them. The two JSTARS surveillance planes sent at the last minute were still considered experimental. The stockpile of guided munitions was small, which helps explain why less than ten percent of the munitions used were guided. Only about ten percent of combat aircraft were capable of delivering guided munitions. The B-2 stealth bomber, in development for a decade and costing almost a billion dollars each, would not make its debut for several years. Satellite-guided munitions that could be used from greater distances in any weather remained extremely expensive and needed to be rationed. And the timely dissemination of real-time intelligence to forces that needed it had yet to be achieved. From a technological standpoint, the Gulf War provided only a hint of what was possible. The post–Desert Storm and post–Cold War environment, however, would pose some unusual problems for realizing the promise of the incipient RMA.

For almost forty years, American defense policy focused on the Soviet Union. Whether it was the Soviet strategic nuclear threat, the conventional balance in Europe, or Soviet support for leftist regimes and movements in the Third World, almost every aspect of U.S. defense policy was viewed through the prism of the superpower conflict. Almost without exception, the military capabilities that defeated Iraq in the Gulf War were designed and justified with an eye toward the Soviet Union. The collapse of communism and demise of the Soviet Union left the United States without a significant strategic challenge or peer military competitor. The United States was left with technologies developed, weapons acquired, and forces trained for an opponent that no longer existed. There were, of course, still some threats: a weakened Saddam who managed to hold on to power and an unpredictable North Korea with nuclear ambitions. But no threats came close to matching the Soviet Union. China was probably the only potential peer competitor, but that challenge was years, perhaps decades, in the future.

Although on many levels the absence of a peer military competitor is a blessing, it does present challenges for defense planning. Paul Yingling explains that "to prepare for war, the general must visualize the conditions of future combat. To raise forces properly, the general must visualize the quality and quantity of forces needed for the next war. To arm and equip military forces properly, the general must visualize the material

---

[2] Michael G. Vickers, "Revolution Deferred: Kosovo and the Transformation of War," in Andrew J. Bacevich and Eliot A. Cohen, eds., *War over Kosovo: Politics and Strategy in a Global Age* (New York: Columbia University Press, 2001), p. 190.

requirements of future engagements. To train forces properly, the general must visualize . . . future battlefields and replicate those conditions in peacetime training."[3] In the immediate post–Cold War period, however, this sort of visualization was extremely difficult, if not impossible. For what sort of battles does the world's largest military, one that spends more than the next twenty-five largest militaries combined, prepare in the absence of a credible military challenger? What weapons does it need to prevail in the next war? How does it exploit and channel incipient RMA capabilities in order to prepare for future missions? There were no easy answers to such questions. The sense of relief, vindication, and even triumph engendered by victory in the Cold War and Desert Storm was accompanied by a large measure of uncertainty and ambiguity. For the first time in a long time, "the Army of the 1990's simply had no idea about what contingencies it would have to be ready for."[4] The most powerful military the world had ever seen was without an enemy or mission.

Technology Advances

Technology was the star of the Gulf War. The war's most immediate lesson was that the technologies worked mostly as promised. Stealth fighters completed their missions unscathed, even in heavily defended areas. Laser guidance increased the accuracy of bombing dramatically with low levels of collateral damage. Cruise missiles went where they were sent, not toward targets of their own choosing. The Gulf War clearly demonstrated the potential of an entire suite of information gathering, precision targeting, and detection avoidance technologies developed since the 1970s and weaved together in war for the first time. This combination of technologies marked the emergence of a "guided-munitions battle network" or "reconnaissance-strike complex" with three basic components: sensors locating and tracking targets; platforms, weapons systems, and munitions able to attack with precision, often from great distances; and command, control, and communications assets linking sensors and "shooters."[5] But whatever its impressive successes, Desert Storm was not an exercise in technological perfection. The war revealed almost as much about the

---

[3] Paul Yingling, "A Failure in Generalship," *Armed Forces Journal* (May 2007). Accessed at: www.armedforcesjournal.com/2007/05/2635198/.

[4] Kagan, *Finding the Target*, p. 204. The point applies equally well for the military as a whole, not just the Army.

[5] The concept of "reconnaissance-strike complexes" was introduced by Soviet military theorists in the early 1980s who sometimes drew a distinction between "reconnaissance-strike" and "reconnaissance-fire" complexes that will not be emphasized here. See Milan Vego, *RECCE-Strike Complexes in Soviet Theory and Practice* (Ft. Leavenworth, KS: Soviet Army Studies Office, June 1990); and Chris Bellamy, *The Future of Land Warfare* (London: Routledge, 1987), p. 65.

limitations of this emerging complex/network and its constituent technologies as it did about their potential. Overcoming these limitations in
munitions, sensors, and command and control was a priority moving
forward.

Munitions

No technology demonstrated its potential more strikingly than PGMs,
particularly the laser-guided bombs (LGBs) emphasized in the war's video
images. LGBs were the public face of the United States' new high-tech way
of war and the most prominent manifestation of a contemporary RMA.
Although LGBs were less than ten percent of all munitions used in Desert
Storm, they were invaluable against targets that were small, hardened,
or located where the risk of collateral damage was high. They were not,
however, without their limitations. Because LGBs require laser designation, either by troops on the ground or from the aircraft delivering them,
they must be deployed from within visual range and are susceptible to bad
weather, clouds, smoke, dust, and sandstorms. If conditions limit visibility, LGBs cannot be used effectively. And because aircraft delivering LGBs
need to be within visual range of the target, their use in heavily defended
areas places planes and aircrews at risk, though the F-117's stealth capabilities reduced the danger in Desert Storm. There were alternatives to
LGBs. Cruise missiles launched from submarines or surface ships relied
largely on satellite guidance and were accurate from hundreds of miles
away. On the first night of Desert Storm, targets in Baghdad were attacked
not only by F-117's and their LGBs but also by Tomahawk cruise missiles launched from the Persian Gulf. In all, between 200 and 300 cruise
missiles were used against Iraq. The United States' inventory of cruise
missiles, however, was much smaller than LGBs, largely because they
cost well over a million dollars each at the time. What the United States
needed was accurate, all-weather, and affordable guided munitions that
could be deployed from beyond visible range. After Desert Storm the Air
Force and Navy set about developing such a weapon.

The result of their efforts was a relatively inexpensive technology that
could convert old-fashioned gravity bombs into guided munitions. The
Joint Direct Attack Munition (JDAM), deemed operationally capable
in 1997, was basically a tail kit attached to existing bombs that relied
on satellites to guide them to fixed targets whose coordinates were pre-
programmed. Berkowitz describes JDAMs as consisting "of just a GPS
receiver, a miniature inertial measurement unit, and a set of control fins.
You could bolt the JDAM to the back of a World War II or Korean War
dumb bomb, and have a smart bomb that cost just $16,000."[6] Reliance

[6] Berkowitz, *The New Face of War*, pp. 96–7.

on satellite guidance eliminated the need for visual recognition, meaning that JDAMs would be unaffected by inclement weather or other visual obstacles. Perhaps best of all, JDAMs were about one-thirtieth the cost of satellite-guided cruise missiles such as the Tomahawk. And though slightly less accurate than LGBs, JDAMs were good enough for most purposes. Referencing the experience of the Gulf War, Lambeth explains the significance of JDAMs:

> On more than one occasion . . . Brigadier General Buster Glosson, chief air campaign planner for Desert Storm, complained that weather was a greater impediment to effective allied strike operations than the Iraqi Air Force. In finally transcending this problem, the introduction of a family of internally guided, GPS-aided bomb kits that provide consistently accurate attack capability against fixed targets regardless of weather has made for a major increase in the combat leverage of conventional air power.[7]

In addition to solving the weather problems associated with laser-guided munitions, JDAMs could also be used from greater distances. Because they require no laser designation, JDAMs can be launched from beyond visual range without any soldiers on the ground to illuminate the target. But because JDAM-equipped bombs lack any independent propulsion, they cannot match a cruise missile's ability to strike from hundreds of miles away. Nonetheless, JDAMs could be deployed from a distance of fifteen miles, which could reduce dramatically the vulnerability of planes and aircrews attacking heavily defended targets. JDAMs appeared to be the Holy Grail of aerial bombing – cheap, reliable, and accurate from far away regardless of weather.

Sensors

Moving planes and their crews further from targets and defenses is one way to keep them safe. Removing them from hostile airspace entirely is another. This is the objective of unmanned aerial vehicles (UAVs), probably the technology displaying the greatest upside potential in Desert Storm. UAVs, also known as drones or remotely piloted vehicles, have a surprisingly long military history. As with the LGBs many associate with Desert Storm, UAVs were used in large numbers for the first time during Vietnam, where the United States flew more than 3,000 UAV sorties for surveillance and battle damage assessment.[8] For various economic, technological, and institutional reasons, however, the development of UAVs was not a priority in the years after Vietnam. It was the Israelis who took the lead in their development, and the successful use of UAVs

---

[7] Lambeth, *The Transformation of American Air Power*, p. 161.
[8] Mahnken, *Technology and the American Way of War Since 1945*, p. 113.

in the Bekka Valley in 1982 rekindled interest in the United States.[9] In the Gulf War, the workhorse UAV was actually the Israeli-designed (but U.S. manufactured) Pioneer, which flew more than 500 sorties over Kuwait and Iraq during Desert Shield and Desert Storm. Demonstrating their value, the development of UAVs did become a priority during the 1990s.

UAVs have several clear benefits over manned aerial surveillance. In comparison to the modified Boeing 707 of JSTARS, for example, UAVs are small, ranging in size from a radio-operated model plane to small private aircraft. Able to operate at altitudes as high as 15,000 feet, UAVs are almost impossible to detect and target. In an era when large manned aircraft are likely to become increasing vulnerable, UAVs present a viable solution to an emerging problem. Although UAVs are not cheap, costing over a million dollars for most models, they are nonetheless much less expensive than any manned aircraft. The lower cost means they are more expendable and can be procured in larger numbers. And perhaps the most significant advantage of UAVs is that by being unmanned, they keep soldiers out of harm's way. Even if the enemy hits one, "unlike a manned aircraft, you don't have to send condolences to loved ones when a UAV gets shot down."[10]

In many respects, the evolution of UAVs mirrors that of their manned predecessors, which at first were also used primarily for surveillance and reconnaissance. The ability to fly over and behind enemy lines was one of the primary military attractions of aircraft in the early twentieth century. It did not take long to realize that planes could also be used offensively if equipped with guns and bombs to attack other planes or ground forces. There was no obvious barrier to a similar progression of missions for UAVs. Rather than just find and identify targets, why not arm UAVs to attack as well? The so-called sensor-to-shooter cycle can be shortened by merging the sensor and shooter into a single platform. With this in mind, the development of UAVs in the 1990s focused on expanding their missions to include war fighting, not merely perfecting their surveillance capabilities. Some military futurists even envision a day when manned aircraft disappear entirely as remotely controlled planes replace manned bombers and fighters.[11] It is not hard to imagine, however, why the prospect of an Air Force without airmen arouses mixed feelings and resistance in certain quarters. Would it be possible, some wonder, to earn medals and promotions by "piloting" unmanned attack aircraft sitting behind a desk hundreds or even thousands of miles away from the fighting? Despite these concerns, advances in technology combined with a determination to minimize casualties seem to be moving us inexorably in the direction of airspaces with more machines and fewer people.

---

[9] Hallion, *Storm over Iraq*, p. 312.
[10] Berkowitz, *The New Face of War*, p. 120.
[11] See, for example, Friedman and Friedman, *The Future of War*, pp. 333–42.

Communications

Sensors such as UAVs and guided munitions constitute the most visible bookends of a reconnaissance-strike complex. The less visible, but equally important, element is composed of the command, control, and communications assets that link sensors, platforms, and munitions. Since the components of any integrated complex work together, changes in one component usually create pressures for changes in others. The vast increase in information resulting from the proliferation of ever more accurate sensors is something of a mixed blessing for the reconnaissance-strike complex. On the one hand, it seems axiomatic that more information is preferable to less. But on the other hand, the variety and sheer quantity of raw data poses challenges. There is always a danger of overwhelming the system's ability to disseminate necessary information to the forces that need it most. Raw data must be processed, analyzed, and filtered into useable information, not just gathered and transmitted wholesale. Everyone, after all, does not need to know everything at every moment. Soldiers engaged with the enemy do not need every bit of information about the entire theater of operations. The problem is magnified when time is of the essence, such as when troops in the midst of battle need to know the location of mobile targets in their immediate area. Allen Hazlegrove explains the age-old problem in the context of new technologies:

Since the beginning of organized warfare, the central problem in command and control has been intellectual; that is, organizing data to transform information into knowledge and then into understanding. The problem is even more daunting in the information age as communications and computers provide a profusion of intelligence and operational reports. In a time-sensitive targeting environment, the challenge is to sift through the volume of data quickly and to make accurate decisions.[12]

Linking together space, air, and ground assets collecting and disseminating information with platforms, commanders, and soldiers needing it was a significant challenge exacerbated in Desert Storm by the size and diversity of the military coalition. Fortunately, the United States had five months between the Iraqi invasion and the start of Desert Storm to create an almost mind-bogglingly complex communications system linking dozens of military and civilian satellites, more than two thousand personnel in fifty-nine communications centers, and tens of thousands of computers and phones. The seven thousand radio frequencies used and twenty-million phone calls made give some indication of the scale of the enterprise.[13] Despite its immense capabilities, the demands on the

[12] Allen P. Hazlegrove, "Desert Storm Time-Sensitive Surface Targeting: A Successful Failure or a Failed Success," *Defense Analysis* Vol. 16, No. 2 (December 2000), p. 123.
[13] Lukasz Kamieski, "Gulf War (1990–1991)," in Christopher Sterling, ed., *Military Communications* (ABC-CLIO, 2007), pp. 201–4.

system were so great that it was occasionally unable to cope. According to one comprehensive study, "the extensive use of PCs, modems, faxes, and other commercially available systems was largely unanticipated, overwhelmed existing communications infrastructure, and became a user-discipline issue ... this resulted in data overload, which in turn meant that in many instances data were ignored, misdirected, or misjudged."[14] There was, however, an even more basic problem than dealing with the volume of information and demands for it.

To maximize the potential of a reconnaissance-strike complex, the components need to communicate with each other. Sensors, platforms, and soldiers can only work together if they are able to send, receive, and understand information in a timely fashion. In technical terms, the components of the complex must be interoperable. This was not always the case in the Gulf War, and the difficulties were not limited to communications with coalition allies who one might expect would possess incompatible systems. Even within the American military there were interoperability problems. The Department of Defense, which gave itself a generally glowing evaluation after Desert Storm, zeroed in on interoperability problems as one of the key weaknesses of its performance. In an initial report to Congress, for example, it noted that "the ATO [Air Tasking Order] transmission process was slow and cumbersome because of inadequate interoperability. This was particularly true in the case of the Navy."[15] More specifically, the ATO (i.e., the daily aerial attack plan), often in excess of 800 pages, had to be physically delivered to ships in the Persian Gulf due to the absence of secure links for digital transmission.[16] As a result, "one lesson learned is that all the services and agencies must deploy with compatible intelligence dissemination and communications systems."[17] Delays and bottlenecks in transmitting information, particularly with regard to time-sensitive targets, diminished the effectiveness of the emerging reconnaissance-strike complex. The war demonstrated that "large problems remained in coordinating large-scale operations and creating a reconnaissance-strike complex that could disseminate critical information to the appropriate shooters."[18] Improving communications interoperability at all levels became a central element of intra- and

---

[14] James A. Winnefeld, Preston Niblack, and Dana J. Johnson, *A League of Airmen: U.S. Air Power in the Gulf War* (Santa Monica, CA: RAND, 1994), p. 213.

[15] Department of Defense, *Conduct of the Persian Gulf War: An Interim Report to Congress*, April 1992, pp. 15-5.

[16] Anthony Cordesman, *The Iraq War: Strategy, Tactics and Military Lessons* (New York: Praeger, 2003), p. 400.

[17] Department of Defense, *Conduct of the Persian Gulf War: An Interim Report to Congress*, pp. 14-1.

[18] Jeremy Shapiro, "Information and War: Is It a Revolution," in Zalamy Khalizad and John White, eds., *Strategic Appraisal: The Changing Role of Information in Warfare* (Santa Monica, CA: RAND, 1999), p. 120.

inter-service "digitization" plans in the 1990s.[19] And now that the problems of surveillance and munitions guidance were largely solved, the RMA agenda would increasingly focus on the challenge of linking sensors, platforms, and soldiers. This would be seen during the 1990s in emerging notions of a system of systems and network-centric (or net-centric) warfare.

Intervention in Somalia, 1992–1993

Not long after the smashing success in Desert Storm and its dazzling display of American technological superiority, the United States was drawn into a very different conflict whose more ambiguous result would dull some of the lingering glow of victory and call into question some claims of a revolution in warfare. In the waning days of his administration, President George H.W. Bush faced an emerging humanitarian crisis in the African nation of Somalia. The immediate cause of the crisis was the civil war that erupted in 1991 following the ouster of long-time dictator Siad Barre in which several political and clan-based factions vied for control. By the end of 1991, violence had spread beyond the capital to most of the country. Diplomatic and media reports of lawlessness, atrocities, and widespread starvation attracted the attention of many in the West. Over the next two years, the United Nations would intervene in a series of escalating missions to deal with the country's humanitarian and political crises with varying degrees of U.S. involvement.

United Nations intervention began in March 1992 when it negotiated a ceasefire among the warring factions and introduced fifty unarmed observers to monitor compliance in what was dubbed the United Nations Operation in Somalia (UNOSOM). Responding to the humanitarian aspects of the crisis, in August, the United Nations approved a relief mission to deliver food throughout Somalia. The United States provided military transport to airlift food into Somalia from bases in Kenya. The delivery and distribution of aid, however, was hindered throughout the fall by continuing violence, leading to a U.N. appeal for military forces that could create a secure environment for the distribution of aid. Faced with the U.N. request and reports of a worsening humanitarian situation, President Bush offered 25,000 troops. The United Nations accepted and American forces, joined by 12,000 troops from other countries, began arriving for "Operation Restore Hope" on December 5, a month after President Bush lost his bid for reelection to Bill Clinton.

---

[19] The *Army Digitization Master Plan* (1995), for example, can be accessed at: http://www .dtic.mil/cgi-bin/GetTRDoc?AD=ADA305855&Location=U2&doc=GetTRDoc.pdf. See also Elizabeth Stanley-Mitchell, "Technology's Double-Edged Sword: The Case of US Army Battlefield Digitization," *Defense Analysis* Vol. 17, No. 3 (December 2001), pp. 267–88.

This initial mission enjoyed the support of the various faction leaders largely because it was viewed as genuinely humanitarian and politically impartial. U.S.-led forces secured ports and accompanied aid convoys to protect them from ambushes. Most view the mission as a success. Johnathan Stevenson notes that,

> After taking control of Mogadishu, with other cities in south-central Somalia, and the routes that connect them to the capital, the U.S.-led forces, known as the United Task Force (UNITAF), did succeed in dramatically improving food distribution.... By the end of December, the number of malnourished children under five in Mogadishu had returned to a near normal 10 percent, compared to the more than 60 percent 5 months before.[20]

UNOSOM (and UNITAF), however, was at best a temporary solution. Since "the famine that gripped Somalia in 1992 resulted from the degeneration of the country's political system and economy," a lasting solution would have to bring the civil disorder and violence to an end.[21] With this in mind, UNITAF and UNOSOM were superseded in May 1993 by UNOSOM II with a much broader mandate of ending the civil war, restoring the rule of law, improving infrastructure, and disarming the warring factions. What had been a humanitarian mission became a political mission of "nation-building." UNOSOM II involved military contingents from more than two dozen nations. Although the new U.S. administration supported the expanded mission, the American military presence was reduced to slightly less than 5,000. In contrast to UNITAF, which was largely an American undertaking, "UNOSOM II forces were inevitably composed of an ill-assorted number of foreign military personnel with disparate training methods and varying degrees of military control."[22]

This expanded mandate removed the veneer of humanitarian impartiality and placed the United Nations on a collision course with Somalia's armed factions, particularly the Somali National Alliance (SNA) led by Mohammed Farrah Aidid, a former Somali army general and Ambassador to India. A critical turning point for the mission occurred in early June when Aidid's forces killed twenty-four Pakistani soldiers in a confrontation as they tried to inspect an arms depot. The United Nations' reaction was swift: the next day the Security Council passed a resolution calling for the arrest of those responsible for the killings, including Aidid himself. This new resolution escalated U.N. involvement further as it was rightly seen as "tantamount to a declaration of war

---

[20] Jonathan Stevenson, "Hope Restored in Somalia?" *Foreign Policy* No. 91 (1993), p. 139.

[21] Walter Clarke and Jeffrey Herbst, "Somalia and the Future of Humanitarian Intervention," *Foreign Affairs* Vol. 75, No. 2 (March/April 1996), p. 74.

[22] John Drysdale, "Foreign Military Intervention in Somalia," in Walter Clarke and Jeffrey Herbst, eds., *Learning from Somalia: The Lessons of Armed Humanitarian Intervention* (Boulder, CO: Westview Press, 1997), p. 134.

against Aidid's militia."[23] U.N. and U.S. forces began attacks on SNA sites in Mogadishu. The result was "four months of war between the U.N. peacemaking forces and a Somali commander and his untrained, underequipped guerilla fighters."[24] And even though U.S. forces were only a small part of UNOSOM II, "the only serious war-fighting forces in Somalia were the 1,200-member Quick Response Force, composed of elite soldiers from the U.S. Army's 10th Mountain Division and several hundred Rangers."[25] As General Anthony Zinni explains, the United States "was now in a counterinsurgency operation, or in some form of war . . . we had defined an enemy and we were fighting and we were going to be involved in taking casualties and killing Somalis."[26]

For the United States, the defining moment of its Somalia intervention came on October 3 and 4 in the so-called Battle of Mogadishu, the critical events of which were later depicted in the popular book and film *Blackhawk Down*. On October 3, U.S. Rangers and Delta force commandos were sent from their base on the outskirts of Mogadishu to abduct/arrest Aidid and some of his top lieutenants. They encountered unexpectedly heavy resistance. During seventeen hours of the most intense urban fighting American forces had faced since Vietnam, two U.S. Army Blackhawk helicopters were shot down, several others were damaged, and eighteen U.S. soldiers were killed with another eighty-four wounded. Pictures of jeering Somali crowds dragging the charred remains of an American Blackhawk pilot through the streets of Mogadishu were broadcast around the world and were seared into the public's consciousness as the iconic images of the war. There had been nothing like this in Desert Storm. For the United States, it was the beginning of the end of its intervention in Somalia. President Clinton authorized an immediate increase in troop levels, though only to facilitate a safe withdrawal of all U.S. forces by the end of March 1994. The United Nations would follow suit a year later.

The Lessons of Somalia

Somalia sparked an intense debate about the wisdom of humanitarian interventions that place American lives at risk when vital national interests are not at stake. Samuel Huntington reflected a widespread skepticism of humanitarian missions, arguing it was "morally and politically indefensible that members of the [U.S.] armed forces should be killed

---

[23] Drysdale, "Foreign Military Intervention in Somalia," p. 132.
[24] Ibid., p. 133.
[25] Clarke and Herbst, "Somalia and the Future of Humanitarian Intervention," p. 76.
[26] General Anthony Zinni interview, *PBS Frontline: Ambush in Mogadishu* (1994). Accessed at: www.pbs.org/wgbh/pages/frontline/shows/ambush/interviews/zinni.html.

to prevent Somalis from killing each other."[27] The perceived failure in Somalia almost certainly played a critical role in dampening support for intervention to stop the Rwandan genocide in 1994. The concept of "nation-building" became almost toxic in discussions of American foreign and defense policy for a decade. Somalia raised concerns about committing American forces to ill-defined missions without clear exit strategies, echoing the Weinberger and Powell doctrines.

In purely military terms, the juxtaposition between Somalia and the Gulf War was hard to avoid: just two years after its overwhelming victory against one the largest militaries in the world, the United States appeared to be defeated, indeed humiliated, by a ragtag militia of no more than several thousand fighters armed with comparatively primitive weapons. How did this happen? What were the military lessons of Somalia, particularly in comparison to Desert Storm? A fairly simple explanation for the difference in outcomes would be the varying levels of commitment. The United States had hundreds of thousands of troops in Desert Storm but fewer than five thousand in Somalia at the time of the Battle of Mogadishu. In Desert Storm the military got whatever equipment it asked for, whereas in Somalia Secretary of Defense Les Aspin made controversial decisions denying military requests for tanks and armored vehicles.[28] Perhaps more troops and equipment would have produced a better outcome. There is, however, a different way of comparing Somalia and Desert Storm that points to some larger lessons.

Andrew Bacevich is not alone in emphasizing that in Desert Storm "Saddam had challenged the United States on terms that could hardly have been less conducive to his own success. It was a war in the preferred American style: a high-tech, high-firepower encounter conducted (for the most part) on a battlefield remote from large civilian populations, in which combatants and noncombatants were (for the most part) clearly differentiated."[29] Desert Storm may have been waged with advanced, perhaps revolutionary, technologies, but it was a fairly traditional conflict involving national military organizations. It was the sort of war the United States had prepared for almost a decade to fight, though the expected adversary had been the Soviet Union, not Iraq. American information gathering and targeting systems were designed to deal with precisely the

---

[27] Michael Smith, "Humanitarian Intervention: An Overview of Ethical Issues," *Ethics and International Affairs* Vol. 12 (1998), p. 63.

[28] See Steve Holmes, "The Somalia Mission: Pentagon; Clinton Defends Aspin on Action Regarding Request for U.S. Tanks," *New York Times* (October 9, 1993); Elizabeth Drew, *On the Edge: The Clinton Presidency* (New York: Simon and Schuster, 1995), p. 358; and Bill Geertz, "Aspin's Decision on Tanks Was Political: Reports Says He Gave in to U.N.," *Washington Times* (October 3, 1995), p. 3.

[29] Andrew J. Bacevich, "Learning from Aidid," *Commentary* Vol. 16, No. 6 (December 1993), p. 32.

sort of opponent faced in Desert Storm. Many of the "specific military problems," to use Kagan's terminology, encountered in fighting Iraq were not much different from what the United States would have faced against the Soviet Union.

The war in Somalia (and it was a war against Aidid in its final months) posed a very different set of military problems. Somalia was not a high-intensity war of firepower against a traditional military opponent. There was no open battlefield, but rather a densely populated urban environment in which the distinction between combatants and noncombatants was anything but clear. Bacevich notes that "as a military commander, Aidid appears to have had one great insight: unlike Saddam, he knew that to play your enemy's game is the height of folly. On the other hand, to engage the opponent on terms that expose his weaknesses is to gain a priceless advantage."[30] This gives Aidid a bit too much credit, because he really did not have the option of playing the United States' game. Aidid did not disperse his battalions and armored personnel carriers as a clever means of avoiding detection by JSTARS: he did not have any to disperse. Ironically, Aidid's technological inferiority worked to his advantage. The technologies and systems that provided valuable information on the location and movement of Iraqi forces in the Kuwaiti desert offered little for finding and following Aidid's militia through the streets and alleys of Mogadishu. Even the most precise weapons could not target snipers, safe houses, and weapons stashes so closely intermingled with the local population without risking politically disastrous civilian casualties. In fact, the fighting in Mogadishu from June to October resulted in many civilian deaths, gradually turning even Somalis who disliked Aidid against the United States and United Nations. At least 500 Somali civilians, for example, lost their lives in the defining battle when 18 Americans were killed.[31] Richard Van Atta summarizes the difficulties of urban combat operations: "the crux of urban warfare is that the effectiveness of standoff sensors and precision weapons is severely diminished in the face of 3D, complex, transient terrain, with its short line-of-sight and overwhelming target discrimination issues."[32] In this war against this opponent even the United States' technological advantages would not allow it to fight from the air or at safe distances. But Aidid did not *choose* to fight this kind of war; he fought the only kind of war he could.

[30] Ibid, p. 32.
[31] Anatol Leivin, "Hubris and Nemesis: Kosovo and the Pattern of Western Military Ascendency and Defeat," in Andrew J. Bacevich and Eliot A. Cohen, eds., *War over Kosovo: Politics and Strategy in a Global Age* (New York: Columbia University Press, 2001), p. 111.
[32] Richard H. Van Atta, "Urban Warfare 2015: The Role of Persistent Assistants in Achieving Capabilities for Small Unit Precision Combat," Paper presented at symposia of the American Association for Artificial Intelligence, 2002.

The larger lesson of Somalia may be that the benefits of technological superiority and capabilities such as precision targeting are not constant but vary by opponent and setting. The technologies and capabilities revolutionizing some kinds of war may have a much less profound effect on others. Writing in its immediate aftermath, Bacevich claimed that "the lost battle for Mogadishu ha[d] shattered the dangerous illusion that the American military prowess displayed in the desert foretold an era of war without the shedding of American or civilian blood." And although the loss of life was tragic, "if General Aidid has deflated some of the wilder expectations derived from Desert Storm, it may be just as well."[33] It is easy to argue that policymakers *should* have paid more attention to the lessons of Somalia. Perhaps the Battle of Mogadishu was more indicative of the military problems the United States was likely to face in the post–Cold War world. But it is not surprising that Desert Storm eclipsed what could be dismissed as a comparatively small-scale elective humanitarian intervention. In retrospect, it is doubtful that the Somali experience had the impact on American military thinking and policy that Bacevich hoped for. But while it may not have deflated many of the expectations arising from Desert Storm, it did highlight several critical challenges for the U.S. military, particularly the Army.

Military Operations Other Than War

Somalia and Desert Storm clearly indicated that the "strategic pause" resulting from the Soviet Union's collapse and absence of a replacement peer competitor would not translate into a lull in military activity. In Iraq, the United States would enforce no-fly zones throughout the 1990s and the Somalia intervention was soon followed by others in Haiti (1994) and Bosnia (1995). As Jablonsky notes, "from the Gulf War to 1997, the pace of US military operations increased by at least 300 percent even as the armed forces were buffeted by cuts in structure, weapons programs, and personnel strength."[34] The challenge, however, was greater than simply carrying out more missions with fewer resources: the military's missions were becoming increasingly diverse as well as more frequent. In the span of little more than a year the military had gone from fighting Iraqi troops in the Arabian Desert to airlifting food supplies throughout Somalia to hunting down Aidid and his aides in the neighborhoods of Mogadishu. In Somalia alone, the mission morphed from humanitarian assistance to peace-keeping to peace-making to urban warfare. There was no way

---

[33] Ibid., p. 34.
[34] David Jablonsky, "Army Transformation: Tale of Two Doctrines," *Parameters* (Autumn 2001), p. 44.

of knowing whether the next military mission would require waging high-intensity war on the Korean peninsula, peace-keeping in Africa, or humanitarian assistance anywhere. As a result, the military needed to prepare not only for different kinds of war but also the full range of military operations other than war (MOOTW), to use the military's inelegant catch-all phrase.

In the 1997 *Quadrennial Defense Review*, Secretary of Defense William Cohen predicted that MOOTW, especially various peace operations, would dominate the military's future missions.[35] This prediction posed particularly severe challenges for the Army because these missions tend to be relatively manpower-intensive and make the greatest demands of soldiers on the ground. Donald Rose explains that peace and humanitarian operations require "skills the Army does not normally practice" and "put unusual demands on forces prepared for combat. Troops engaged in such missions have helped refugees return to their homes, protected relief convoys, maintained order in refugee camps, disarmed and demobilized former fighters, trained and monitored civilian police, and monitored respect for human rights."[36] The question was whether the same force could be trained and equipped to excel at major combat operations *and* all of these other missions or was there some trade-off between versatility and excellence. There was little agreement on the response to this challenge: "Some recognized that involvement in those operations was inevitable and began adjusting doctrine and training programs. Others continued to think of peace operations as the Army had thought of counterinsurgency in the 1990s – as a less important contingency for which any well-trained conventional force is automatically prepared."[37]

The Army's other major challenge stemmed from uncertainty about the location of future missions. When its primary objective was deterring a Soviet invasion of Western Europe, the Army enjoyed the benefit of bases in Germany where troops, equipment, and ammunition could be prepositioned. In the absence of forward bases, the logistical challenges of deploying large numbers of ground forces and their heavy equipment (e.g., tanks and armored personnel carriers) by sea and air are substantial. While in 1991 the U.S. military was able to move over half a million troops and their supplies to the Persian Gulf, certainly an impressive logistical accomplishment, it did take some time. Had Saddam moved against Saudi Arabia in August or early September 1990, the United States would have been forced to rely on air power and whatever ground forces the Saudis

35 William S. Cohen, *Report of the Quadrennial Defense Review* (Washington DC: Department of Defense, 1997), Section 3.
36 Donald G. Rose, "Peace Operations and Change in the US Military," *Defense Analysis* Vol. 17, No. 2 (2001), p. 141.
37 Ibid., p. 141.

could muster to stop him. Peter Spiegel provides a vivid description of those first weeks:

At a planning meeting in Saudi Arabia shortly after Iraq invaded Kuwait in 1990, General Charles Horner, commander of all US air force squadrons in the region, turned to General John Yeosock, his army counterpart, and asked what kind of protection the army could provide for air force bases in the region. Gen Yeosock, a straight-shooter with large, wire-rimmed glasses, reached into his uniform pocket and pulled out a small penknife. Such was the situation in the summer of 1990. With few forces based in the region and the bulk of the US Army's tanks and armoured personnel carriers thousands of miles away, American ground forces had little to offer the air force or their Saudi allies by way of protection. The 82nd airborne division, the army's elite air assault troops, with no armoured Bradley fighting vehicles or Abrams battle tanks . . . were all that stood between Saddam Hussein and the Saudi oil fields for more than a month.[38]

Desert Storm highlighted the comparatively limited strategic mobility of the Army. Lewis notes that the Army's biggest problem remained the same as that "identified by Ridgway and Taylor in the 1950s: the inability to get to battlefields around the world in a timely manner, in days as opposed to months."[39] In an environment where both the nature and location of the next mission were unpredictable, a similar delay could be disastrous the next time.

The solutions to the problem of strategic mobility were obvious, if not easily implemented: increase dramatically sea and airlift capabilities, figure out how to carry out its missions with fewer troops, and/or reduce the weight of tanks, personnel carriers, and other heavy equipment. The size and weight of the ground forces deployed to the Gulf suggested to some that the Army was, to be blunt, an RMA laggard intent on fighting industrial age wars with massive manpower and firepower. There seemed nothing revolutionary about the Army deployed to the Gulf or the war plan it carried out. The Army may have been assisted by a handful of revolutionary technologies such as GPS navigation, but the ground forces and war plan were utterly traditional. The western "Hail Mary" flanking maneuver may have been bold, audacious, and wildly successful, but it was a classic move that would have made sense to Patton or Napoleon. It is difficult to disagree with Linn's observation that "the RMA benefited the other services, particularly the air force, far more than the army."[40] Less clear are the reasons for this disparate impact: was it

---

[38] Peter Spiegel, "The US military's continued inability to move heavy equipment may force war planners to go with a smaller, lighter ground force than the Pentagon had planned," *Financial Times* (March 17, 2003), p. 19.
[39] Lewis, *The American Culture of War*, p. 387.
[40] Brian McAllister Linn, *The Echo of Battle: The Army's Way of War* (Cambridge, MA: Harvard University Press, 2007), p. 226.

the result of some inherent feature of land warfare or the army's institutional resistance to transformation?

The Army's predicament was not lost on its Chief of Staff, General Gordon Sullivan. Even though "the Army's fundamental character is to fight and win the nation's wars and protect its vital interests," Sullivan recognized that "events around the world – in Somalia, Korea, Haiti, Kuwait, and the former Yugoslavia – amply demonstrate the post-Cold War expansion, in category, frequency and geographic dispersion, of missions we may be called upon to accomplish."[41] The army that prepared to fight the Soviet Union and defeated Iraq was not ready for the diversity of missions it was likely to face in the years ahead. In response, Sullivan launched several initiatives (e.g., Force XXI) to spark a debate about the Army's future that would ultimately lead to changes in organization and doctrine. Sullivan was an active participant in the debate, arguing that "we are on the eve of new era ... the industrial age is being superseded by the Information Age, the Third Wave, hard on the heels of the agrarian and industrial eras. Our present Army is well-configured to fight and win in the late-industrial age." It was not prepared for the information age and needed "to move into Third Wave warfare, to evolve [into] a new force for a new century – Force XXI."[42] In somewhat more concrete terms, "our future vision must ... design and develop rapidly expansible, strategically deployable and effectively employable forces capable of achieving decisive results in war and operations other than war."[43] The implicit message was clear: the army was not "readily expansible, strategically deployable and effectively employable." Sullivan advanced several reform objectives that would become staples of debates about the army's future – a more organizationally flexible army whose components could combine in a manner appropriate to the mission, a fully digitized army exploiting advances in information technologies to achieve complete battlespace awareness, and a lighter army less reliant on heavy equipment that could be deployed quickly anywhere in the world from bases in the United States. Knowledge, versatility, and mobility became the mantras of army transformation.

There is little doubt that Sullivan got the debate he hoped for. There even appeared to be widespread support for the general objectives he articulated. Whether this debate led to real change is another matter. Linn is among those who offer a harsh assessment, seeing more sloganeering and rhetoric than meaningful reform. "When Sullivan retired,"

[41] Gordon Sullivan, "A Vision for the Future," *Military Review* Vol. 75, No. 3 (May/June 1995), p. 6.
[42] Gordon Sullivan, "Force XXI," *The Collected Works of the Thirty-Second Chief of Staff of the United States Army: June 1991–June 1995* (Washington, DC: CMH, 2004), p. 316.
[43] Gordon Sullivan, "A Vision for the Future," p. 6.

Linn argues, "the army still had made no substantial effort to adapt to the chaotic nonstate warfare it had encountered in Somalia and would encounter again in the Balkans and postinvasion Iraq."[44] In all fairness, however, one needs to remember that Sullivan retired in 1995, less than two years after initiating Force XXI. It is probably not realistic to expect much reform in such a short period, especially given the magnitude of the challenge of organizing, training, and equipping a force capable of rapid deployment anywhere in the world for any mission ranging from high-intensity warfare to peace-keeping and humanitarian operations. This was not something to be achieved in the short-term, and jury was still out as to whether it could be achieved even in the long-term.

The RMA and Net-Centric Warfare

Sullivan's Toffleresque rhetoric about the transition from industrial to information-age warfare was symptomatic of the mindset that infused military discourse in the decade after the Gulf War. The success of Desert Storm helped expand discussions about a possible RMA beyond the narrow range of academics and military theorists who debated it before the war. The notion that the Gulf War marked the beginning of a new RMA became the new commonly accepted wisdom. Kagan is probably correct in observing that after the Gulf War "the RMA bug . . . infected the armed forces, the Clinton administration, and Congress."[45] Somalia did nothing to halt the infection's spread. The language, buzzwords, and jargon of the RMA were ubiquitous in military vision statements and congressional testimony. Every weapon system needed to be justified in terms of its contribution to transforming the military in accordance with the RMA. It was nearly impossible to pick up a military journal without at least one article on some aspect of the RMA. *Joint Force Quarterly* even sponsored an RMA essay contest. Although it is easy to ridicule the more extreme RMA rhetoric that sometimes seemed a caricature of itself, there were serious attempts to come to grips with nature of the changes in warfare signaled by the Gulf War. If perfecting the reconnaissance-strike complex was the major technological challenge after Desert Storm, the intellectual challenge was in some sense even greater. If a new RMA was under way, what kind of revolution was it? Precisely how would the character of warfare change? What conceptual/doctrinal edifice would rest on the technological foundation of a reconnaissance-strike complex? Toward the middle and end of the 1990s the paradigm of net-centric warfare and related concepts such as information warfare and "Shock and Awe" would dominate American military thinking on the eve of the terrorist attack of September 11, 2001, and the United States' second war with Iraq.

44 Linn, *The Echo of Battle*, p. 227.
45 Kagan, *Finding the Target*, p. 219.

The System of Systems

Vice Chairman of the Joint Chiefs of Staff Admiral William Owens was among the RMA's most enthusiastic advocates. He was convinced that information technologies were altering the character of warfare and that radical changes in military organization and doctrine were needed for the United States to gain the maximum advantage from the RMA. His major contribution was conceptualizing the RMA in terms of a "system of systems" that would employ information technologies to integrate previously disparate forces and weapons systems into a coherent whole whose unprecedented battle space awareness and speed of decision making would provide a decisive edge over opponents. For Owens, the RMA boils down to two essential imperatives: information and jointness.

Owen sees the ability to collect, disseminate, and act on information as the decisive factor in modern warfare. He makes his case in typically bold terms:

> There is profound information technology available in America. This technology would allow our country the capability *for the first time in history of man*, to be able to "see" a very large strategic battlefield with great definition. That means that 24 hours a day, in real-time, all weather, we could have the ability . . . to *see every activity and facility* which might be of interest to our warfighting, peace-making or peacekeeping effort . . . if we are able to view a strategic battlefield this way and prevent an enemy from doing so, we have dominant battlefield awareness, and we are *certain to prevail* in a conflict.[46]

Skeptics, of course, were quick to pounce. The notion that sensors could completely eliminate the fog of war (i.e., "see *every* activity and facility") was easily dismissed as an RMA fantasy. The proposition that information dominance guarantees victory was rejected as simplistic nonsense. Unfortunately, Owens' tendency toward hyperbole, a common trait of RMA proponents, often made it easy for his critics to pile on. But at other times his claims were more modest and restrained. He cautioned, for example, that "the system-of-systems does not offer omniscience or omnipotence. It has demonstrated the ability to reduce the fog and friction of war and promises to do even more so in the future."[47] The proposition that technological advances are substantially *reducing*, as opposed to *eliminating* the fog of war is more defensible. Similarly, he claimed that "if you know everything you possibly can about your enemy and prevent him from knowing much about you, then you have an advantage. Whether it's a battlefield in Somalia . . . or whether it's the next Desert

---

[46] William Owens, Prepared Statement for the U.S. Senate Budget Committee, February 12, 2001, emphasis added. Accessed at: www.budget.senate.gov/democratic/testimony/2001/owens_defhrng021201.pdf.

[47] William Owens, "The Emerging U.S. System of Systems," *Strategic Forum* No. 63 (February 1996). Accessed at: www.ndu.edu/inss/Strforum/SF_63/forum63.html.

Storm, if there are 'smart' systems that give us a picture of the real battlefield, then we have a decided edge."[48] Again, this is a more reasonable
position than his assertion that victory is certain.

The magnitude of the advantage information dominance affords depends on the military's ability to think, plan, and act jointly as a single
force rather than a collection of services. The benefits of technology and
jointness are synergistic: information technologies facilitate joint operations by making it easier to communicate and share information, and the
ability to use information efficiently magnifies its advantages. The goal
of a system of systems is the seamless linkage of commanders, forces,
platforms, and sensors, with everyone sharing the most complete picture
of the battlespace possible so that tasks can be allocated to whatever elements of the architecture are best positioned to carry them out. Dominant
battlespace knowledge combined with jointness permits what Freedman
refers to as "Near-Perfect Mission Assignment."[49] Whether a target is
best attacked by nearby artillery, an F-117 fighter in the area, or a cruise
missile launched from a ship 200 miles away, the system of systems will
make it possible to choose the most effective option.

By properly exploiting the benefits of information dominance and jointness, wars could be waged in a fundamentally different way. In what
would become one of the central themes of military transformation,
Owens argued that it would be possible to think in terms of mass effects
rather massive forces. When information and jointness are combined with
standoff precision weapons, a relatively small number of distant and dispersed forces can concentrate massive firepower on short notice. "We
have to understand," he argued, "that it's not mass, it's dominant knowledge that is most important to our success, whether it's success in Somalia
or in fighting terrorism in this country and abroad. It is knowledge that
counts."[50] The skillful exploitation of knowledge, jointness, and precision weapons will allow "the United States to step away from the tenets
of attrition warfare, with its emphasis on overwhelming mass, e.g. large
numbers of ships, tanks, aircraft, and troops."[51]

The military advantage of Owens's system of systems derives not only
from the unprecedented *amount* of information it provides but also from
the *speed* with which it is provided. The rapid collection and dissemination of information makes it possible to act quickly. The notion that
information technologies can accelerate decision making and increase the
tempo of military operations is a recurring theme of RMA proponents

[48] William Owens, interview, *The Carnegie Reporter* Vol. 1, No. 4 (Spring 2002). Accessed
at: www.carnegie.org/reporter/04/interview/interview.html.
[49] Freedman, *The Revolution in Strategic Affairs*, p. 12.
[50] Interview with William Owens, *PBS Newshour* (February 29, 1997). Accessed at:
www.pbs.org/newshour/bb/military/Adm_Owens_3-1.html.
[51] Owens, "Prepared Statement for the U.S. Senate Budget Committee," February 12, 2001.

going all the way back to John Boyd's idea that whoever can complete the OODA (observe, orient, decide, and act) loop more rapidly gains the upper hand. It is hard to miss Boyd's influence in Owens claim that with a system of systems "we truly will be able to operate within the opponent's decision cycle." As a result, speed became a defining characteristic of the RMA along with dominant battle space knowledge, jointness, and standoff precision engagement.

The major obstacles to the achievement of Owens's vision were institutional and cultural, not technological. The enemy of jointness was parochialism, the tendency for individual services to think of themselves as distinct entities with their own weapons systems and doctrines. Owens complained that "in the US, service parochialism has far more influence on force planning than it should. Episodic efforts to balance it with a stronger joint perspective ... did not break the crystalline stovepipes that channel service planning. Nor have they succeeded in changing the basic planning assumption of each military service; namely, that they are engaged in a zero sum game among the other military services." Taken to its logical conclusion, and Owens provided no reason why it should not, his case for jointness is truly radical as it suggests not merely the reduction of cultural and institutional service barriers but their elimination, a military in which the divisions between the services are no greater than those within them. Although it might be possible to achieve some type of RMA even in the face of lingering parochialism, its full potential would remain unrealized.

Rapid Dominance: "Shock and Awe"

Most Americans have probably never heard of the RMA, and fewer still know anything about a system of systems, but mention "Shock and Awe" and one is likely to see some sign of recognition. The familiarity stems from the run up to the 2003 Iraq War when the doctrine enjoyed its fifteen minutes of fame as military pundits speculated that it would form the basis for the American plan of attack. The term "Shock and Awe" was coined in 1996 by Harlan Ullman and James Wade who led a group of retired military officers searching for an alternative to what they viewed as the military's unimaginative war fighting concepts.[52] Interestingly, Ullman points to Charles Horner, who led the Gulf War air campaign and was part of the group, as providing the project's impetus: "Horner often remarked that during Desert Storm he simply did not know where to 'put the needle' in order to bring down the enemy. We went about searching

---

[52] The definitive statement is Harlan Ullman and James Wade (with L.A. Edney, Fred Franks, Charles Horner, Jonathan Howe, and Keith Bradley), *Shock and Awe: Achieving Rapid Dominance* (Washington, DC: The National Defense University, 1996).

for those needles and the appropriate entry points to defeat an adversary with minimal effort and presumably at the least cost to us and to the other side."[53]

As Ullman's observation indicates, Shock and Awe resulted from an effort to move beyond the very general, abstract, and esoteric theorizing so prevalent in discussions of the RMA to formulate a new concept of war that would "bring down the enemy," a war-fighting doctrine for the information age. Often caricatured by its critics, Shock and Awe was complex and difficult to summarize, incorporating almost every major element of RMA theory from Boyd to Warden to Owens: knowledge dominance, precision targeting, rapid decision making, speed of operations, jointness, standoff engagement, strategic and tactical paralysis, casualty avoidance, and collateral damage minimization. At times it almost appears as if they were trying to cram as much RMA jargon as possible into a single passage:

Rapid Dominance requires a sophisticated, interconnected, and interoperable grid of netted intelligence, surveillance, reconnaissance, communications systems, data analysis, and real-time deliverable actionable information to the shooter. This network must provide total situational awareness and supporting nodal analysis that enables U.S. forces to act inside the adversary's decision loop in a manner that on the high end produces Shock and Awe among the threat parties.[54]

The doctrine's two elements were conceptualized in almost sequential terms. The initial attacks are designed to be so shocking that they create "paralysis, impotence and a feeling of helplessness. In other words, it mean[s] overcoming an enemy so quickly and rendering that enemy incapable so as to make any resistance futile or impossible." Subsequent attacks, if necessary, translate "the initial shock into an enduring quality," instilling awe by "demonstrate[ing] to the adversary our endurance and staying power, that is, the capability to dominate over as much time as is necessary."[55] Shock and Awe's closest doctrinal predecessor is probably Warden's notion of parallel attacks on the enemy's centers of gravity to create decisional paralysis and induce surrender. There are some differences, most significantly the absence of any explicit claim that Shock and Awe could be accomplished with air power alone. Ullman and Wade were careful to note that Shock and Awe would be achieved by "the rapid and simultaneous application (or threat of application) of land, sea, air, space, and special operating forces against the broadest spectrum of the adversary's power base and center or centers of gravity."[56] It is clear, however,

[53] Harlan Ullman, "Slogan or Strategy: Shock and Awe Reassessed," *The National Interest* No. 84 (Summer 2006), p. 45.
[54] Wade and Ullman, *Shock and Awe*, p. 45.
[55] Ibid., p. 45; and Ullman and Wade, *Shock and Awe*, pp. 13–14.
[56] Wade and Ullman, *Shock and Awe*, p. 12.

that at a minimum air power would have to play a disproportionately large role in any Shock and Awe campaign.

The often extravagant claims for Shock and Awe were tempered with notes of caution. Wade and Ullman conceded that Shock and Awe's effectiveness, as with any military doctrine, would depend in part on the nature of the enemy and conflict. Even if the United States had the ability to implement Shock and Awe in Vietnam, for example, it probably would have made no difference in the war's outcome because "there are certainly situations such as guerilla war where . . . most means of employing force to obtain Shock and Awe may simply prove inapplicable."[57] And even when circumstances are conducive, there is no guarantee that Shock and Awe would succeed. If Shock and Awe fails and "the enemy still resist[s], then conventional forms of attack would follow."[58] The major shortcoming of Shock and Awe, however, is its unfulfilled promise, the failure to "identify the needles" that would bring down a country like Iraq. After more than 100 pages, one is left wondering what the critical needles are. What other targets could the United States have attacked in 1991 to shock and awe Saddam Hussein into withdrawing his forces from Kuwait? One searches in vain for an answer to this basic question. It is difficult to see how Horner's frustration was relieved.

The authors of *Shock and Awe* believed that the RMA was just beginning and its implications were even more radical than many of its proponents realized. They worried that existing doctrine and vision statements merely grafted new technologies onto traditional industrial age war-fighting assumptions. Although it never became an official doctrine, many saw the influence of Shock and Awe in the 2003 Iraq War, even if Ullman thinks it did not come close to what they recommended. Shock and Awe is best seen as a critical juncture in the evolving debate over the RMA because it brought together the various strands of thought about the nature and elements of the RMA, even if the somewhat unfortunate and gimmicky label obscured the seriousness of the analysis. Whatever its shortcomings as a doctrine, Shock and Awe was a sort of intellectual progress report, a road map of where the debate had been as well as where it was heading.

Net-Centric Warfare

Toward the end of the 1990s, RMA advocates and theorists began to coalesce around the concept of network-centric warfare, the intellectual origins of which are usually traced to William Owens. David J. Betz notes that net-centric warfare (NCW) "is rooted – as are most derivative

[57] Ibid., p. 26.
[58] Ibid., p. 14.

concepts of the RMA – in the idea of a 'system of systems' as described by Admiral William Owens."[59] The term itself is more closely associated with Admiral Arthur Cebrowski, who maintained a career-long interest in the military applications of computers, transistors, and digital technology going back to the 1970s.[60] For almost two decades he was convinced that the military was failing to exploit the potential of the information technologies revolutionizing business and society as a whole. As Owens was articulating his system of systems in the mid-1990s, Cebrowski was serving as the Joint Staff's Director of Command, Control, Communication, and Computers. The two found in each other a kindred spirit sharing a belief that military success would increasingly depend more on agility and the management of information than mass and overwhelming firepower. But the notion that net-centric warfare is "rooted" in the system of systems understates the case. Perhaps because Owens and Cebrowski were already on the same intellectual wavelength, it is almost impossible to see any difference between the system of systems and net-centric warfare. Common definitions of the two are virtually indistinguishable. One would be hard-pressed, for example, to determine whether the following refers to net-centric warfare or the system of systems:

its power [is derived] from the strong networking of a well-informed but geographically dispersed force. The enabling elements are a high-performance information grid, access to all appropriate information sources, weapons reach and maneuver with precision and speed of response, value-adding command-and-control (C2) processes – to include high-speed automated assignment of resources to need – and integrated sensor grids closely coupled in time to shooters and C2 processes.[61]

The RMA debate, like the military as whole, has a tendency to generate new concepts, labels, and jargon even when there is not much need for them. Such is the case with net-centric warfare, which is better seen as a pithy and clever relabeling of RMA orthodoxy than a reconceptualization. Net-centric warfare is the system of systems. There is no point in parsing out credit: Owens and Cebrowski probably arrived at the same

---

[59] David J. Betz, "The More You Know, the Less You Understand: The Problem with Information Warfare," *The Journal of Strategic Studies* Vol. 29, No. 3 (June 2006), p. 511.

[60] The first use of "network-centric warfare" was probably in Arthur K. Cebrowski and John H. Garstka, "Network-Centric Warfare: Its Origins and Future," *Proceedings of the US Naval Institute* Vol. 124, No. 1 (January 1998). For an excellent overview of Cebrowski's career and thinking see James Blaker, "Arthur K. Cebrowski: A Retrospective," *Naval War College Review* Vol. 59, No. 2 (Spring 2006), pp. 129–45 and the chapter on Cebrowski in P.W. Singer, *Wired for War: The Robotics Revolution and Conflict in the 21st Century* (New York: Penguin Press, 2009) entitled "The Big Cebrowski and the Real RMA," pp. 179–204.

[61] Cebrowski and Gartska, "Network-Centric Warfare," p. 34.

intellectual point on their own but used different labels to describe what they were thinking.

By the time Owens retired in 1998 and Cebrowski became net-centric warfare's most prominent advocate, it was well on its way to being "widely accepted, *at least verbally*" within the Department of Defense.[62] The influence of the system of systems and net-centric warfare was evident in *Joint Vision 2010* (1996) and *Joint Vision 2020* (2001). These were glossy Department of Defense documents filled with colorful charts and pictures purporting to be "conceptual template[s] for how America's Armed Forces will channel the vitality and innovation of our people and leverage technological opportunities to achieve new levels of effectiveness in joint warfighting."[63] All the key elements of RMA theorizing were ubiquitous – jointness (hence the titles), information dominance, rapid communications, interoperability, precision targeting, speed of operations, and so on. Phrases such as "seamless joint architecture" and "massed effects from dispersed forces" were sprinkled throughout. The following passages leave little doubt about the influence of RMA theorizing:

Throughout history, gathering, exploiting, and protecting information have been critical in command, control, and intelligence. The unqualified importance of information will not change in 2010. What will differ is the increased access to information and improvements in the speed and accuracy of prioritizing and transferring data brought about by advances in technology. While the friction and the fog of war can never be eliminated, new technology promises to mitigate their impact.

Information operations will tie together high fidelity target acquisition, prioritized requirements, and command and control of joint forces within the battlespace. This combination will provide a greater assurance of delivering the desired effect, lessen the risk to our forces, and minimize collateral damage.

The organizational concept of dominant maneuver is a prescription for more agile, faster moving joint operations, which will combine air, land, and maritime forces more effectively to deliver decisive combat power.[64]

Both vision statements were broad frameworks with extremely general operational concepts (e.g., dominant maneuver and precision engagement) mixed with a decent measure of cheerleading and vacuous sloganeering. They were intentionally not war-fighting doctrines. Nonetheless, Kagan views *Joint Vision 2010* as "little more than *Shock and Awe* watered down."[65] This seems a bit strong. Although *Joint Vision 2010*

[62] The quite is from Andrew Krepinevich in Adam Bernstein, "Adm. Arthur Cebrowski Dies: Led Pentagon Think Tank," *Washington Post* (November 15, 2005), p. B6.
[63] Chairman of the Joint Chiefs of Staff, *Joint Vision 2010* (Washington, DC: U.S. Department of Defense, 1996), p. 1.
[64] Ibid., pp. 16 and 21.
[65] Kagan, *Finding the Target*, p. 230.

and 2020 are perfectly consistent with Shock and Awe, they are so vague as to be consistent with a number of possible doctrines. Like so many documents written by a committee trying hard not to upset any constituency, the *Vision* statements read like Rorschach tests in which people can see what they want.

In the end, the *Joint Vision* statements and others like them revealed more about how people were thinking, or perhaps only what they were saying, than what they were doing. They are a testament to the dominance of RMA theorizing on military thought (or at least rhetoric) in the decade after Dessert Storm. Translating vision into reality, however, is not always easy, or even intended.

Kosovo: NATO's "Curious Little War"[66]

Nowhere in Europe did the demise of communism create more problems than in Yugoslavia. A collection of diverse ethnicities and nationalities that never managed to forge a common identity, Yugoslavia encompassed the republics of Bosnia-Herzegovina, Croatia, Macedonia, Montenegro, Serbia (which included Kosovo and Vojvidina), and Slovenia. The republics were kept together in a delicate balancing act by Yugoslavia's leader, Josip Broz Tito, from the end of World War II until his death in 1980. Attempts to devise a political formula that would preserve the union after Tito's passing proved problematic as nationalist sentiment intensified and demands for greater autonomy and even independence increased. Against this backdrop, Slobodan Milosevic, considered as a strong Serbian nationalist determined to resist such demands, became president of Serbia in 1989. Shortly thereafter, Yugoslavia began to unravel. In 1991 Slovenia and Croatia declared independence, a move most European countries recognized. Bosnia-Herzegovina's declaration of independence in 1991 and the referendum supporting it in 1992 were opposed by Serbia and ethnic Serbs in Bosnia-Herzegovina. The resulting conflict led to three years of war, including a brief NATO bombing campaign in September 1995, following the "Srebrenica massacre" of thousands of Bosnian men and boys by Bosnian Serb forces that summer. The Bosnian conflict was brought to end with the Dayton Agreement of December 1995.

Memories of events in Bosnia and atrocities in Srebrenica were still fresh as tensions increased between Serbia and Kosovo, an autonomous province of the Republic of Serbia in the former Yugoslavia. Ethnic Albanians dominated in Kosovo, constituting about ninety percent of the population compared to the minority Serbs with eight percent. To

[66] This description is taken from Stephen Biddle, "The New Way of War? Debating the Kosovo Model," *Foreign Affairs* (May/June 2002), p. 138.

strengthen Serbian control, Milosevic curtailed dramatically Kosovo's autonomy in 1989. This did not sit well with the Kosovar Albanians. Despite a 1990 declaration of independence that was recognized only by neighboring Albania, Serbian forces remained in Kosovo. A violent opposition emerged as the Kosovo Liberation Army (KLA) began a guerrilla campaign to force out the Serbs. In early 1998 Serbia cracked down on the KLA, worsening the violence and attracting international attention. Western rhetoric was strong and calls for restraint and a ceasefire common, but other than some weak sanctions action was lacking and the violence escalated. Unfortunately, it was difficult to see the common ground on which a settlement could be reached: the Kosovar Albanians wanted independence, and Serbia viewed the KLA as an illegal secessionist movement that needed to be crushed. In the summer of 1998, Serbia stepped up its attacks and "Serb military, paramilitary, and interior police forces left little unscathed. In August alone, 100,000 Kosovars were forced to flee their homes," raising the specter of ethnic cleansing.[67] In September the U.N. Security Council passed Resolution 1199 unanimously (China abstained), calling for an end to actions against civilians in Kosovo, international monitoring, unimpeded access for humanitarian organizations, the return of refugees forced from their homes, and meaningful negotiations to find a diplomatic solution.[68] The problem, of course, was the absence of agreement on how to achieve the resolution's objectives. Since everyone expected Russia and/or China to veto forceful action, attention shifted to NATO.

NATO devised a number of military options, all involving air strikes, as background threats to spur diplomacy and possibly punish particular acts of misconduct. Although there was little diplomatic progress, the situation in Kosovo calmed a bit as winter approached. On January 16, 1999, however, the situation took a turn for the worse when forty-five people were found dead in the Kosovar town of Racak. The "massacre," proclaimed by some on the scene as a crime against humanity, was immediately blamed on the Serbs.[69] The violence seemed to be spiraling out of control. There could not be another Srebrenica. The time to act had come. A conference was convened in Rambouillet, France, which included the Serbian government in Belgrade (Milosevic chose not to attend) and the Kosovar Albanians. Perhaps to demonstrate NATO's resolve and pressure the sides to an agreement, the alliance's North Atlantic Council

---

[67] Ivo H. Daalder and Michael E. O'Hanlon, *Winning Ugly: NATO's War to Save Kosovo* (Washington, DC: Brookings Institution Press, 2000), p. 40.

[68] Ibid., p. 42.

[69] The validity of these charges remains in dispute. A Finnish forensic team, for example, found no evidence of a massacre at Racak. See Dag Henricksen, *NATO's Gamble: Combining Diplomacy and Airpower in the Kosovo Crisis, 1998–1999* (Anapolis, MD: Naval Institute Press, 2007), pp. 162–4.

authorized air strikes if no agreement was reached. As diplomats talked in France, Serbian action in Kosovo continued unabated. In the end, the Serbs refused to sign the final accords and the talks collapsed on March 18. Within days, and just a few weeks before its fiftieth anniversary, NATO would be at war with Serbia.

Operation Allied Force

Even with reports of ethnic cleansing and human right abuses, support for using force against Serbia remained shaky in many NATO countries, and there was little stomach for the introduction of ground troops. Even President Clinton, who pushed for military action, ruled out the possibility of a ground war early on, though his position would eventually change. As NATO planned military action against Serbia, the assumption (or hope) was that air power would be sufficient, with the debate centering on how it would be applied. Some, such as NATO's air warfare commander Lt. Gen. Michael Short, preferred a Wardenesque approach modeled on Desert Storm: a massive aerial assault with parallel attacks on a wide range of strategic targets. NATO Supreme Commander General Wesley Clark, however, realized that this was untenable because "his political masters would never agree to opening the war with a Desert Storm-style all-out assault on Belgrade."[70] Instead, the war plan involved a gradual escalation of attacks in three phases:

Phase 1 would establish air superiority over Kosovo and degrade command and control throughout Yugoslavia. Phase 2 would attack military targets in Kosovo and those Yugoslav forces providing reinforcement into Kosovo south of 44 degrees north latitude. Phase 3 would expand air operations against a wide range of military and security targets throughout Yugoslavia, including the capital city Belgrade.[71]

When the war began on March 24 there was an "almost universal assumption among NATO's leaders that the operation would last no more than two to four days."[72] Despite the formal plan for gradual escalation, "the *real* plan rested on a single unstated assumption: As soon as Milosevic saw that NATO meant business, he would sue for terms."[73] This was not to be. Milosevic apparently thought he could sit out the air campaign and wait for the inevitable civilian casualties and collateral damage to

[70] William M. Arkin, "Operation Allied Force: 'The Most Precise Application of Air Power in History,'" in Andrew J. Bacevich and Eliot A. Cohen, eds., *War over Kosovo: Politics and Strategy in a Global Age* (New York: Columbia University Press, 2001), p. 5.
[71] Ibid., p. 4.
[72] Benjamin Lambeth, *NATO's Air War for Kosovo: A Strategic and Operational Assessment* (Santa Monica, CA: RAND, 2001), p. 232.
[73] Arkin, "Operation Allied Force," p. 7.

split the fragile alliance.[74] After the first few days of bombing failed to induce capitulation, NATO implemented Phase 2 and the air campaign stretched into April amidst justified and growing concern that it was not going well. There was no indication that Milosevic would buckle and Serbian actions against the Kosovar Albanians only intensified and refugee flows increased.

Several problems were increasingly apparent. First, politically imposed limitations and restrictive rules of engagement meant that "the air effort as a whole remained but a faint shadow of Operation Desert Storm."[75] As a point of comparison, "it took NATO 12 days to complete the same number of strike sorties that had been conducted during the first 12 hours of Desert Storm."[76] Second, the Serbs were skilled in keeping parts of their air defence system in operation, especially mobile heat-seeking SAMs that remained a threat throughout the war, often forcing allied aircraft to fly at higher altitudes. Third, Serb forces in Kosovo were almost impossible to target because they dispersed and mixed in with the civilian population. And unlike the open desert of Iraq, Kosovo provided lots of forest, mountains, valleys, and caves that made concealment easy. Finally, bad weather and heavy cloud cover throughout most of March and April "forced the cancellation or failure of more than half of all bombing sorties on 20 of the first 35 days of air attacks."[77] Thus, when NATO's representatives gathered in Washington on April 23 to mark the alliance's anniversary, the focus was on the war rather than the celebration. Far from being over as most originally expected, the air war was being lost. The alliance's credibility was at stake, and there was a consensus that NATO could not fail. The target list grew as the allies focused increasingly "on what NATO officials had come to characterize as the four pillars of Milosevic's power – the political machine, the media, the security forces, and the economic system."[78] There was also increasing talk about a ground war.

As the air campaign entered its sixth week, the tide began to turn. The expanded target list, more attack aircraft, and improving weather allowed NATO to intensify its efforts. The split in the alliance Milosevic had hoped for failed to materialize, in part because of continuing Serbian action in Kosovo. NATO finally went after the targets some had urged all along, including "oil refineries, petroleum depots, road and rail bridges over the Danube, railway lines, communications sites, and factories capable

[74] See Barry Posen, "The War for Kosovo: Serbia's Political-Military Strategy," *International Security* Vol. 24, No. 4 (Spring 2000), pp. 51–2.
[75] Lambeth, *NATO's Air War for Kosovo*, p. 31.
[76] Ibid., pp. 27–8.
[77] Ibid., p. 37.
[78] Ibid., p. 39.

of producing weapons and spare parts."[79] On May 3, restrictions on targeting the electrical grid were lifted and attacks on five transformers left seventy percent of Serbia in the dark. Even the accidental bombing of the Chinese embassy in Belgrade on May 7 did nothing to diminish the campaign's increasing intensity. As a result of "the speedy erosion of constraints on NATO's target selection," Posen notes that "Serbia faced for the first time the possibility that its infrastructure might be systematically destroyed." Indeed, "the Serb nation was now in great danger."[80] As if this were not bad enough for Serbia, sentiment within NATO increasingly favored an invasion if the air war proved insufficient. Daalder and O'Hanlon note that "even though NATO never explicitly threatened a ground invasion.... key allies signaled a growing interest in the idea.... and did so in way that no careful observer, including Milosevic, could fail to notice."[81]

On May 27, former Russian Prime Minister Viktor Chernomyrdin traveled to Belgrade and advised Milosevic to accept NATO's terms, particularly the demand that Serbian forces leave Kosovo and be replaced with an international/NATO force. As the Russians generally sided with Serbia, this was a significant indication that Russian support had been lost. He apparently also warned that NATO would resort to a ground invasion if Serbia failed to accept. Milosevic balked and the bombing continued. On the same day Milosevic was indicted for war crimes by the International Criminal Tribunal in the Hague. Chernomyrdin returned to Belgrade on June 2 joined by Finnish President Martti Ahtisaari. They laid out NATO's terms for an end to the bombing, the key conditions being: (1) an end to the violence in Kosovo, (2) a rapid withdrawal of all Serbian forces, (3) the deployment of an international security force in Kosovo under the banner of the United Nations, (4) the return of all refugees, and (5) the participation in a political process for Kosovo self-government (not independence). Milosevic was told this was the best deal he could get. He agreed. Seventy-eight days after the first attacks Operation Allied Force (OAF) came to an end.[82] NATO would not have to make the tough decision to launch a ground invasion.

Evaluating OAF

Given the disparity of power between NATO and Serbia, the outcome of OAF, like Desert Storm, was not very surprising. If anything, the gap

---

[79] Ibid., p. 39.
[80] Posen, "The War for Kosovo," pp. 73 and 82.
[81] Daalder and O'Hanlon, *Winning Ugly*, p. 155.
[82] Ibid., p. 173.

in military power was greater in 1999 than it had been in 1991. Posen reminds us of the magnitude of the mismatch:

The bald facts of Serbia's strategic situation were discouraging. NATO's combined gross domestic product is nearly 900 times that of Yugoslavia. NATO's combined defense budgets sum to 300 times that of Yugoslavia. NATO's combined population sums to nearly 70 times that of Yugoslavia. NATO represents an assemblage of countries with the most advanced military capabilities in the world. NATO is next door, operating from a base structure built up over nearly a half century of superpower competition.[83]

As a result, "victory in this very small war against a small backward country without powerful friends willing to act on its behalf was never seriously in doubt."[84] Of course, victory in war often seems inevitable after the fact. There was no guarantee, however, that even with the aggregate power disparities the alliance would prevail. If the bombing resulted in numerous civilian casualties or widespread collateral damage, the split in the alliance Milosevic hoped for might very well have emerged. The alliance's vulnerable "center of gravity" was always its political will, which is difficult to capture in quantitative measures of power.

Of course, the reason NATO's center of gravity held was the total absence of allied combat deaths and the low civilian casualties in Serbia and Kosovo. For this we can credit the alliance's extremely restrictive rules of engagement and increased reliance on guided munitions. Lambeth notes that OAF involved a historically "unprecedented use of precision-guided munitions." Whereas in Desert Storm only about ten percent of U.S. combat aircraft could deliver guided munitions, ninety percent had this capability in OAF. It was not just a matter of more guided munitions but also new types, particularly JDAMs. Vickers explains that "with the initial combat employment of the Joint Direct Attack Munition (JDAM), the war for Kosovo further accelerated the shift toward all-weather, GPS-guided munitions. The $14,000 JDAM outperformed laser-guided bombs and cruise missiles that are 10 to 70 times more expensive, and became the weapons of choice for the most sensitive targets."[85] These munitions help explain why "the most intense and sustained military operation to have been conducted in Europe since the end of World War II" resulted in no more than 528 civilian casualties in Serbia and Kosovo.[86] A journalist in Belgrade described the bombing's accuracy in almost haunting terms: "Like ice-pick punctures in the neck, the chilling quality of the strikes

[83] Posen, "The War for Kosovo," pp. 49–50.
[84] Michael G. Vickers, "Revolution Deferred," p. 191.
[85] Ibid., p. 194.
[86] Lambeth, *NATO's Air War for Kosovo*, p. 219 and Human Rights Watch, "The Crisis in Kosovo." Accessed at: www.hrw.org/legacy/reports/2000/nato/Natbm200–01.htm.

was not their size but their placement. We stopped at an intersection in the heart of the city. At each corner of the intersection, but only at each corner, were the ruins.... The precision of the destruction suggested a war with an invisible, all-seeing enemy."[87] But as with Desert Storm, it is easy to exaggerate. In fact, the majority of bombs used in OAF were old-fashioned unguided munitions: of the roughly 28,000 munitions used, fewer than 7,000 (29%) were guided. Although this is unprecedented, it is important to point out that the vast majority of munitions used in OAF were old-fashioned free-fall bombs. But given the relatively small number of civilian casualties, guided munitions were obviously successful when precision was needed most. Without this capability it is difficult to imagine NATO waging a successful air war within the political constraints its member governments faced. Precision weapons allowed NATO to create hardship for the Serbian people and promised a lot more without large-scale civilian casualties to provoke outrage.

Precise targeting, as mentioned several times already, is worthless without precise information. On this score, OAF offers encouraging as well as cautionary lessons. NATO's ability to locate and bomb stationary targets was excellent. In addition to systems such as JSTARS, the proliferation of UAVs "provided commanders and planners with the frequent advantage of real-time video imagery without any accompanying danger of aircrew losses."[88] The Serbs, however, were well aware of American capabilities. They saw what was accomplished in Desert Storm. As a result, they exploited the limitations of existing surveillance technologies by using a variety of deception techniques to avoid detection or confuse NATO targeting. Serb forces in Kosovo, for example, moved in small groups that could not be detected by JSTARS. They comingled with the local population, making both detection and targeting nearly impossible. Only on the rare occasions when Serb forces had to mass to fight the KLA were NATO air strikes very effective. Serb forces even deployed primitive decoys disguised as tanks or artillery that successfully fooled NATO. Thomas relates how the Serbs "knowing when reconnaissance flights would be conducted ... would preposition armored vehicles to be picked up as targets. Then the Serbs would move the actual targets: in some instances they would put in the target's place an old tractor with a telephone pole attached to make it look like a tank from 15,000 feet."[89] Serb efforts illustrated the ability of a technologically inferior but clever

[87] Blaine Harden, "The Milosevic Generation," *New York Times Magazine* (August 29, 1999), p. 34.
[88] Lambeth, *NATOs Air War for Kosovo*, p. 94.
[89] Timothy L. Thomas, "Kosovo and the Current Myth of Information Superiority," *Paramaters* Vol. 30, No. 1 (Spring 2000), p. 24. He notes a number of other problems, particularly with respect to the timely transmission of information on mobile targets, that denied allied forces the benefits of information superiority. See also "Kosovo: Allies

foe to deny complete battlespace awareness.[90] The fog of war was not completely lifted.

What surprised observers most, however, was not NATO's military performance or Serb ingenuity but rather the alliance's ability to force concessions using only air power. The prominent military historian John Keegan, for example, claimed that "there is a new turning point to fix on the calendar: June 3, 1999, when the capitulation of President Milosevic proved that a war could be won by air power alone."[91] Reflecting the extent to which this upset traditional military assumptions, he conceded that he felt "rather as a creationist Christian . . . being shown his first dinosaur bone."[92] Keegan was not alone in his surprise. Daalder and O'Hanlon also offered a postwar mea culpa: "Like many of the analysts looking at the war in Kosovo, we were (fortunately) wrong . . . the air campaign succeeded. NATO achieved its objectives without launching a ground invasion or changing its demands."[93] Days after the war's end, General Merrill McPeak, the Air Force Chief of Staff, was asked whether "some of the nay sayers who said that air power just couldn't do this were proved wrong?" Not surprisingly, he responded, "Yes. A lot of defense pundits have egg on their face at this point." He warned, however, that "they will find reasons for explaining away this – this decisive use of air power."[94]

McPeak's warning proved correct. The assertion that air power alone won the war was challenged: a few questioned whether NATO really "won," while many others doubted that "air power alone" brought victory. Critics were quick to point out that "NATO threats and bombing did not halt the ethnic terror for seventy-eight days, more than enough time for Serbia to displace almost a million Kosovar ethnic Albanians and kill thousands in Kosovo."[95] General Klaus Naumann, the German Chairman of the NATO Military Council, was not surprised by this failure, arguing "they are asking for the impossible, they want us to stop the individual murderer going with his knife from village to village and carving up some Kosovars; that you cannot do from the air."[96] This

---

Still Lack Real-Time Targeting," *Jane's Defense News*, accessed at: http://www.janes. com/defence/news/kosovo/jdw990407_01_n.shtml\.

[90] It seems clear in retrospect that NATO officials exaggerated the success of bombing against Serb artillery, tanks, and armored personnel carriers in Kosovo. See John Barry and Evan Thomas, "The Kosovo Coverup," *Newsweek* (May 15, 2000). Accessed at: www.newsweek.com/id/84044?tid=relatedcl.

[91] Hallion, *Storm over Iraq*, p. ix.

[92] Lambeth, *NATO's Air War for Kosovo*, p. 220 (n. 4).

[93] Ivo Daalder and Michael E. O'Hanlon, "Unlearning the Lessons of Kosovo," *Foreign Policy* (Fall 1999), p. 128.

[94] Merrill McPeak interview, *PBS Newshour* (June 16, 1999). Accessed at: http://www .pbs.org/newshour/bb/europe/jan-june99/lessons_6-16.html.

[95] Byman and Waxman, "Kosovo and the Great Air Power Debate," p. 16.

[96] Henricksen, *NATO's Gamble*, p. 192.

is among the reasons Michael Mandelbaum goes so far as to label the war a "perfect failure."[97] Others, such Barry Posen, note that the final terms were somewhat more favorable to Serbia than those on the table at Rambouillet, suggesting NATO did compromise.[98] The vast majority of analysts, however, appear to share Daalder and O'Hanlon's assessment that "NATO achieved its objectives... all Serbian forces left Kosovo, some 50,000 NATO troops have entered in their wake, and more than 1 million refugees and displaced persons returned home."[99] Most postwar debate has focused on a different question: victory or failure, was "air power alone" responsible for the war's outcome?

The debate over OAF is the latest installment in the running controversy over the potential and uses of air power relative to other forms of military power. In previous cases, such as Desert Storm, the issue was complicated because they involved air and ground campaigns, thus requiring analysts to untangle the relative contributions. In contrast, OAF featured no ground war; therefore, the air war must seemingly be credited with the win. This logic has been questioned on two fronts: first, while there may have been no NATO invasion of Kosovo, the KLA was fighting the Serbs on the ground. NATO may have fought solely from the air, but the Serbs faced opponents in the air and on the ground; and second, as the air war entered its twelfth week, even NATO members that initially ruled out a ground campaign came around to support one if the air war failed to cow Milosevic. This is the question on which debate is most intense: was it the air war or the *threat* of a ground invasion that finally brought Milosevic to his knees?

Robert Pape is perhaps the most prominent skeptic of the air-power-alone thesis and has consistently argued that strategic air campaigns aimed at decapitation or eroding enemy resolve do not work. He is unequivocal: "no strategic bombing campaign has ever yielded decisive results."[100] For Pape, air power is most effective when combined with ground forces and focused on degrading the opponent's fielded forces. In OAF, however, aerial attacks on Serb forces in Kosovo had little effect. Lambeth reflects the consensus that "in contrast to Desert Storm... Allied air attacks against dispersed and hidden enemy forces were largely ineffective... hence, Serb atrocities against the Kosovar Albanians increased even as NATO air operations intensified."[101] Pape makes no attempt to argue otherwise. Pape also admits that "the KLA remained far too weak

[97] Michael Mandelbaum, "A Perfect Failure: NATO's War Against Yugoslavia," *Foreign Affairs* Vol. 78, No. 5 (September/October 1999), pp. 2–8.
[98] Posen, "The War for Kosovo," pp. 79–81.
[99] Daalder and O'Hanlon, "Unlearning the Lessons of Kosovo," p. 128.
[100] Robert Pape, "The Limits of Precision-Guided Air Power," *Security Studies* Vol. 7, No. 2 (Winter 1997/98), p. 99.
[101] Lambeth, *NATO's War for Kosovo*, p. 225.

to seriously threaten the Serbian army" and "had not recorded a single offensive success." But if aerial attacks on Serbian forces were largely inef-fective, and KLA ground efforts were unsuccessful, what explains Milo-sevic's capitulation? In Pape's view, Milosevic gave in because NATO was finally preparing for a ground invasion: "in early June 1999, NATO countries were about to formalize a decision to mount a ground inva-sion of Kosovo... [and] the United States and the United Kingdom also took strong measures to make the threat credible." Pape points to the timing of Milosevic's decision, arguing that it is no coincidence it came at the meeting where Chernomyrdin and Ahtisaari warned that NATO was going to invade. As a result, "the more likely explanation... is that Milosevic surrendered from fear that NATO would invade Kosovo, with the devastating help of precision air power."[102] The air campaign would not have induced a Serbian withdrawal from Kosovo in the absence of a credible invasion threat.

For advocates of the air-power-alone thesis, Pape underestimates the consequences of the air war while exaggerating the threat of a ground invasion. Support for a ground attack may have been growing, but the signals were decidedly mixed and public opinion in NATO countries was deeply divided at best. Although some preliminary preparations were in progress, an invasion was clearly not imminent. It would likely have taken until September for NATO to position the necessary forces, and NATO was not close to an invasion when Milosevic surrendered. This raises the obvious question: if NATO's bombing was not sufficiently coercive nor the invasion imminent, why would Milosevic not wait to see if NATO had the political will to move forward with an invasion before he conceded? As Stigler notes, "from Milosevic's perspective, it should have been obvi-ous that a ground invasion would require a lengthy buildup. The media could be counted on to report the start of the necessary preparations."[103] Stephen Hosmer makes the same point, explaining that "Milosevic and his advisers probably regarded invasion as a more distant threat – one that would provide weeks of strategic warning before it evolved."[104] Pape would have us believe that Milosevic's decision to withdraw from Kosovo resulted not from weeks of bombing and the prospect of many more but rather from the threat of ground invasion that had yet to be approved and was months away. Fareed Zakaria can barely contain his incredulity with such arguments: "NATO flew 37,465 sorties, relentlessly destroying every major military, industrial and communications site in

[102] Robert Pape, "The True Worth of Air Power," *Foreign Affairs* Vol. 83, No. 2 (March/April 2004), p. 124.
[103] Andrew L. Stigler, "A Clear Victory for Air Power: NATO's Empty Threat to Invade Kosovo," *International Security* Vol. 27, No. 3 (Winter 2002/03), p. 143.
[104] Stephen T. Hosmer, *Why Milosevic Decided to Settle When He Did* (Santa Monica, CA: RAND, 2000), p. 110.

Serbia. But if you thought this was what made Milosevic fold, you're wrong. Soon after the war, commentators decided that it was a couple of phrases that Bill Clinton muttered about the possibility of ground troops that did the trick. Who knew that words could be so powerful?"[105]

As Zakaria's sarcasm suggests, many find Pape's argument implausible. Instead, they believe that NATO's attacks, particularly once escalated to military, leadership, and infrastructure targets, were beginning to take their toll.[106] By bringing the war home to Serbia's people and political leadership, support for the war was beginning to erode. Byman and Waxman explain that "initially the air strikes bolstered the Yugoslav's president's stature . . . over time, however, NATO air strikes appear to have contributed to discontent in the federation."[107] Indeed, "by the end of the seventh week, there began to be reports of Yugoslav officials openly admitting that the country was on the verge of widespread hardship because of the air war's mounting damage to the nation's economy."[108] And although it was precisely the sort of mistake that should have given NATO a pause, even the bombing of the Chinese embassy did nothing to diminish the onslaught. The weeks between the embassy bombing and Milosevic's meeting with Chernomyrdin and Ahtisaari saw the most intense bombing of OAF. Arkin notes that while "an average of 362 weapons were dropped per day" throughout the war, "70 percent or more of the bombs were dropped is the war's final three weeks."[109] So when Milosevic met with Chernomyrdin and Ahtisaari on July 2, he faced an escalating air war that was inflicting significant damage on the country's infrastructure without any end in sight. As a result, Stephen Hosmer notes, "When explaining the decision to accept NATO's terms, Milosevic and other senior officials have consistently asserted that the primary reason was to avoid the destructive bombing that a failure to yield would have inevitably unleashed."[110]

Questions about whether air power "won" the war in Kosovo and debates about the existence of an RMA are not one in the same. The case for a new RMA does not rely on the supposition that air power can now win wars on its own. Nonetheless, one of the major themes in arguments

[105] Fareed Zakaria, "Face the Facts: Bombing Works," *Newsweek* Vol. 138, No. 23 (December 3, 2001), p. 54.
[106] See, for example, Lambeth, *NATO's War for Kosovo*, especially pp. 77–86; and Stigler, "A Clear Victory for Air Power," pp. 124–57.
[107] Byman and Waxman, "Kosovo and the Great Air Power Debate," p. 19.
[108] Lambeth, *NATO's War for Kosovo*, p. 41.
[109] Arkin, "Operation Allied Force," p. 21. See also Lambeth, *NATO's War for Kosovo*, pp. 64–5. Interestingly, Pape portrays the air campaign as diminishing in intensity, claiming that "by the time Milosevic surrendered, the rate of attacks on new strategic targets was declining sharply, especially in the weeks after NATO embarrassed itself by bombing the Chinese embassy" ("The True Worth of Air Power," p. 124). The critical qualifier in this description appears to be "new strategic targets."
[110] Hosmer, *Why Milosevic Decided to Settle When He Did*, p. 92.

for a new RMA is that technological advances have had a disproportionate impact on the effectiveness and lethality of air power compared
to other forms of military power. It is important to remember that not
all components of military power need be equally revolutionized in an
RMA. If new technologies led to new ways of fighting wars that fundamentally alter the traditional mix of various aspects of military power,
this in itself can be considered revolutionary and could represent a change
in the nature of warfare as significant as past RMAs. This appears to be
what Pape has in mind. Although he is critical of many claims of air
power enthusiasts, particularly regarding the value of strategic attacks,
he admits that "precision air weaponry has revolutionized warfare, as
its advocates claim." The revolution in warfare involves a fundamental
increase in the leverage of air power compared to other elements of mili
tary power: "air power used to play a supporting role. Bombing's greater
accuracy means that now, and in the future, these roles are likely to be
reversed."[111]

Air-Centric versus Network-Centric Warfare

For some RMA/NCW advocates, the most important lessons of OAF
were offered not by the forces and weapons that won the war, but rather
those that never even got into the fight. Shortly after NATO's bombing campaign began on March 23, General Clark requested U.S. Army
Apache helicopters to assist in attacks on Serbian targets, particularly
tanks, in Kosovo. President Clinton approved the deployment, known as
Task Force Hawk, on April 4. What followed became one of the most
controversial aspects of OAF.

　　The ill-fated task force faced challenges from the outset. The original
basing plan had to be altered when the Macedonians refused permission
to launch offensive operations from their territory. The location then
shifted to Albania, where existing facilities were inadequate to support
the force or accommodate the large cargo aircraft that would deliver it.
Partly for this reason, it took more than three weeks for the twenty-four
Apache helicopters to arrive, and then another two weeks passed before
they were ready for action. Renovating the air base was not the only cause
of delay. The Apaches were also accompanied by more than 6,000 troops,
12 M1A1 tanks, 42 Bradley fighting vehicles and 37 other helicopters, and
moving all this manpower and equipment to a somewhat remote airfield
in Albania was a complex, time-consuming, and an expensive logistical
task.[112] And even once the task force was on the ground in Albania,
there were further problems. The Army would have been hard-pressed,

[111] Pape, "Hit or Miss: Pape Replies," pp. 162–3.
[112] Vickers, "Revolution Deferred," p. 198.

for example, to make any use of the M1A1 tanks that were delivered. At more than seventy tons a piece, "Army planners discovered that moving tanks from Albania into Kosovo would have required four heavy engineering battalions working for four months to reinforce a dozen bridges along the route."[113] For those who saw a need to create a lighter force with greater strategic mobility, none of this was encouraging. Lawrence Korb characterized Task Force Hawk as "a metaphor for how heavy the army is," pointing out that "if you can't get it to where you want to, it's no good."[114]

An additional concern, less noted at the time but particularly galling for advocates of NCW, was the problems of interoperability in incorporating Army helicopters into a largely Air Force effort. Even more basic than the absence of adequate pilot training for such a joint mission was the inability of Army and Air Force systems to communicate. A postwar Government Accounting Office's analysis of Task Force Hawk highlighted the problem:

> The older mission planning and targeting system used by the Apache unit in Albania was also not compatible with the Air Force system. The Air Force has a single digital battlefield command system. The Apache unit in Albania, using its older equipment, could not readily share data directly with the Air Force. In addition, the intelligence system being used by the Army at the unit level and at the liaison level could not directly exchange information with the Air Force.[115]

Owens found it inexcusable that "sixteen years after Grenada – during which the Army ground troops found themselves unable to communicate with Navy carrier aircraft providing close-air support on the battlefield – the Army and Air Force units rushed to Kosovo could still not communicate with one another."[116]

Despite the effort and expense of deploying Task Force Hawk, the Apaches never saw combat in Kosovo. The reasons for this were many, including fears that their vulnerability to enemy fire and the difficult terrain might lead to unacceptably high loss rates and casualties.[117] Since OAF was probably the most casualty-sensitive military campaign ever waged, this was a major concern. As a result, at the end of the war the deployment of Task Force Hawk seemed like a complete waste of

---

[113] Richard J. Newman, "After the Tank," *U.S. News and World Report* Vol. 129, No. 11 (September 18, 2000), p. 42.

[114] Interview with Lawrence Korb, *PBS Frontline: The Future of War* (2000). Accessed at: www.pbs.org/wgbh/pages/frontline/shows/future/interviews/korb.html.

[115] *Kosovar Air Operations: Army Resolving Lessons Learned Regarding the Apache Helicopter* (Washington, DC: U.S. General Accounting Office, 2001), p. 14.

[116] Owens, *Lifting the Fog of War*, p. 199. See also, Bruce R. Nardulli, Walter L. Perry, Bruce Pirnie, John Gordon, and John McGinn, *Disjointed War: Military Operations in Kosovo* (Santa Monica, CA: RAND, 2002), especially pp. 57–98.

[117] See Daalder and O'Hanlon, *Winning Ugly*, pp. 125–6.

resources. "All in all," Adams notes, "it was a miserable performance followed by a great deal of finger pointing."[118] And for RMA/NCW advocates like Owens, "the Task Force Hawk incident was a telling example of how the revolution in military affairs remains hobbled by the paralyzed U.S. military bureaucracy and infrastructure."[119] The technologies associated with the RMA may benefit air power disproportionately, but waging war only from the air is not the be-all and end-all of the RMA. OAF may have been an "air-centric" war, but this did not mean it was a "net-centric" war. It revealed how far the United States had come in exploiting some technologies, but also how far it had yet to go with others.

Conclusion

The United States emerged from the Cold War and Desert Storm without a significant strategic rival or peer military competitor. This defining strategic reality of the 1990s is critical for understanding not only the American defense policy, but also the potential for realizing an RMA. Murray and Knox argue that previous "revolutions in military affairs have emerged from evolutionary problem-solving directed at specific operational and tactical issues in a specific theater against a specific enemy. Successful innovators have always thought in terms of fighting wars against *actual* rather than *hypothetical* opponents." Historical RMAs, in their analysis, have "depended on the existence of concrete adversaries against which to frame innovation."[120] Desert Storm came at the end of just such a period when the Soviet Union was the actual opponent framing American military innovation. Focusing on the Soviet Union's demise and the end of the Cold War, Kagan emphasizes the same point, arguing that "there is virtually no example in history of a revolution in military affairs being conducted *successfully* in such a strategic vacuum."[121] In the absence of a credible threat, military planners lack the information, resources, and motivation that usually drive successful innovation: military challenges are vague, defense spending tends to decline, and the sense of strategic urgency diminishes.

Murray and Knox suggest an interesting dichotomy between *actual* and *hypothetical* opponents. And since the American military lacked an actual opponent in the 1990s, they implicitly assume the need for a hypothetical opponent to drive innovation. But this construct may not provide the best way to characterize the options. Perhaps it is better to think in terms of *specific* versus *generic* opponents rather than actual and hypothetical.

---

[118] Adams, *The Army After Next*, p. 61.
[119] Owens, *Lifting the Fog of War*, pp. 199–200.
[120] Murray and Knox, *The Dynamics of Military Revolution*, pp. 181 and 192.
[121] Kagan, *Finding the Target*, p. 200, emphasis added.

That is, if it is impossible to identify and prepare for a specific opponent, it might be reasonable to make a judgment about the *type* of opponent one is most likely to encounter. Indeed, that might be the only sensible approach. This may not yield equally specific information about operational and tactical issues that need to be addressed, but it provides general guidance about what kinds of problems one might anticipate in a future conflict. It is difficult to know what else can be done in a strategic vacuum. An actual opponent cannot be willed into existence for the convenience of defense planners. There is no value in imposing a false specificity on an uncertain and ambiguous strategic environment.

Kagan laments that during the 1990s "none of the visionaries tied their programs to any particular threat or the solution to any pressing military problem." That is, theorists such as Owens and Cebrowski advanced visions of warfare and proposals for innovation without reference to any actual enemy. Kagan goes so far as to claim that their ideas were "without careful connection to reality."[122] On one level, of course, Kagan is absolutely correct. Net-centric warfare, for example, was not tied to a specific opponent in the same way that AirLand Battle in the 1980s focused on the Soviet Union. There is a good reason for this: there were no major opponents or pressing military problems, only minor opponents and less-than-pressing military problems. That is the nature of strategic vacuums. In the absence of a specific opponent and specific tactical and operational issues in a specific theater, these visions assumed a generic conventional opponent and linked innovation to solving the generic tactical and operational challenges of conventional warfare. Intelligence gathering, communications, and target acquisition were viewed as valuable capabilities against any conventional military enemy – perhaps a mistaken assumption, but hardly a disconnect from reality. Whether the resulting innovations were successful remained to be seen.

[122] Ibid., p. 362.

5 AFGHANISTAN AND THE SECOND IRAQ WAR, 2001–2003 – A REVOLUTION CONFIRMED?

Bush, Rumsfeld, and Military Transformation

When his campaign for the presidency began, George W. Bush's foreign and defense policy views were something of mystery. There was little indication that he had devoted much thought to international issues of the day, and as a two-term governor of Texas, there was no need for him to do so. To be taken seriously as a future commander-in-chief, however, he could not remain a blank slate, especially since Senator John McCain was expected to be his chief rival for the Republican nomination. Given McCain's distinguished military career and nearly two decades in the Senate, he was sure to paint Bush as a foreign and defense policy neophyte, although whether this line of attack would carry much weight in the relatively serene international environment of the late 1990s was unclear. But Bush did not wait long to stake out his position, using a speech at the Citadel military academy in September 1999 to provide the first indications of his vision for American foreign and defense policy.[1]

Bush's speech began unremarkably, consisting largely of widely voiced conservative criticisms of the Clinton era. Bush promised to "renew the bond of trust between the American President and the American military," suggesting, of course, that the antimilitary and borderline draft-dodging Clinton had severed the bond. Claiming that "not since the years before Pearl Harbor has our investment in national defense been so low as a percentage of GNP," he pledged to reverse the decline in defense spending begun by his father and continued under Clinton. He lamented the military's low morale, blaming low pay and, somewhat ironically given future events, "back-to-back deployments" on "vague" and "aimless" missions. This would become a standard Bush campaign theme: under Clinton the military was underpaid, inadequately equipped,

---

[1] George W. Bush, "A Period of Consequences," September 23, 1999. Transcript available at: www.citadel.edu/pao/addresses/pres_bush.html.

poorly funded, and overstretched by misguided peace-keeping and nation-building missions that had little to do with the nation's security. All of this was pretty standard fare in Republican circles, the sort of thing any candidate for the party's nomination might say. Were this all he had to say, Bush's address would have been a forgettable stump speech. But when he turned his attention to defense policy, eyebrows began to rise as he offered a ringing endorsement of military transformation and the RMA.

In Bush's view the American military was "still organized more for Cold War threats than for the challenges of a new century." The time had come to "begin creating the military of the next century . . . [and] a new architecture of American defense for decades to come" that exploited the "revolution in the technology of war, . . . [a] revolution [that] perfectly matches the strengths of our country – the skill of our people and the superiority of our technology." What was the nature of this revolution? What would the new architecture look like? Bush's outline could easily have come from the pen of Marshall, Owens or Cebrowski:

Power is increasingly defined, not by mass or size, but by mobility and swift-ness. Influence is measured in information, safety is gained in stealth, and force is projected on the long arc of precision-guided weapons. . . . Our forces in the next century must be agile, lethal, readily deployable, and require a minimum of logis-tical support. We must be able to project our power over long distances, in days or weeks rather than months. Our military must be able to identify targets by a vari-ety of means – from a Marine patrol to a satellite. Then be able to destroy those targets almost instantly, with an array of weapons, from a submarine-launched cruise missile, to mobile long-range artillery. On land, our heavy forces must be lighter. Our light forces must be more lethal. All must be easier to deploy. And these forces must be organized in smaller, more agile formations, rather than cumbersome divisions.

Even this might not seem terribly earth shattering, but to those in the know the RMA buzzwords and themes were impossible to miss. As Nicholas Lemann noted, "if you owned a secret decoder ring, the speech was highly significant: Bush had just endorsed the Revolution in Military Affairs."[2] His speech represented "the most emphatic pro-transformation statement yet from a national leader."[3] Bush's enthusiastic embrace of the RMA was probably due in no small part to Donald Rumsfeld, one of the campaign's senior defense policy advisers and, in the words of one critic, "a notorious addict of RMA/NCW fantasies."[4]

[2] Nicholas Lemann, "Dreaming About War," *The New Yorker* (July 16, 2001), p. 32.
[3] Thomas K. Adams, *The Army After Next: The First Postindustrial Army* (Stanford: Stanford University Press, 2008), p. 95.
[4] Mike Davis, "Wal-mart Revolution in Slouching Toward Baghdad: It's All in the Net-work," *San Francisco Chronicle* (March 9, 2003).

Bush's selection of Rumsfeld as Secretary of Defense was the first of several personnel decisions reflecting his commitment to military transformation. RMA advocates had reason to hope that at long last there might be sufficient political will at the top to achieve the radical changes needed to fully exploit the benefits of the RMA. Shortly after taking office, Rumsfeld tapped Andrew Marshall, father of the RMA, to lead the team conducting the congressionally mandated 2001 Quadrennial Defense Review, an "assignment [that] rang through the Pentagon like a distress signal."[5] Any lingering doubts that the RMA's moment had arrived vanished when Rumsfeld created a new Office of Defense Transformation headed by none other than Arthur Cebrowski. A new regime had clearly arrived, and not everyone was happy about it. RMA advocates were thrilled, of course, but skeptics worried that those in power had imbibed a bit too much of the RMA kool-aid.

Rumsfeld was not the first defense secretary to speak favorably of the RMA and endorse many of its key elements: his predecessor, William Cohen, occasionally offered grandiose assessments of the transformative potential of modern technology. Rumsfeld stands out primarily in the zeal and single-mindedness with which he pursued an RMA agenda that was his "singular priority."[6] Rumsfeld was determined to create, not merely pay lip service to, a smaller, lighter, mobile, and more lethal military force that exploited its overwhelming advantages in information, stealth, and precision to achieve rapid mass effects without massive forces and firepower. He had also taken to heart the argument that new technology alone would not bring a revolution if it was merely incorporated into existing force structures and doctrine. The military would need to reorganize and rethink how it employed force for the RMA to be realized. Like Owens, Rumsfeld viewed the military itself as the greatest obstacle to genuine transformation. As a result of service cultures, institutional interests, and bureaucratic inertia, changes in force structure and doctrine lagged behind advances in technology. In one presentation, Rumsfeld talked about "an adversary that poses a threat, a serious threat, to the security of the United States." The adversary "attempts to impose its demands across time zones, continents, oceans and beyond." Its bureaucracy "stifles free thought and crushes new ideas...plac[ing] the lives men and women in uniform at risk." Rumsfeld's Pentagon

[5] Peter Boyer, "Downfall: How Donald Rumsfeld reformed the Army and lost Iraq," *The New Yorker* Vol. 82, No. 38 (November 20, 2006), p. 58.

[6] Mark G. Czelusta, *Business as Usual: An Assessment of Donald Rumsfeld's Transformation Vision and Transformation's Prospects for the Future*, Occasional Paper Series, Marshall Center for Security Studies, No. 18 (June 2008), p. 4. On Rumsfeld's vision, see also Dale R. Herspring, *Rumsfeld's Wars: The Arrogance of Power* (Lawrence, KS: University Press of Kansas, 2008), pp. 22–67; and Donald Rumsfeld, "Transforming the Military," *Foreign Affairs* Vol. 81, No. 3 (May/June 2002), pp. 20–32.

audience could not have been happy when the suspense was lifted and the enemy revealed: "it's the Pentagon bureaucracy."[7] In effect, the enemy was the very institution he led, and Rumsfeld was declaring war on it.

The rhetoric of military revolution and transformation, already dominant before his arrival, became almost oppressive under Rumsfeld. Because anything that did not advance his agenda appeared to be in danger, there was a mad rush to portray everything as transformational. Systems in development for years were suddenly repackaged and repositioned at the vanguard of military transformation. The pervasiveness of his transformational mantra, however, should not be taken as acceptance of Rumsfeld himself, who proved to be a divisive and polarizing figure. Charging that the Pentagon was placing the lives of its soldiers at risk did not win him any popularity contests. These substantive views were compounded by a personal style that many found abrasive, overbearing, and occasionally demeaning, even to the most senior military officers. After only a few months in office there were rumblings that his days might be numbered. As Adams explains, "by the summer of 2001, the secretary appeared headed for an early departure. The question was not whether President Bush would let Rumsfeld go, but when. As early as April, the on-line magazine *Slate* offered a Rumsfeld 'death watch.'" But on September 11, less than twenty-four hours after Rumsfeld delivered his speech identifying its bureaucracy as the nation's greatest adversary, the Pentagon came under attack by a hijacked jetliner. Al-Qaeda was now the nation's greatest adversary, even if the Pentagon bureaucracy remained the major obstacle to military transformation. The attacks also meant that the first test of Rumsfeld's ideas about military transformation would come sooner than anyone expected as the United States turned its sights on the regime that harbored those responsible. The Rumsfeld "death watch" was now on hold.

The Afghan Prelude

Although there was some support in the administration for pursuing Saddam Hussein again immediately after September 11, the president delayed any action against Iraq and instead focused on Afghanistan, where the fundamentalist Taliban regime harbored those responsible for the attacks. Because no one expected the regime to comply with demands to hand over Al-Qaeda leaders, a military option was needed, and quickly. The approach of winter and the political imperative to take some action in response to the attacks left little time, perhaps only a few weeks. Not surprisingly, the Pentagon had no contingency plans on the shelf

---

[7] Michael R. Gordon and Bernard Trainor, *Cobra II: The Inside Story of the Invasion and Occupation of Iraq* (New York: Pantheon, 2006), p. 9.

for an invasion of Afghanistan, and the obstacles to using force against a country dubbed the "graveyard of empires" appeared daunting.[8] Distant, landlocked, mountainous, forbidding, and lacking any neighbors likely to permit the United States to use their territory as a base for attack, Afghanistan presented a unique set of challenges.

Charged with devising a plan to overthrow the Taliban and attack Al-Qaeda, the Joint Chiefs of Staff (JCS) proposed a fairly traditional invasion that would have required months to move the necessary army divisions, thereby delaying an invasion until the spring at the earliest. The idea of waiting half a year, however, before responding to the September 11 attacks was a nonstarter. For advocates of military transformation, the JCS approach was not only politically worthless but also depressingly conservative and unimaginative, the very sort of staid thinking they wanted to change. The CIA, which had experience in Afghanistan and contacts with local forces that had fought the Soviets, countered with a proposal relying on CIA operatives and special operations forces (SOF) operating in conjunction with the indigenous Northern Alliance supported by American air power.[9] The Northern Alliance, which controlled about ten percent of the country, was a loose conglomeration of tribal forces that had been fighting the Taliban for years with little success. The CIA's approach had several things to recommend it. Unlike the JCS plan, it could be put together in only a few weeks, satisfying the political imperative for quick action. If the plan worked, it might preclude the need to introduce large numbers of ground forces, thus avoiding a Soviet style quagmire. Finally, it was an innovative war plan that exploited the United States' technological advantages and resonated with advocates of the RMA and transformation. The CIA carried the day, and the administration moved forward with what would become known as the "Afghan model."

The "Afghan Model"

The Afghan war began in late September with the introduction of CIA agents carrying large amounts of cash tasked with contacting leaders of the Northern Alliance to draw them into a joint effort with the United States to topple the Taliban. The Northern Alliance, however, was hesitant to move against the Taliban until it knew the Americans were committed to the fight. A little cash and the word of a few CIA agents was not enough. The Northern Alliance had no desire to move against the Taliban only to be abandoned. Attacking Taliban targets from the air

---

[8] Milton Bearden, "Afghanistan, Graveyard of Empires," *Foreign Affairs* Vol. 80, No. 6 (November/December 2001), pp. 17–30.

[9] See Gary C. Schroen, *First in: An Insider's Account of How the CIA Spearheaded the War in Terror in Afghanistan* (New York: Ballantine, 2005).

would enable the United States to jumpstart the war and demonstrate its intentions. President Bush learned in early October that sufficient forces and supplies had been deployed to bases in Saudi Arabia, Kuwait, Qatar, Diego Garcia, and Uzbekistan as well as aircraft carriers in the Persian Gulf. Bombers from as far away as England and Whiteman AFB in Missouri would join these local combat aircraft. It was time to move. Operation Enduring Freedom (OEF) began on the morning of October 7, less than a month after the terrorist attacks. If the Taliban expected a long buildup of American forces in advance of an attack, they were mistaken. This was not to be a replay of 1991.

Although the Taliban represented a very different and less formidable opponent than Iraq, the basic structure and objectives of the U.S. air campaign were similar to that waged in 1991. George Friedman explains that "U.S. doctrine was that wars begin with the United States seizing air superiority, which means that it can carry out attacks without danger to its aircraft. Then command and control facilities must be attacked in order to paralyze enemy forces, followed by attacks on ground forces. Operation Enduring Freedom opened with a textbook display of this doctrine."[10]

Achieving air superiority was to come easily: the Taliban's air force contained nothing but a few obsolete aircraft, and its air defenses consisted of a few fixed SAM sites that were promptly knocked out with a few strikes. Attacks then shifted to command and control targets as well as Taliban and Al-Qaeda forces. Initial results were disappointing because of delays in introducing SOF units into Afghanistan. For a variety of reasons, including bad weather, they did not start arriving until October 19 and would not be in place in large numbers until the end of the month. Adams explains that "without the SF teams to 'lase' ground targets with their laser designators there was little application for the air delivered PGMs, and no tactical progress was being made."[11]

Although barely three or four weeks into the war, impatience was growing in the United States, and the word "quagmire" was already being bandied about. John Mearsheimer, prescient in his 1991 predictions of a quick victory, expected failure this time. "American airpower," he warned in an editorial published November 4, "is of limited use because there are few valuable targets to strike in an impoverished country like Afghanistan." Attacks on Taliban and Al-Qaeda forces were unlikely to succeed "because, in the absence of a formidable ground opponent, they can easily disperse." The Northern Alliance did not qualify as such an opponent as "it is despised by many Afghans (and Pakistanis), and the Taliban outnumber it by about three to one. Alliance soldiers are poorly

[10] George Friedman, *America's Secret War: Inside the Hidden Worldwide Struggle Between America and Its Enemies* (New York: Broadway, 2004), p. 169.
[11] Adams, *The Army After Next*, p. 114.

led, trained and equipped." Furthermore, "despite recent talk about how the Northern Alliance would capture Mazar-i-Sharif and Kabul, it has launched no major offensives. Indeed, the Alliance may be losing ground to the Taliban, even with American air support."[12] Mearsheimer's pessimism would very soon be overtaken by events.

The introduction of SOF units in late October marked the decisive turning point. From that point on, "SOF-directed precision airpower transformed the U.S. campaign by radically improving the ability of airpower to destroy the Taliban's fielded forces; once the new tactics were brought to bear, Taliban forces were quickly overwhelmed."[13] The combination of Northern Alliance forces fighting on the ground with SOF units coordinating American air strikes placed the Taliban on the horns of dilemma with no good solution. If massed to take on the Northern Alliance, Taliban forces became the target of devastating aerial bombardment. But when the Taliban responded logically by hiding and dispersing, "they lost most of their ability to conduct conventional operations, rendering them all but ineffective in their main mission of fighting rebel forces."[14]

With all the pieces in place, the offensive against Mazar-i-Sharif commenced just as the ink was drying on Mearsheimer's editorial. Five days later on November 9, the Northern Alliance, thanks to the assistance of SOF units and American air power, captured the city, yielding "the first tangible victory in Enduring Freedom."[15] A quick progression of successes followed. After the capture of Mazar-i-Sharif, the Northern Alliance turned its attention to Kabul and drove Taliban forces from the city in days. With the fall of Kabul on December 7, "the resistance now controlled nearly three-quarters of the country, as contrasted with only 10 percent in the northernmost reaches before the start of the campaign just a few weeks before."[16] Next in line was Kandahar, the Taliban's last remaining stronghold and its real center of power. By the end of the first week of December, only two months after the start of OEF, the Taliban fled from Kandahar as well, leading Hamid Karzai to declare, "Taliban rule is finished. As of today, they are no longer part of Afghanistan."[17] The speed of Taliban collapse was remarkable: "in the course of two months, 316 SOF and 110 CIA paramilitary officers, working with native

[12] John Mearsheimer, "Guns Won't Win the Afghan War," *The New York Times* (November 4, 2001), Section 4, p. 13.

[13] Richard B. Andres, Craig Wills, and Thomas E. Griffith, "Winning with Allies: The Strategic Value of the Afghan Model," *International Security* Vol. 30, No. 3 (Winter 2005/2006), p. 134.

[14] Ibid., p. 133.

[15] Benjamin S. Lambeth, *Air Power Against Terror: America's Conduct of Operation Enduring Freedom* (Santa Monica, CA: RAND, 2005), p. xvii.

[16] Ibid., p. xix.

[17] Patrick Cockburn and Andrew Buncombe, "'Taliban rule is finished,' says Karzi as Kandahar falls," *The Independent* (December 7, 2001). Accessed at: www.independent .co.uk/news/world/asia/the-taliban-rule-is-finished-says-karzai-as-kandahar-falls-619314.html.

insurgents and backed by massive amounts of air power, brought the Taliban regime down and denied Al Qaeda the use of the country as a safe haven."[18] Even the most optimistic supporters of the CIA could not have expected that the Taliban would fall in such short order.

After Kandahar, the war entered a new phase focused on finding Osama Bin Laden and wiping out Al-Qaeda in the western mountainous region along the border with Pakistan to which they had fled. The bulk of the fighting occurred in Tora Bora, and by all accounts this phase of the war was not nearly as successful in part because "it became more difficult for U.S. forces to motivate the Northern Alliance to continue to prosecute the fight against Al Qaeda." The United States' surrogates "were not concerned with fighting Al Qaeda ... Afghan soldiers arrived in Tora Bora with little equipment and even less motivation to pursue Al Qaeda in such a harsh environment."[19] This highlighted one of the limits of the Afghan model: it works only so long as the objectives of external and indigenous actors are aligned. When local forces engaged Al-Qaeda fighters they found an opponent that fought with greater ferocity and skill than the Taliban. Furthermore, caves and valleys in the region helped Al-Qaeda avoid detection. Even with all the intelligence assets at its disposal, the United States struggled to locate small bands of fighters determined to escape. By the time American ground forces were sent, Bin Laden and many others had probably escaped into Pakistan, leading to endless second-guessing about whether the battle in Tora Bora was mismanaged, causing the United States to miss its golden opportunity to capture Bin Laden.

Evaluating the "Afghan Model"

In OEF, the United States joined an ongoing conflict in Afghanistan in which the Northern Alliance had been battling the Taliban and their Al-Qaeda allies for control of the country. Prior to 2002, the Northern Alliance had been held at bay, controlling only a small part of northeast Afghanistan. But then in a matter of only a few weeks the introduction of a few hundred American special operations forces able to call in precision air strikes transformed the conflict, completely reversing the Northern Alliance's fortunes as the Taliban regime was chased from power.[20] For RMA proponents it was a stunning turn of events. As was the case in the Gulf War, the sheer rapidity and ease of victory was taken as evidence of fundamental change. After all, was there any parallel in the history

---

[18] Mahnken, *Technology and the American War of War*, p. 197.

[19] Brian E. Mead, *The Future of the Afghan Model: Unconventional Application of Conventional Counterland Doctrine* (Maxwell AFB, April 2008), p. 16.

[20] See Eliot A. Cohen, "Stephen Biddle on Military Power," *The Journal of Strategic Studies* Vol. 28, No. 3 (June 2005), pp. 421–2.

of warfare? Would such a campaign have been possible even a decade earlier? Andres, Wills, and Griffith were typical of RMA proponents in arguing that "the military operation the United States conducted to overthrow the Taliban...represents something new in warfare," a "new way of war."[21] Military analyst Andrew Krepinevich declared the war "a wake-up call for transformation...exhibit A in the list of evidence that warfare is changing."[22] And Max Boot thinks "Afghanistan showed how successful a netwar could be."[23]

Not surprisingly, the administration shared this view. As the Taliban were fleeing Kandahar, Bush returned to the Citadel and presented Afghanistan as an example and vindication of the "revolution in our military...[that] promises to change the face of battle." Commanders and special forces on the ground benefited from technologies that provided a "a real-time picture of the entire battlefield" and an ability "to get information from sensor to shooter almost instantly." The war broke new ground in that "this combination – real-time intelligence, local allied forces, and precision air power – ha[d] never really been used." This model demonstrated how "innovative doctrine and high-tech weaponry can shape and dominate an unconventional conflict." It was but the latest example of how "warfare will be truly revolutionized" as a result of new technologies and war-fighting doctrine.[24]

On one level the revolutionary or transformational nature of the Afghan war derives from the continued exploitation of the now familiar technologies and capabilities that form the foundation of the RMA. In terms of guided munitions, for example, "whereas only 9 percent of the munitions expended during the Gulf War featured precision guidance and 29 percent of the munitions employed during the air war over Kosovo were guided, during Operation Enduring Freedom two years later nearly 60 percent were guided."[25] Their declining cost and the political imperative of avoiding civilian casualties and collateral damage dictated an increasing reliance on guided munitions. The quantity and quality of intelligence continued to improve with more and better sensors on the ground and overhead. Lambeth focuses on this aspect of the Afghan war, arguing "for the first time in the history of modern warfare, Operation Enduring Freedom was conducted under an overarching intelligence, surveillance, and reconnaissance (ISR) umbrella that stared down relentlessly in search of enemy activity." Improvements in the ability to share and disseminate information was perhaps most important because "this multiplicity of interlinked and mutually supporting sensors...allowed

[21] Andres, Wills and Griffith, "Winning with Allies," pp. 124 and 127.
[22] In Kagan, *Finding the Target*, p. 311.
[23] Boot, *War Made New*, p. 382.
[24] In Kagan, *Finding the Target*, pp. 305–6.
[25] Mahnken, *Technology and the American Way of War*, p. 200.

for greater connectivity not only between sensors and shooters, but also between those with execution authority at the point of contact with the enemy and more senior decision makers."[26] The ability of SOF units to laser designate targets or transmit coordinates using GPS to aircraft delivering munitions was essential to the success of the Afghan model.

For RMA enthusiasts the most remarkable aspect of the Afghan campaign was not only the volume of information or reliance on guided munitions but also the unprecedented level of jointness involved in the coordination of SOF units and air power. This indicates, albeit on a small scale, the kind of organizational change supposedly needed to achieve a genuine RMA. For Cebrowski, "network-centric warfare combines the four military branches into a seamless, joint warfighting force."[27] This was one of the major criticisms of military transformation in the 1990s: it was too focused on technology and too little on organizational and doctrinal change. In this vein Marine Lt. Col. Paul Van Riper saw in Afghanistan "a unique combination, a new organization, in which special operational forces were working directly with what in the past would have been assets we would have identified as strategic air assets – B-52 bombers in particular. You had something nobody had envisioned before."[28] Cebrowski made the same observation in broader terms:

the conflict was not the Special Operations force doing thus and so, or the U.S. Marine Corps doing thus and so. Rather it was a commander of U.S. Central Command as a joint commander operating his joint force. Nobody did anything by themselves. It was a level of teamwork that was far grander and more sophisticated than anything we had seen before.... In Afghanistan we found a level of teamwork that led us all to believe that we were looking at indicators of a new level of jointness, a new concept of joint interdependency that we hadn't seen before. That was one of the more stunning lessons.[29]

The transformational nature of the Afghan war did not impress everyone. Stephen Biddle was among the dissenters who saw little revolutionary in its conduct. He does not deny that certain aspects of the war were indeed "quite new: the fire support came almost exclusively from the air; the air strikes were directed mostly by commandos whose methods,

[26] Lambeth, *Air Power Against Terror*, pp. 253–4.
[27] Arthur Cebrowski and Thomas P.M. Barnett, "The American Way of War," *Transformation Trends* (January 13, 2003). Accessed at: www.au.af.mil/au/awc/awcgate/transformation/trends_165_transformation_trends_13_january_2003_issue.pdf.
[28] Interview with Paul Van Riper, *PBS Nova: Battle Plan Under Fire* (2004). Accessed at: www.pbs.org/wgbh/nova/wartech/nature.html. Van Riper is not, however, an RMA enthusiast. In the same interview he rejects the RMA, asserting that the nature of war never changes. Of course, RMA theorists posit a change in the character of war, not its nature.
[29] Interview with Arthur Cebrowski, *PBS Nova: Battle Plan Under Fire* (2004). Accessed at: www.pbs.org/wgbh/nova/wartech/transform.html.

equipment, and centrality to the outcome were *unprecedented*, and the ground armies were mostly not countrymen of the commandos and air forces who provided the firepower."[30] The war plan "surely surprised the Taliban" because even though "neither SOF nor PGMs were new, they had *never* been combined in quite this way before, presenting a *novel* problem for the defenders."[31] In the end, "the outcome of this territorial struggle was affected *profoundly* by SOF-directed precision air power – this ultimately made the difference between stalemate and victory."[32] And when it comes to advances in "firepower's range, precision, round-the-clock lethality, responsiveness and flexibility," Biddle agrees that the "changes have been *revolutionary* if considered chiefly in terms of their effect on the way fires have been provided."[33,34] Indeed, Biddle goes so far as to agree with RMA proponents in claiming "the introduction of precision air power is what turned a stalemated civil war into a decisive defeat for the Taliban."[35] Although this would appear to support the case for a contemporary RMA, Biddle nonetheless warns that it would be "a mistake to see Afghanistan as radical break with prior military experience."[36] Despite the admittedly novel combination of forces and firepower, the Afghan war was actually a "surprisingly *orthodox* air-ground campaign."[37] The lesson Biddle takes away from Afghanistan is that "the key to success, whether in 1916 or 2002, is to team heavy, well-directed fires with skilled ground maneuver."[38] The war confirmed "the necessary synergy between fires and maneuver [that] has been at the heart of most great power military doctrines since 1918."[39] So, despite the radical advances in technology during the previous century, Biddle sees the continuities between World War I and the invasion of Afghanistan as more significant than the differences.

Biddle reaches this conclusion because he thinks any military campaign combining ground maneuver and firepower is merely another manifestation of the modern system that emerged in the final years of World War I. He consistently points out that OEF failed to demonstrate an ability

---

[30] Stephen Biddle, *Afghanistan and the Future of Warfare: Implications for Army and Defense Policy* (Carlisle, PA: U.S. Army War College, 2002), p. 6, emphasis added. See also Stephen Biddle, "Afghanistan and Future of Warfare," *Foreign Affairs* Vol. 82, No. 2 (March/April 2003), pp. 31–46.
[31] Ibid., p. 19, emphasis added.
[32] Ibid., p. 44, emphasis added.
[33] Ibid., p. 48, emphasis added.
[34] Ibid., p. 48, emphasis added.
[35] Biddle, *Military Power*, p. 202.
[36] Biddle, *Afghanistan and the Future of Warfare*, p. 49.
[37] Ibid., p. 6.
[38] Ibid., p. viii.
[39] Ibid., p. 44.

of maneuver or firepower to win battles or wars on their own, implicitly adopting this as the criterion for revolutionary change. Making the
case for continuity, he places OEF in a larger historical context: "The
Afghan campaign – like the Western Front in World War I, the invasions
of France, Poland or Russia in 1939–41, the Northwest European campaign of 1944–45, the Mideast Wars of 1956–1982, or any dozens of
other, similar examples – was a joint air-land war in which the ability to
combine fire and maneuver by diverse arms made the difference between
success and failure."[40] There was no radical or revolutionary change
because "what technology has *not* done is to enable us to succeed using
firepower or maneuver alone."[41] In Biddle's view, "the key to success in
Afghanistan *as in traditional joint warfare* was the close interaction of
firepower and maneuver, neither of which was *sufficient* alone."[42]

This analysis of the Afghan war reveals the same absolutist framing
of military change evident in Biddle's discussion of the modern system,
which he claimed could only be revolutionized by technology making
terrain "irrelevant" and any form of concealment or cover impossible. His
standard here appears equally demanding: only a war waged exclusively
with ground maneuver or firepower could be considered revolutionary. As
long as there is some combination of the two, whatever their character,
source, effectiveness, or relative contribution, there is no radical break
with the past. For RMA proponents, however, it strains credulity to
emphasize continuity over change merely because both the Germans in
1916 and the Americans in 2002 coordinated maneuver and firepower
on the battlefield. Cohen characterizes this argument as "a case of seizing
on the trees so as to avoid looking at the forest. . . . a conclusion that
common sense rejects."[43]

The Second Iraq War, 2003

By the middle of 2002, "the war in Afghanistan had largely settled down
to sniping, skirmishes and intermittent rocket and mortar attacks . . . [and]
the situation appeared to be largely contained."[44] With the toppling of
the Taliban and the introduction of limited American ground forces into
Afghanistan to conduct postwar stabilization and pursue remnants of
the Taliban and Al-Qaeda, those in the administration who wanted to
go after Iraq from the start renewed their efforts. Now that the first
order of post-9/11 business was almost out of the way, it was time to
move on.

[40] Ibid., p. 49.
[41] Ibid., p. 49.
[42] Ibid., p. 6, emphasis added.
[43] Cohen, "Stephen Biddle on Military Power," p. 422.
[44] Adams, *The Army After Next*, p. 132.

The Battle Over the War Plan

Rumsfeld and others in the Department of Defense such as Richard Perle and Paul Wolfowitz began evaluating plans for war against Iraq as early as November 2001. Unlike Afghanistan, however, they did not have to start from scratch. Since the United States had already fought one war with Iraq and engaged in low level military action against it throughout the 1990s, the prospect of another Iraq war not far-fetched. But when briefed on Central Command's (CENTCOM) contingency plan, Rumsfeld did not like what he heard. Last revised in 1998, the CENTCOM plan called for approximately 500,000 troops, not what Rumsfeld had in mind.[45]

Rumsfeld saw several problems with CENTCOM's plan, the most glaring being the number of troops. It appeared to be a replay of the Gulf War without any recognition of the significant changes in the intervening decade. As a result of the Gulf War and subsequent economic sanctions, Iraq's military was now a shadow of its former self, and advances in surveillance capabilities and guided munitions had enhanced American military power despite a reduction in overall troop strength. The ongoing Afghan campaign demonstrated what a small handful of technologically advanced forces combined with devastating air power could accomplish. Although some toyed with the idea of applying the Afghan model to Iraq, most realized that it could not be used without modification, largely because the Iraqi regime was much stronger than the Taliban and there was no Iraqi equivalent of the Northern Alliance. As Steven Metz explains, "Hussein's Army was nearly twenty times the size of the Taliban force... [and] despite American funding for Iraqi resistance movements, none were militarily effective."[46] The success in Afghanistan did, however, indicate that there was no need to recreate the military behemoth deployed to the Gulf in 1991. A somewhat less evident problem with the CENTCOM plan was that required a long deployment phase. Rumsfeld wanted something shorter, perhaps as little as thirty days, that could be implemented as early as spring 2002. The plan as it stood, required a massive logistical effort in support of a deployment that could take half a year, as in 1991. This would not do. The plan was not military transformation but rather a conservative and unimaginative relic of the staid pre-RMA thinking that Rumsfeld had come to Washington to challenge.

General Tommy Franks, the CENTCOM commander, was not unsympathetic to Rumsfeld's concerns. He had also been struck by the success of the war in Afghanistan and agreed that 500,000 troops seemed excessive. He did not object when Rumsfeld instructed him to develop a new approach. Reevaluating the plan, however, was no easy task. There had

[45] Kagan, *Finding the Target*, p. 342; and Gordon and Trainor, *Cobra II*, p. 4.
[46] Steven Metz, *Iraq & The Evolution of American Strategy* (Washington, DC: Potomac Books, 2008), p. 110.

been no official decision for war and everything needed to be done quietly. Franks had to deal with major uncertainties. He had no idea, for example, what bases in the region would be available or whether the United States would have any allies and what their contributions might be. Nonetheless, by early December he had whittled the number down to about 380,000 troops, still way too high for Rumsfeld. Sent back to the drawing board, by the end of December Franks proposed an invasion force that would reach 275,000. Franks presented his plan to President Bush during a December 28 briefing with Rumsfeld listening in by teleconference. Rumsfeld clearly remained dissatisfied, jumping in to assure the President that "the number Tom is giving you is still soft."

The number would remain "soft" for some time. Over the next year, as the administration made its case to build support domestically and internationally, the tug of war over troop levels continued behind the scenes. The numbers debate reflected deeper disagreements on two interrelated, and often difficult to disentangle, questions: First, how many troops would be required to defeat the Iraqi military and oust Saddam Hussein? Second, what would be needed for postwar stabilization and reconstruction? These were very different tasks, and though it might be convenient if the requirements were the same, there was no a priori reason to assume this would be the case. When General Eric Shinseki gave his infamous congressional testimony that so enraged Rumsfeld and the Pentagon civilians indicating a need for "several hundred thousand soldiers" in Iraq, he was addressing the challenges of postwar occupation. This figure derived from his experience with NATO's stabilization efforts in Bosnia-Herzegovina in the 1990s. If the same population-to-force ratios were applied to Iraq, 480,000 troops would be needed. There is no indication that Rumsfeld envisioned a specific alternative to the CENTCOM plan. The Afghan model impressed him, but Franks convinced him that Iraq was not comparable to Afghanistan. In December, Rumsfeld also suggested that Franks familiarize himself with Wade and Ullman's *Shock and Awe*. It appears as if Rumsfeld had an outline of what he wanted, not a detailed blueprint. His basic vision reflected most of the now familiar elements of the RMA: a rapidly deployable small invasion force that would exploit American advantages in information, speed, precision, and air power to bring about a rapid collapse of Saddam Hussein's regime with a minimum of casualties and collateral damage. It is not clear how small an invasion force Rumsfeld thought would be sufficient, though some suggest it may have been as low as 60,000. Such was Rumsfeld's general answer to the first question – that is, the requirements for defeating Iraq and deposing Saddam.

More problematic was Rumsfeld's approach to the postwar phase. Rumsfeld clearly rejected Shinseki's assumption that hundreds of thousands of troops would be required to stabilize post–Saddam Iraq. Rumsfeld responded to Shinseki almost immediately: "The idea that it would take several hundred thousand U.S. forces, I think, is far from the mark."[47] The most pointed criticism of Shinseki came two days later from Paul Wolfowitz:

There has been a good deal of comment – some of it quite outlandish – about what our postwar requirements might be in Iraq. Some of the higher end predictions we have been hearing recently, such as the notion that it will take several hundred thousand U.S. troops to provide stability in post-Saddam Iraq, are wildly off the mark ... It is hard to conceive that it would take more forces to provide stability in post-Saddam Iraq than it would take to conduct the war itself and to secure the surrender of Saddam's security forces and his army – hard to imagine.

It was, of course, quite easy for some to imagine of why it might require more troops to stabilize and secure a country the size of California than it would require to defeat its battered, overmatched, unmotivated, and poorly led military. Wolfowitz failed to explain why there should be any relationship between the requirements for winning a war and the requirements for stabilizing the peace. Nothing about RMA supported such a conclusion. The RMA was about a revolution in warfare, not postwar stabilization. Technologies that substitute for mass in war do not necessarily substitute for mass in situations other than war.

Why did Wolfowitz and Rumsfeld find it so hard to imagine that more troops might be needed to police the peace than conduct the war? No doubt there was a strong political imperative for rejecting Shinseki's analysis. As the administration desperately tried to marshal support for war, conceding the need for a large and lengthy postwar military presence would have been political poison. But this political motive was combined with a series of optimistic – some would say rosy – assumptions about postwar Iraq, such as the expectation that other nations, even those opposed to the war, would participate in postwar efforts out of self-interest. In his testimony contradicting Shinseki, for example, Wolfowitz speculated that "that even countries like France will have a strong interest in assisting Iraq's reconstruction." Rumsfeld suggested that Arab states might agree to peacekeeping operations in postwar Iraq. Wolfowitz also assumed there would be little need for stabilization. Because the Iraqis would welcome Saddam's demise, American forces and the introduction of democracy, they would not create much instability. "I am reasonably certain that [the Iraqis] will greet us as liberators," he predicted famously, which would "help us to keep [stabilization] requirements down." Nor did the administration contemplate an extensive military role in policing and rebuilding Iraq because this smacked of the nation-building and peacekeeping missions for which Clinton had been criticized. In the administration's view, the military's mission was to fight

[47] Metz, *Iraq & The Evolution of American Strategy*, p. 120. See also Eric Schmitt, "Pentagon Contradicts General on Iraq Occupation's Force Size," *The New York Times* (February 28, 2003).

and win the nation's wars, and any distractions from this mission were to be avoided. Metz speculates that "the Bush administration assumed that Iraq was much like Eastern Europe's communist states.... a functioning society with a pathological and parasitic regime perched on top." Once the regime fell, the society would continue to function, though not without some adjustment pains. "In reality," Metz argues, "Iraq was a deeply wounded nation held together and kept alive by a pathological regime" whose removal would create monumental problems.[48] But these judgments about postwar Iraq constituted political assessments, albeit it ones with military consequences, unrelated to the RMA.

Throughout 2002, the military percolated an almost dizzying proliferation of war plans with names like "Generated Start," "Running Start," "Vigilant Guardian," and "the Hybrid." In the struggle between CENTCOM and Rumsfeld, the size of the invasion force expanded and contracted like an accordion from a low of 18,000 to a high of 275,000.[49] Rumsfeld consistently pushed for the leanest possible force that could win and be deployed on short notice. CENTCOM leaned more toward overwhelming power and worried about having enough forces to protect supply lines, secure WMD sites, and preserve order in postwar Iraq. Secretary of State Powell, former Chairman of the JCS, shared these concerns and expressed them to the President. In several iterations Franks tried to satisfy both camps, suggesting an initial invasion force on the small side with reinforcements scheduled to arrive if needed.

The number of troops was not the only difference among the war plans. They also varied in the timing and weighting of the air and ground components. Some followed the example of Desert Storm in calling for weeks of aerial attacks on strategic targets and Iraqi forces before ground troops moved in, while others envisaged the air and ground campaigns commencing simultaneously. All versions, however, had the same basic objectives for the air campaign. The first priority was establishing air supremacy. Given the state of the Iraqi Air Force and air defenses, this was not expected to last long. The United States would enjoy air superiority from the war's first moments. The second priority was to either eliminate or paralyze the regime through massive but precise attacks on leadership and command and control targets. With an eye toward postwar rebuilding, infrastructure and critical economic assets (e.g., the electrical grid) would be off limits. This war was going to focus as much as possible on the regime, not the nation. Finally, while the Iraqi Army and the Republican Guard would be targeted, the goal was not to destroy the Iraqi military unless it chose to fight. The hope was that either the regime would collapse

[48] Metz, *Iraq & the Evolution of American Strategy*, p. 133.
[49] Gordon and Trainor, *Cobra II*, p. 88.

quickly or the Iraqi commanders and soldiers would opt not to fight and die for a despised and doomed regime.[50]

The final plan may have called for a larger invasion force than Rumsfeld preferred, but in many critical respects it embodied much of his RMA vision. The two most important elements of the plan came directly from the RMA playbook: simultaneity and speed. The plan called for a three (or four) pronged ground invasion. Three would come from the south of Kuwait, two north to Baghdad up both sides of the Euphrates River and another to secure the oil fields in southeast Iraq. A fourth front would be opened in the north, provided Turkey, the only predominately Muslim member of NATO, consented. With the exception of the forces destined for the oil fields, the invading armies were to move as rapidly as possible toward Baghdad. Thomas Ricks explains that "Rumsfeld had come out of the Afghan war believing that speed could substitute for mass in military operations. Franks had bought into this, summarizing it in the oft-repeated maxim 'Speed kills.'"[51] Of course, given Rumsfeld's prior commitment to the RMA, the Afghan war only confirmed his belief in the military, tactical, and operational value of speed. Combined with simultaneous aerial attacks on Iraqi leadership, command, and control targets, the goal was to create the paralysis envisaged by Warden while getting inside the Iraqi decision cycle as suggested by Boyd. Scales and Murray explain that according to the war plan, "the secret to winning quickly was to strike the enemy across the entire extent of his territory in many dimensions – air, land, and sea – in the shortest period of time. The objective of simultaneity was as much psychological as physical. The pattern of assaults against the Iraqis aimed a paralyzing a command structure that moved at a glacial pace."[52] If the regime could be deposed or paralyzed quickly by aerial attacks and rapidly advancing ground forces, the military hoped it could avoid the nightmare scenario it feared most: Iraqi use of chemical weapons and urban, close order, street-by-street fighting in Baghdad.

Although the war planners debated the details of the coming invasion, political debate raged as the administration tried to lure international allies and build domestic support, whereas in Iraq the cat and mouse game of inspections for weapons of mass destruction continued. The administration's rationales for war – Iraqi WMD, connections to terrorism, threats to regional stability, and the venal nature of the regime – met with mixed success. Domestically, the administration built sufficient

[50] On the debates over air power in planning for the 2003 Iraq War, see Lewis, *The American Culture of War*, p. 417.

[51] Thomas Ricks, *Fiasco: The American Military Adventure in Iraq* (New York: Penguin, 2006), p. 75.

[52] Williamson Murray and Robert H. Scales, *The Iraq War: A Military History* (Cambridge, MA: Harvard University Press, 2003), p. 248.

support and in October secured positive votes of 296–133 in the House and 77–23 in the Senate. Internationally, the administration's efforts met with mixed results. In November, the U.N. Security Council voted 15–0 in favor of a resolution threatening "serious consequences" if Iraq failed to cease its chemical, biological, and possible nuclear weapons programs; however, final United Nations approval for the use of force was not forthcoming. Some allied governments were supportive (e.g., Spain, Italy, and Australia), even if their publics were not. Militarily, only a single ally was able and/or willing to make a significant contribution, Great Britain. The "coalition of the willing" was more a political and rhetorical fig leaf than a military reality.

It is difficult to pinpoint exactly when President Bush decided to invade Iraq. As early as August 2002 the administration produced a secret document laying out its objectives in the event of war with Iraq.[53] In December 2002, Bush took a major step toward war when he signed off on the deployment of 200,000 troops to the region. Some accounts report that Bush pulled Colin Powell aside after an NSC meeting on January 13, 2003, telling him, "I really think I'm going to have to take this guy out."[54] On February 9 Powell made a rare appearance at the Security Council to present the case against Iraq in the hopes of securing a final resolution unambiguously endorsing the American position. Despite his dramatic presentation, this was not to be: a draft resolution had to be withdrawn once it became clear that it would fail, leaving the administration to argue that previous resolutions constituted sufficient authorization. In a March 6 press conference, Bush announced that time was running out for diplomacy and U.N. inspections. On March 17 Bush delivered a nationally televised address indicating that the time for diplomacy had passed. His ultimatum could not have been clearer: "Saddam and his sons must leave Iraq within 48 hours. Their refusal to go will result in military conflict commenced at a time of our choosing." No one seriously expected them to leave. Within seventy-two hours, the United States would once again be at war with Iraq.

The Opposing Forces

The war would once again be a mismatch: if anything, the disparity in military power was greater than in 1991. The American military may have been smaller as a result of substantial reductions in troop strength since the end of the Cold War, but because it was better equipped with the technologies and weapons that provided such an advantage in the last Iraq War, it was probably a more lethal force. Iraq, on the other hand, was

53 Gordon and Trainor, *Cobra II*, p. 72.
54 Herspring, *Rumsfeld's Wars*, p. 112.

almost certainly a less formidable opponent. The lingering effects of its military beating in 1991 combined with a decade of economic sanctions and intermittent air attacks had taken their toll. But as in 1991, there are some differences of opinion on the issue of Iraqi military power. Murray and Scales, for example, present a dire picture, judging that Iraq "had virtually no military capabilities left after an air war of attrition lasting over twelve years."[55] Anthony Cordesman, on the other hand, describes Iraq as "the largest and most effective military power in the Gulf at the start of the Iraq War, despite its defeat in the Gulf War and the loss of some 40 percent of its army and air force."[56] Although it is not logically impossible for the region's "largest and most effective military power" to have "virtually no military capabilities," such characterizations are difficult to reconcile. Disagreements also surfaced on the more objective question of Iraqi troop strength. Thomas Ricks is on the high end, estimating the Iraqis "fielded about 400,000 troops."[57] Cordesman approaches Ricks with a figure of "some 350,000 actives."[58] John Keegan suggests there is more uncertainty, claiming that "even the Iraqi government seems to have lacked a clear picture of the Army's strength: perhaps 200,000 at the most, or as few as 150,000."[59] Details aside, it is difficult to identify any significant disagreement with Keegan's general assessment of the opposing forces: "In February 1991 a very large high quality Western army confronted a equally large but low quality Iraqi army.... In March 2003 a much smaller but even higher quality Western army confronted an Iraqi army degraded and enervated by its earlier defeat and by twelve years of isolation from its foreign sources of supply."[60] Or, as William Arkin put it, if Iraq was a military paper tiger in 1991, in 2003 it was a tissue paper tiger.

Iraqi ground forces comprised three elements: the Army, Republican Guard, and Fedayeen. The regular Iraqi Army, though the largest of the three, was not expected to provide much resistance. "Composed largely of Shiite conscripts" motivated more by fear than loyalty, the Iraqi Army was universally seen as "poorly led, trained and equipped."[61] The United States conducted a massive psychological operations campaign designed to exploit this presumed lack of commitment and motivation. Millions of leaflets detailing the regime's vile nature and the inevitably of defeat were dropped on Iraqi forces urging them to either join the battle against

[55] Murray and Scales, *The Iraq War: A Military History*, p. 183.
[56] Anthony Cordesman, *The Iraq War*, p. 40.
[57] Ricks, *Fiasco*, p. 117.
[58] Cordesman, *The Iraq War*, p. 40.
[59] Keegan, *The Iraq War*, p. 129.
[60] Ibid., p. 127.
[61] Metz, *Iraq & Evolution of American Strategy*, p. 111.

Saddam or at least not fight the Americans. Many appear to have taken the latter advice.

As in 1991, the main concern centered on the more capable, better equipped, and loyal elite Republican Guard whose 60,000 men (including the Special Republican Guard) were divided into six divisions deployed closer to Baghdad, three each to the north and the south. As a result, the fiercest resistance was expected as American troops approached the capital. A new and more unknown military quantity that didn't even exist in 1991 was the so-called Fedayeen Saddam. An irregular paramilitary organization founded in 1995 by Saddam's son Uday, the Fedayeen included the regime's most fanatical and brutal supporters that helped the Husseins enforce their will and intimidate (and murder) political opponents.[62] Given the Fedayeen's focus on domestic enforcement, no one knew what role, if any, it would play in resisting the coming invasion. In fact, American military planners hardly ever mentioned the Fedayeen in the lead up to the war.

The War: Operation Iraqi Freedom

To defeat these forces, the United States originally planned nearly simultaneous air and ground assaults. The ground invasion would come from the north and south, forcing Iraq to fight on two fronts. The invasion in the south out of Kuwait would be a three-pronged offensive. The Army's fifth Corps, including the heavy third Infantry Division (ID), would head toward Baghdad up the western side of the Euphrates while the first Marine Expeditionary Force (MEF) would do likewise up the eastern side. British forces, assisted by the U.S. marines would move to the northeast and take Basra (see Map 5.1). Approximately 140,000 troops – Army and Marine contingents of 60,000 each with an additional 20,000 British troops – were in place to attack from the south.[63] The Army's fourth Infantry Division, perhaps the best equipped from a technological standpoint, was slated to invade from Turkey in the north. This part of the plan never materialized. After intense debate, on March 1 the Turkish Parliament denied the United States permission to invade from Turkish soil. This last minute refusal forced redeployment to the south, preventing the fourth ID from seeing action until mid-April, weeks into the invasion.[64] To tie down some Iraqi forces, SOF would team up with Kurdish rebels

---

[62] See Martin Lumb, "The Fedayeen: Saddam's Loyal Force," *BBC News Service*. Accessed at: www.news.bbc.co.uk/2/hi/middle_east/2881889.stm.

[63] Ricks, *Fiasco*, p. 117. These figures refer to troops directly involved in the invasion. Overall, about 450,000 American troops were deployed to the region as of the end of April in support of OIF, including logistical, maintenance and support forces (as well as twenty-one Air Force historians). See T. Michael Moseley, *Operation Iraqi Freedom – By the Numbers* (USCENTAF: Assessment and Support Division, 2003).

[64] Adams, *The Army After Next*, pp. 154–5.

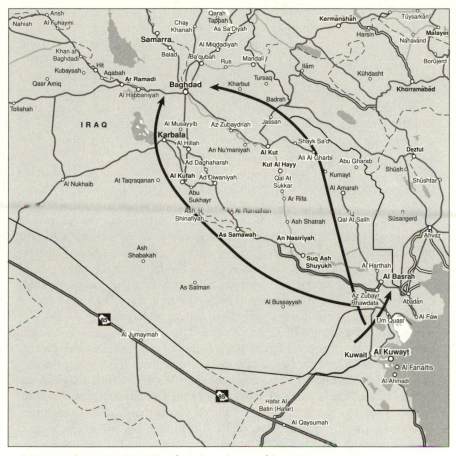

Map 5.1. Operation Iraqi Freedom (2003) ground invasion.

and American air power in a sort of mini-Afghan model.[65] Despite the Turkish setback, the invasion remained on schedule to begin on March 21 as planned. Overall, the final plan "was consistent with a classical breakthrough operation, and, although not radical, it was innovative in some areas, notably in the speed with which the invading force would proceed to Baghdad, the significant use of special operations forces, and the simultaneity of air and ground operations."[66]

On March 19, the CIA received a tip indicating that Saddam Hussein was at a house in the Dora Farms section of Baghdad. There was little time to take a decision. Should the United States rely on the information to

[65] For an analysis of the northern campaign as an example of the Afghan model, see Andres, Wills and Griffith, "Winning with Allies," pp. 141–4.

[66] Risa Brooks, *Shaping Strategy: The Civil-Military Politics of Strategic Assessment* (Princeton: Princeton University Press, 2008), p. 240.

pursue Saddam or stay with the plan? The prospect of eliminating Saddam in the ultimate decapitation strike and winning the war with a single bombing raid proved too tempting, and Bush took the gamble. Two F-117 stealth fighters were sent to Baghdad and destroyed the house with laser-guided bombs. The mission appeared successful. If Saddam died, the war might be over before it even began. Saddam's appearance on Iraqi television dashed such hopes. The weapons hit the right target, but Saddam was not in the house, demonstrating once again that precision weapons are only useful if combined with accurate information. The gamble having failed, the countdown to war continued.

When intelligence suggested that Iraqi oil fields were being sabotaged, Franks wanted to start the invasion a day early.[67] Since Iraq's oil would be a vital resource for postwar reconstruction, the wells and infrastructure needed to be protected. Although the ground forces were ready, the air commanders indicated that the intricately planned campaign could not be moved up. Franks decided to go anyway. The first ground forces moved into Iraq before dawn on March 20, though more than thirty SOF teams had been inserted into Iraq in the days before the formal ground invasion began. The air war would begin the next day. The simultaneity of the air and ground wars surprised many, perhaps even the Iraqis, who expected a replay of Desert Storm. The absence of a separate air campaign is often highlighted as one of the key differences between the two wars. Such comparisons, however, are slightly misleading. In the name of enforcing no-fly zones after the Gulf War, the United States had "waged a twelve year air campaign against Iraq's air defense system before the first shot was fired" in 2003.[68] This air war intensified in the summer of 2002 with an expanded target list including Iraqi air defenses and communications facilities as "a way of compensating for the possibility that the air commanders might have little time to set the stage for a ground invasion."[69] In the months leading up to the March 2003 invasion, the United States and Britain waged a slow motion "secret" air campaign, flying more than 20,000 sorties against a range of targets in preparation for a possible war.[70]

As the American and British ground forces moved through southern Iraq with little resistance from the Iraqi Army, the air campaign got under way. Dramatic images of attacks on targets throughout Baghdad were broadcast around the world, the fireballs seemingly confirming the shock and awe campaign everyone expected, an intimidating display of power and technology. In reality, the range of targets was quite limited,

[67] Boot, *War Made New*, p. 391.
[68] Murray and Scales, *The Iraq War*, pp. 162–3.
[69] Gordon and Trainor, *Cobra II*, p. 69.
[70] Michael Smith, "General Admits to Secret Air War," *The Sunday Times*, London (June 26, 2005). Accessed at: www.timesonline.co.uk/tol/news/uk/article537580.ece.

much more so than in 1991. Fearing civilian casualties that might alienate an Iraqi populace soon to be under American control, severe limits were placed on aerial attacks in Baghdad. While planning the air war "the strategic strikes were narrowed to three specific categories: 59 'leadership' targets ... 112 communications targets; and 104 offices and facilities of the ruling Baath Party and Saddam's security services."[71] There was no attempt to attack the nation's infrastructure, a point driven home by the eerie sight of the lights remaining on throughout Baghdad even as leadership and government targets were being destroyed one by one. As administration officials would emphasize repeatedly, this was a war against Saddam Hussein and his regime, not the Iraqi people: "the aim was explicitly to spare the country's economic infrastructure while disrupting the ability to top commanders to issue orders."[72] If Saddam hoped that widespread civilian casualties and devastation of essential infrastructure would rally the populace to his cause and outrage world opinion, he was sadly disappointed.

By the time most of the strategic targets had been hit on March 23, the third ID had already advanced almost 180 miles, halfway to Baghdad. Army and Marine units were constantly urged to move faster, avoiding Iraqi cities and forces in their rush to the capital. The relentless demand for speed in harsh desert conditions was "brutal on humans and machines alike."[73] The logistical challenges of keeping rapidly advancing forces supplied with food, water, fuel, and spare parts were substantial. The advance was so rapid that front-line forces "sometimes outran even the most basic supplies including bottled water and packaged rations.... fuel was a constant problem ... many units spent all 21 days of continuous combat operations without receiving a single repair kit."[74] More importantly, contrary to the popular slogan, "speed didn't kill the enemy – it bypassed him."[75] As Citino explains, "the lightening drive on Baghdad left behind it not 'occupied territory,' but a yawning void, a vacuum into which irregular forces like the 'fedayeen Saddam' soon filtered."[76]

In fact, one of the war's first major engagements began on March 23 when troops supplying the rapidly advancing third ID mistakenly entered the town of Al Nasiriyah about 150 miles south of Baghdad, finding themselves behind enemy lines and under attack from the Fedayeen. Eleven Americans were killed and another seven taken hostage. U.S. Marines were sent to secure the city, resulting in another 29 Americans deaths.

[71] Budiansky, *Air Power*, p. 437.
[72] Ibid., p. 437.
[73] Adams, *The Army After Next*, p. 148.
[74] Ibid., pp. 147 and 148.
[75] Ricks, *Fiasco*, p. 128.
[76] Citino, *From Blitzkrieg to Desert Storm*, p. 298.

Many feared that the battles with the Fedayeen in Nasiriyah were but a small taste of what awaited them in Baghdad. Subsequent Fedayeen attacks on supply lines would become one of the war's most unexpected obstacles. In general, however, seventy-two hours into the war everything seemed to be going about as well as could be expected in the race to Baghdad, which some referred to as the "Baghdad 500." But the situation was about to take a turn for the worse. While Fedayeen attacks and a lack of supplies for front-line units may have been sufficient to slow the advance on Baghdad, these problems were soon exacerbated by a new and unanticipated obstacle.

It is a cliché that no war plan survives first contact with the enemy: the enemy, as they say, always gets a vote. Even the most carefully crafted plans cannot predict accurately everything on which success depends. But the opponent's actions are not the only element of uncertainty. There is also the weather. In many respects March was a good time to invade because American forces could avoid the scalding heat of the Iraqi summer. Unfortunately, it was also sandstorm season, and on March 25 "a sandstorm lasting three days engulfed Iraq. . . . stalling advancing forces in what General Petraeus described as 'a tornado of mud.'"[77] In the United States critics seized upon this "operational pause" as evidence that the war was "bogging down." Retired generals appeared on round-the-clock news networks using words like "quagmire," blaming the lack of sufficient forces. In reality, the sandstorm was a mixed blessing. Unpleasant as it was, the storm gave many American forces a chance to rest. Although Iraqi forces may have viewed the storm as an opportunity to do likewise or reposition themselves under the cover of swirling sand, they were in for a rude awakening.

By the time the sandstorm moved into Iraq, the focus of the air campaign had already shifted and "nearly all of the roughly one thousand strike sorties were being flown against Iraqi fielded forces."[78] As a result of detection and targeting technologies providing the United States with an all-weather strike capability, attacks on Iraqi forces continued unabated. Whereas in 1991 a comparable sandstorm would have shut down the aerial assault, in 2003 "it was during that horrendous sandstorm that the most significant Air Force action took place."[79] There was no rest for Iraqi forces: "M-1 tanks and M-2 Bradleys, thanks to their thermal sights, could still fire on any gathering Iraqi irregulars. Up above, JSTARs could still pick out the movement of ground units. . . . targeting information could still be forwarded to orbiting U.S. aircraft, armed with

[77] Ricks, *Fiasco*, p. 125.
[78] Budiansky, *Air Power*, p. 437.
[79] Lewis, *The American Culture of War*, p. 431.

GPS-guided JDAMs to destroy any Iraqi units."[80] "With infrared sensors and radars that allowed aircraft to see through the swirling sand," Budiansky explains, "there was no 'pause' in the air war; on the contrary, as one official commented later, coalition air forces knew the location of the Iraqi Republican Guard units better than their own commanders did."[81] As a result, large portions of the Iraqi Army simply shed their uniforms and melted away, leaving the battlefield and taking their weapons with them. Only the Fedayeen adopted an effective strategy, dispersing and blending in with the civilian population, a form of low-tech stealth.

Al Nasiriyah was not the only battle. In the south, the fight for Basra continued as the British took a cautious approach, fearing that a full-force entry into the city would lead to unacceptable military and civilian casualties. Up north, the third ID battled with regular and irregular Iraqi forces in Najaf, less than 100 miles south of Baghdad. By March 29, however, American forces had Baghdad in their sights. This was expected to be the most difficult and costly part of the invasion. Not only were elite Republican Guard divisions stationed around the capital, but intercepted Iraqi communications mentioned a "Red Zone," which many assumed to signify the area which the Iraqis would defend with everything they had, including chemical weapons.[82] Although the Republican Guard divisions had been bombed for almost two weeks, no one knew how much fight was left in them. Chemical weapons, however, were the greatest fear and unknown. While Saddam refrained from using them in Desert Storm, in 1991 he knew his regime faced no immediate danger as long as coalition forces did not continue to Baghdad. His regime could survive a defeat in Kuwait. But in 2003 everything was different. The point would come when the regime would know it was doomed, when it had nothing left to lose. It was reasonable to conclude that a desperate regime would hold nothing back.

To get to Baghdad, American forces needed to break through the Karbala Gap to the west before capturing the international airport and entering the city. Once again, the Iraqis made the job easier than it should have been. Partly as a result of deliberate American deception efforts, Saddam's son Qusay was convinced the main assault would come from the north: the Turkish refusal and the advance from the south were a ruse. Against the advice of military commanders, Qusay ordered some Republican Guard units sent north to defend against the nonexistent threat. On April 2 the third ID advanced into the Karbala Gap, fearing the worst.

---

[80] William Terdoslavich, "From Shock and Awe to Aw Shucks," in Eric L. Haney, ed., *Beyond Shock and Awe: Warfare in the 21st Century* (New York: Berkley Caliber, 2006), pp. 27–8.

[81] Budiansky, *Air Power*, p. 438.

[82] Gordon and Trainor, *Cobra II*, p. 363.

For reasons that became clear after the war, there was no chemical attack. The Americans did not just walk through unmolested, however. Elements of the Republican Guard's Medina division offered futile resistance, but the battle was one-sided, and Iraqi forces were devastated. Although not easy, the Americans "had not expected the move through the Karbala Gap to go so quickly ... as the soldiers advanced, they passed unimaginable scenes of carnage inflicted by their air force brethren on the Iraqis."[83]

On the evening of April 3, American forces entered Saddam International Airport. Surprisingly, there was no resistance. The airport appeared deserted. The calm did not last long. The Fedayeen were close by and the following morning they struck, attacking in undisciplined and unorganized waves. Their fanaticism and intensity was matched only by their ineffectiveness. Given the disparity in skill and weapons, the Fedayeen had no chance and were slaughtered. In this type of setting their mission was suicidal. Although "the ferocity of the Fedayeen surprised US commanders," they displayed "no understanding of firepower and maneuver." At the airport that morning as elsewhere, "the fedayeen and other irregulars made little difference. Courage, tenacity and poor planning were not enough against some of the best-trained and best-motivated troops in the world."[84] The outcome was consistent with Murray and Scales' assessment: while Fedayeen attacks were certainly unwelcome, "the results were the same: dead Iraqis and live Americans, largely unhurt but appalled and unnerved by the lunacy of their attackers."[85]

American forces now had Baghdad in their sights. Rather than enter the city full force, they opted for more limited probes, so-called thunder runs, to test the Iraqis and see what to expect for the final assault on the capital. The first run took place on April 5 as a column of tanks supported by A-10 "warthogs" and attack helicopters providing close air support entered the city. Once the Iraqis realized what was happening, the column was "met with a fusillade of Iraqi rocket propelled grenade (RPG) and small arms fire, at effectively point blank range, along nearly the entire route."[86] A UAV loitering overhead provided the commander outside the city with real-time images as the run progressed. When American forces returned to the airport later that evening, it was obvious that they had been in fight. Col. David Perkins, the run's leader, recalls the scene: "So you see this force come rolling in the airport on fire. We had some casualties ... Talking to those that were there, I think it was kind of traumatic,

[83] Murray and Scales, *The Iraq War*, p. 206.
[84] Ahmed Hashim, *Insurgency and Counter-Insurgency in Iraq* (Ithaca: Cornell University Press, 2006), pp. 14–16.
[85] Murray and Scales, *The Iraq War*, p. 102.
[86] Stephen Biddle, "Speed Kills? Reassessing the Role of Speed, Precision, and Situation Awareness in the Fall of Saddam," *The Journal of Strategic Studies* Vol. 30, No. 1 (February 2007), p. 13.

to kind of see us rolling in on fire and [with] machine gun spent cartridges, vehicles with holes in them [that] had [been] hit by, RPGs and stuff like that."[87] Although a column of burning tanks no doubt looked bad, the news was actually good. In their foray into Baghdad Perkins and his men "met far less resistance than they might have imagined... because the Iraqi regular army more or less crumbled. Saddam and his commanders were not in adequate control. The generals didn't want to give Saddam true information about how bad things were. The Iraqi forces just were not up to the task."[88] While Biddle is correct that "every single vehicle in the brigade was hit at least once," Murray and Scales note that "not a single tank was destroyed... It was a demonstration of U.S. might on the eve of the thrust into the heart of the capital, and it achieved the intended result: shocking Iraqi defenders and weakening their resolve."[89]

The second run came two days later when the Americans did not enjoy the same element of surprise. The Iraqis were a little better prepared: there were more obstacles (e.g., overturned trucks in the roads to slow an advance), and the fighting was equally intense. But by the end of the day Perkins was in downtown Baghdad. Rather than return to the airport as planned, he asked to remain in the city. His superiors agreed. That night American soldiers stayed in one of the presidential palaces where Saddam used to sleep. The Fedayeen and other irregulars attacked during the night, but thermal sensors made it easy to pick them off before they posed any real danger. This was the turning point. According to Murray and Scales, "the successful occupation of downtown Baghdad over the night of April 7–8 essentially broke the back of Iraqi resistance.... By morning, sporadic suicide attacks were all that remained."[90] On April 8, the Marines entered Baghdad from the east with minimal resistance. The regime had collapsed. Reflecting some surprise that "the anticipated Stalingrad-like battle for Baghdad never took place," Lewis quotes one soldier observing that "by the end of April 8 and the beginning of April 9, we were sort of looking at each other as if to say 'Is that it?'"[91] Of course, there was much more to come and several major cities still needed to be secured. Within hours Baghdad would descend into chaos with rampant looting. A new regime was needed to take the place of the old. And six years later Americans would still be fighting on the streets of Baghdad. But when American soldiers used their tanks to help a crowd of

[87] Interview with David Perkins, *PBS Frontline: The Invasion of Iraq* (2004). Accessed at: www.pbs.org/wgbh/pages/frontline/shows/invasion/interviews/perkins.html#medina.

[88] Interview with Todd Purdum, *PBS Frontline: The Invasion of Iraq* (2004). Accessed at: www.pbs.org/wgbh/pages/frontline/shows/invasion/interviews/purdum.html#iraqi.

[89] Adams, *The Army After Next*, p. 152.

[90] Biddle, "Speed Kills?" p. 13; and Murray and Scales, *The Iraq War*, p. 218.

[91] Lewis, *The American Culture of War*, p. 434.

Iraqis topple a giant statue of Saddam in the heart of Baghdad on April 9, victory appeared to be theirs.

Evaluating the Second Iraq War

Operation Iraqi Freedom (OIF) was a wildly asymmetric affair in which the most powerful military the world has probably ever known took on an ill-equipped, poorly motivated, and incompetently led opponent. Despite a handful of intense battles, it is difficult to disagree with Martin Van Creveld's conclusion that "the three-hundred mile, three-week campaign that cost the Americans 138 deaths" was "a walkover."[92] As in 1991, however, the war's brevity and low casualties were surprising. After the end of major combat operations, most observers expressed astonishment at the speed of the American advance on, and capture of, Baghdad. The eminent military historian John Keegan, who by 2003 was in the habit of being amazed every time the United States took to the battlefield, remarked that in taking Baghdad in less than three weeks "the Americans achieved a pace of advance unprecedented in history, far outstripping that of the Germans towards Moscow in the summer of 1941 and even that of the British from the Seine to the liberation of Brussels in the victorious summer of 1944."[93] Victor Davis Hanson agreed that "by any fair standard of even the most dazzling charges in military history, the Germans in the Ardennes in the spring of 1940 or Patton's romp in July of 1944, the... race to Baghdad [was] unprecedented in its speed and daring and in the lightness of its casualties."[94] Max Boot was the more succinct: "No army had ever travelled faster with fewer casualties."[95]

Rumsfeld, of course, basked in the afterglow of a victory, seeing it as vindication of his vision of a smaller force leveraging its advantages in situational awareness, stealth, precision, and speed. More generally, the war was also "a progress report on the revolution in military affairs."[96] As with Desert Storm, the ease of victory at low cost was taken as *prima facie* evidence that an RMA was underway. According to Mahnken, for example, "the swift and lopsided outcome of the war in Iraq provided additional evidence of change in warfare."[97] But did the war provide the vindication Rumsfeld claimed and/or evidence of an RMA?

---

[92] Martin Van Creveld, *The Changing Face of War: Lessons of Combat from the Marne to Iraq* (New York: Ballantine Books, 2006), pp. 247–8.

[93] Keegan, *The Iraq War*, p. 186.

[94] Quoted in Greg Jaffe, "For Military, a Lesson in Speed – Rumsfeld's Vindication Promises to Change Tactics and Deployment of Troops," *Wall Street Journal* (April 10, 2003), p. A1.

[95] Boot, *War Made New*, p. 400.

[96] William Nolte, "Keeping Pace with the Revolution in Military Affairs," *Studies in Intelligence* Vol. 48, No. 1 (2004), p. 1.

[97] Mahnken, *Technology and the American Way of War*, p. 212.

Rumsfeld Vindicated?

On a superficial level Rumsfeld's claims of vindication were certainly plausible. With better technology but only half the troops that liberated Kuwait in 1991, American forces advanced rapidly and struck precisely with an unprecedented degree of situational awareness to eliminate the Baathist regime in short order. As Rumsfeld would note after the war, "just over 100,000 American forces...overwhelmed the enemy...by overmatching [it] with advanced capabilities, and using those capabilities in innovative and unexpected ways."[98] His vision had been implemented, and the outcome was extremely favorable. While Rumsfeld's critics had been proven wrong, not everyone agreed that matters were so simple and straightforward. The most common criticism is by now quite familiar: even if Rumsfeld's plan deserves credit for Saddam's rapid and decisive defeat, it left the United States woefully ill-equipped to deal with the mess that came after. Some, however, remain unconvinced that Rumsfeld deserves much credit even for the success of major combat operations.

Frederick Kagan for one was unwilling to give Rumsfeld much credit, noting that "the Iraqi military was so weak that just about any American plan would have succeeded in driving Saddam from power."[99] Although probably true, this somewhat misses the point. Rumsfeld and other transformation advocates saw validation in the war's speed and low cost, not the mere fact of victory. It is Biddle who offers the most thorough analysis of this issue. He poses two questions: "Do speed, precision and situational awareness account for the low cost of Saddam's ouster in 2003? And if so, does this imply that the US military should be transformed in ways so many now advocate?" Biddle's initial judgment is blunt: "the answers to these questions are no."[100] That is, speed, precision, and situational awareness *do not* account for the war's low casualties. Rumsfeld's self-congratulation was unwarranted. As Biddle's analysis progresses, however, a more nuanced assessment emerges in which speed, precision, and situational awareness are indeed important, if not *sufficient*, for explaining the war's low cost.

Biddle acknowledges the obvious at the outset: "the Coalition moved very rapidly, its weapons were very precise, and its knowledge of the battlefield, though imperfect, was far better than the Iraqis."[101] This doubtlessly translated into genuine battlefield advantages as "speed, precision, and situation awareness did leave much of the Iraqi military

---

[98] In Kagan, *Finding the Target*, p. 346.
[99] Ibid., p. 346.
[100] Biddle, "Speed Kills?" p. 5.
[101] Ibid., p. 11.

out of position, unwilling to fight, or destroyed by deep strikes."[102] Consequently, it is no surprise that the Iraqis did not kill many Americans. The critical question for Biddle is not *whether* speed, precision, and situational awareness helped keep casualties low, but "*how much* did they contribute to the low cost of Saddam's ouster?"[103] Since American casualties were low even in close ground combat, where the benefits of speed, precision, and situational awareness were minimized, there has to be more to the equation.

To explain the war's low casualties, Biddle argues that American strengths in speed, precision, and awareness must also be evaluated in the context of Iraqi shortcomings. The United States was able to fully exploit its advantages because it faced an unskilled and incompetent opponent that made mistake after mistake at all levels. The Iraqis missed numerous opportunities to lengthen the war and impose higher costs. The answer to the puzzle of low casualties "lies in the interaction between the Coalition's strengths and the Iraqis' military weaknesses ... [the] skilled use of modern Coalition technology interacted synergistically with Iraqi errors to produce extreme lethality and a radically one-sided military confrontation."[104] So, Biddle's initial assertion that speed, precision, and situational awareness did not account for low casualties was somewhat misleading. He eventually concludes that they were indeed important factors. "The evidence suggests," he tells us, "that their causal influence, though *important*, was both incomplete and importantly conditional."[105] Biddle's more nuanced argument is that "speed, situation awareness, and precision [were] *insufficient* to explain the low cost of Saddam's ouster."[106] Although Biddle is almost certainly correct on all these points, it is hard to know who he is arguing with because he provides not a single example of anyone arguing that speed, situation awareness, and precision awareness were *sufficient* to explain the war's outcome.

It is certainly valuable to point out how Iraqi weaknesses and errors magnified the benefits of American speed, precision, and awareness. Biddle correctly warns that the capabilities credited with producing a quick and low-cost victory in Iraq might not lead to a similarly favorable outcome against a more skilled and competent opponent. Speed, precision, and situational awareness offer no assurance of a quick, low-cost victory. For Biddle, the danger is overgeneralizing the lessons of the war: "if one cannot guarantee inept enemies in the future," he warns, "then one must be cautious in drawing implications from this conflict."[107] But

[102] Ibid., p. 16.
[103] Ibid., p. 11.
[104] Ibid., p. 22.
[105] Ibid., p. 11.
[106] Ibid., p. 22.
[107] Ibid., p. 41.

even by this analysis, Rumsfeld and other transformation advocates can claim at least partial vindication in the sense that they waged the right kind of war against the enemy they faced.

Even many initially skeptical of Rumsfeld's plan came to admit that it fared better than they expected. James Fallows judges the major combat phase of OIF was "a brilliant success," noting that "its only problems were when the U.S. military got so far ahead that its supply lines were extended." In terms of the war to depose Saddam, "Donald Rumsfeld's vision... was vindicated."[108] Yet this apparent success does not prevent others from offering a harsher evaluation. Thomas Ricks, for example, predicts "that history's judgment will be that the U.S. invasion of Iraq in the spring of 2003 was based perhaps on *the worst war plan in American history.*"[109] Although it may seem odd, there is no inherent contradiction in viewing the war as both a brilliant success and a horrible failure. This somewhat paradoxical assessment of the war as a "brilliant failure" requires differentiating the tactical, operational, and strategic levels of warfare.

The widely shared assessment of OIF is that American forces performed exceptionally well in their battles with the Iraqis as they executed a well-coordinated advance on Baghdad. In Murray and Scales' judgment, "the second Iraq War displayed a combination of tactical and operational virtuosity that obliterated the Baathist regime."[110] Those elements of the war were a brilliant success. But as any student of military history knows, tactical and operational success does not always translate into strategic success. Strategically, the aim of OIF was regime *change*, not regime *removal.* The objective was to replace the existing regime with a stable, and hopefully democratic, government that would threaten neither its neighbors nor the United States and its interests. The elimination of the Baathist regime was not an end itself, but rather a first step toward the larger strategic goal. By this analysis, the war plan was incomplete and any claims of victory or vindication premature. For the narrow purpose of defeating the Iraqi military and toppling Saddam, the war plan may have been crafted and implemented brilliantly, but "there was a disconnect," as Ricks explains, "between the stated strategic goal of transforming the politics of Iraq... and the plan's more limited aim of simply removing Saddam Hussein's regime."[111] Even among supporters of the war it is difficult to find anyone who disagrees with Ricks on this point. The interesting question is why was there such a disconnect? On this there is much less agreement.

---

[108] Interview with James Fallows, *PBS Frontline: The Invasion of Iraq* (2004). Accessed at: www.pbs.org/wgbh/pages/frontline/shows/invasion/interviews/fallows.html.
[109] Ricks, *Fiasco*, p. 115.
[110] Murray and Scales, *The Iraq War*, p. 13.
[111] Ricks, *Fiasco*, p. 116.

Frederick Kagan is among those who argue that postwar failures were rooted in the transformational agenda. Interestingly, Kagan begins his critique of the war by agreeing that "from a purely military perspective, th[e] pressure to keep the force small was wise. . . . U.S. air power with its current level of superiority obviates the need for enormous armies to steamroller the enemy."[112] Transformation advocates would agree completely. Nonetheless, Kagan finds it difficult to fathom why "it did not occur to [Rumsfeld] that the presence of only 100,000 troops in Iraq when Baghdad fell was a major contributing factor to the violence."[113] In essence, Kagan argues that the United States should have deployed more forces than were militarily essential for the task of deposing Saddam so that it could deal with the political problems sure to follow his demise. This essentially mirrors Ricks' argument: the war plan was incomplete. But why did the administration settle on a plan that largely ignored the predictable postwar challenges? In Kagan's view it was the transformation vision that "helped blind military and political leaders to a serious focus on the political objective of the war."[114]

For Kagan, the fatal flaw in the dominant paradigm of military transformation embraced by Rumsfeld and others was its technologically driven obsession with identifying and destroying enemy assets as the key problem of warfare, hence the title of his book, *Finding the Target*. The "blindness" to the political objectives was "induced in part by more than a decade of military dogma arguing for the primacy of destruction over planning for political outcomes." An inability to think about war as anything other than a "targeting drill," to use Kagan's favorite phrasing, "largely explains the amazing failure to take obvious post-war dangers and problems into account in the development of the military campaign."[115] There are two critical elements to this argument: first, the war plan's authors were blind to the war's political objectives; and second, this blindness was induced by a vision of military transformation that equated warfare with targeting and efficient destruction. But what is the evidence that Rumsfeld and others were "blind" to the war's political objectives? Rumsfeld and Franks seemed well aware that the goal of the war was the creation of stable, democratic, and nonthreatening regime. Unfortunately, they engaged in naïve, uninformed, wishful thinking about the difficulty of the task ahead, and as a result they made a string of mind-bogglingly bad political and strategic judgments unrelated to visions of military transformation. There is no connection, for example, between any vision of transformation and the frequently articulated assumption that allies

---

[112] Kagan, *Finding the Target*, p. 329.
[113] Ibid., p. 347.
[114] Ibid., p. 359.
[115] Ibid., p. 359.

would make significant contributions to the postwar effort. One can easily accept everything Owens and Cebrowski say about military transformation/net-centric warfare yet still conclude that more troops would be needed to stabilize and rebuild postwar Iraq than to bring down Saddam Hussein.

OIF and the RMA: Precision, Information, Jointness, and Parallel War

Most casual observers first became aware of guided munitions in Desert Storm. The attempt to portray that war as an exercise in precision targeting, however, was somewhat misleading. The United States had relatively few guided munitions in its arsenal and most of its planes lacked the capability to deliver them. More than ninety percent of the munitions used in 1991 were traditional, unguided gravity bombs. It was not until Afghanistan in 2001 that the United States would wage a war in which the majority of munitions were guided. By then the United States possessed a large inventory of laser- and satellite-guided weapons that could be delivered by virtually all of its attack aircraft. As a result, between Desert Storm and OIF the reliance on guided munitions increased almost tenfold, from seven to sixty-eight percent, with the satellite-guided JDAM being the weapon of choice[116] While some might think Desert Storm was the first precision war, Stephen Wrage is probably correct in arguing that, "the Second Gulf War was the first major-scale test of all precision air power. In this war, as in Afghanistan, 'smart' guided weapons predominated almost to the exclusion of 'dumb' gravity bombs."[117]

The continued improvement in precision strike capability was accompanied by a host of new intelligence and communications systems that dramatically increased situational awareness. In 1991, for example, there were only two (still experimental) JSTARS to track Iraqi ground movements, whereas by 2003 there were enough to provide complete round-the-clock surveillance. These JSTARS were joined by a fleet of new, improved UAVs equipped with better sensors that could fly longer and higher while lingering over potential targets. Murray and Scales judge that these "UAVs accounted for much of the improved sensor capabilities" during the war.[118] Lt. Gen. T. Michael Moseley, the commander of air forces in OIF, was so impressed that in one briefing he was moved to declare, "I love UAVs!"[119] By 2003, some UAVs had even made transformation from purely surveillance assets to attack platforms

---

[116] See CENTCOM's *Operation Iraqi Freedom – By the Numbers*, p. 11.
[117] Stephen Wrage, "Precision Air Power in the Second Gulf War," *Defense & Security Analysis* Vol. 19, No. 3 (September 2003), p. 277. Wrage slightly overstates the case, however, claiming that ninety percent of the weapons used in OIF were guided.
[118] Murray and Scales, *The Iraq War*, p. 163.
[119] Budinasky, *Air Power*, p. 438.

as some Predators were able to launch Hellfire missiles at the targets they identified.

OIF also saw the first large-scale use of the so-called Blue Force Tracking (BFT) system, which the Army rushed to install on as many vehicles as possible beginning in October 2002. Using onboard computers and display screens linked to satellite antenna and GPS receivers, BFT allowed American forces to see the location and track the movement of friendly (i.e., blue) forces in their area. As a result, "Army units fought enabled by a digital network that allowed them to see their units and their activities, which led to situational understanding. Confident that they knew the location of their units, commanders could decide rapidly where, when, and how they would be employed."[120] Hopefully, knowledge of blue force locations would also reduce friendly fire incidents, which accounted for almost one quarter of coalition casualties in Desert Storm.

Precise information and weapons are of little use on their own: the two need to be connected so that the former gets to the latter in time to attack targets effectively, which is critical for time-sensitive, mobile targets common in a dynamic battlefield environment. RMA advocates have long emphasized the need to develop and deploy systems that allow for the near instantaneous transmission of real-time intelligence so that the sensor-to-shooter cycle is as short as possible. This was a central element of Owens' system of systems and Cebrowski's net-centric warfare: connecting the elements of a military architecture into a single, networked, and integrated whole capable of rapid decision making and action.

One sign of progress on this front was the shortening of the sensor-to-shooter cycle evident in OIF, particularly in comparison to Desert Storm. Kober explains that "advanced command and control systems, as well as improved intelligence, surveillance and reconnaissance (ISR) capabilities, considerably shortened the process of spotting a new target, assigning a weapon to hit it, and finally hitting it – from three days in the Gulf War to less than 40 minutes, both in Afghanistan and Iraq."[121] There was even a "Time Sensitive Targeting Cell" in Saudi Arabia that could attack targets within twelve minutes of their identification.[122] The ability to relay targeting information to attack aircraft was such that "for the first time in aviation history, it became commonplace for pilots to take off with only a vague idea where they were headed and then wait for

---

[120] Gregory Fontenot, E.J. Degen, and David Thon, *On Point: The United States Army in Operation Iradi Freedom through 01 May 2003* (Fort Leavenworth, KS: Combat Studies Institute Press, 2004), p. 417. The authors prefer the description of "net-enabled" instead of "networked," though it is difficult to see the difference. The study can be accessed at: www.globalsecurity.org/military/library/report/2004/onpoint/.

[121] Kober, "Does the Iraq War Reflect a Phase Change in Warfare?" p. 124.

[122] Andrew F. Krepinevich, *Operation Iraqi Freedom: A First-Blush Assessment* (Washington, DC: Center for Strategic and Budgetary Assessments, 2003), p. 17.

instructions about where to drop their munitions."[123] Gartska estimates that in Afghanistan "75 percent of the time aircraft did not even know what their targets would be before they took off."[124] Boot illustrates the technologies that made this possible:

In 2003 . . . a Predator or another drone could provide a video feed of the target directly to the air operations center along with GPS coordinates. A detailed grid map of Iraq had already been entered into the computer network, so an air operations officer could immediately click on the target location to see a picture and get other information, such as whether it was considered to be a 'high collateral damage" location . . . with a few more clicks, an officer could determine what assets were available to attack the target. . . . then, without leaving his desk, this officer could enter an internet chat room or use the internet telephony to get approval to hit the target, and a weapons controller could instantly relay that approval to an aircraft already on its way.[125]

Of course, the combination of intelligence and precision did not always work as planned (or hoped). Attempts to target particular individuals, for example, were spectacularly unsuccessful. While most are familiar with the failed attack on Saddam before the war began, this was only the beginning of an ambitious decapitation effort that some hoped might win the war by eliminating Iraq's top leadership. In the end, the effort came to naught and "not one of the top 200 figures in the regime was killed by an air strike."[126] Although it is not clear how many really believed that these attacks could win the war, the idea of an ultimate, decisive decapitating strike remained deceptively attractive. As Kober speculates, "had the precision fire aimed at decapitating key Iraqi leadership figures at the initial stage of the war been successful in eliminating them, the Coalition might have been able to avoid most of what followed."[127] But even if attacks on leadership targets did not succeed in killing individuals, they could still be effective as part of a broad based aerial and ground assault that would intimidate, isolate, disorient, and/or disrupt the regime, preventing it from coordinating and implementing a coherent and effective response to the invasion. As Adams notes, "although not expecting a quick regime collapse, CENTCOM was apparently convinced that relentless pressure on multiple fronts could overwhelm the Iraqi ability to react."[128] The leadership itself was one of those fronts.

While Iraqi leaders managed to escape the air attacks with their lives, the same cannot be said of Iraqi ground forces, except for those who chose to desert and go home rather than fight. Fully 79 percent of the

[123] Boot, *War Made New*, p. 363.
[124] In Berkowitz, *The New Face of War*, p. 115.
[125] Boot, *War Made New*, p. 396.
[126] Gordon and Trainor, *Cobra II*, p. 177.
[127] Kober, "Does the Iraq War Reflect a Phase Change in Warfare?" p. 125.
[128] Adams, *The Army After Next*, p. 145.

more than 29,000 bombs and missiles used in OIF was directed against Iraqi ground forces.[129] The combination of unprecedented surveillance assets, communications, and all-weather guided munitions allowed the United States to "pick up virtually any vehicular ground movements and pass that information along to army and air force stations on the ground. Commanders could then warn ground forces of a possible attack, while at the same time committing aircraft to wiping out the Iraqi units."[130] As a result, "Iraqi battalions were destroyed from the air without ever encountering an enemy they could harm." While coalition forces prevailed whenever they encountered Iraqi units on the ground, it was "air power, not ground power that destroyed the Iraqi Republican Guard."[131] The incredible destruction American forces saw as they advanced through the Karbala Gap resulted from devastating air strikes, not ground artillery. Even in comparison to the successful tank plinking of 1991, in 2003, air power "demonstrated a capability only glimpsed in Operation Desert Storm, the ability to rapidly destroy enemy armored forces in detail."[132] Cebrowski speculated that OIF marked the emergence of "a new air-land dynamic. It's as if we discovered a new sweet spot... through the tighter integration."[133]

For RMA advocates this "new air-land dynamic" derived not only from technology but also from organizational cooperation. The jointness that so impressed Cebrowski and others in the Afghanistan was not a fluke. At long last the organizational changes and adaptations needed for a full exploitation of the RMA began to emerge. The comparisons between OIF and Desert Storm are striking. In Desert Storm, problems of technical incompatibility and institutional parochialism led to a war that resembles discrete, uncoordinated campaigns. Richard Weitz explains that in 1991 "CENTCOM's loose command structure led the components to compete with each other over their preferred method of operations and tactics, and over the distribution of military assets in the theater. Their autonomy also encouraged them to develop their own war plans, which reflected their preferred manner of conducting military operations."[134] Army and Marine complaints about the excessive focus on strategic targets and downtown Baghdad at the expense of Iraqi forces in the field were the most obvious manifestation of these problems in 1991. "Whereas the

---

[129] Budiansky, *Air Power*, p. 438; and Boot, *War Made New*, p. 396.

[130] Ibid., p. 165.

[131] Wrage, "Precision Air Power in the Second Gulf War," pp. 277 and 279.

[132] Lewis, *The American Culture of War*, p. 431.

[133] David A. Fulghum, "The Pentagon's Force-Transformation Director Takes an Early Swipe at What Worked and What Didn't in Iraq," *Aviation Week and Space Technology* Vol. 158, No. 17 (April 28, 2003), p. 34.

[134] Richard Weitz, "Jointness and Desert Storm: A Retrospective," *Defense & Security Analysis* Vol. 20, No. 2 (June 2004), p. 135.

Gulf War had been conducted as two sequential, almost separate campaigns in the air and on the ground," in 2003 "U.S. commanders planned from the beginning an operation that melded Army, Navy and Air Force units into a single, integrated network."[135] Murray and Scales emphasize "advances in the capacity (and willingness) of the air force to connect with ground forces and concentrate its precision killing power on Iraqi army targets."[136] Even the often skeptical Stephen Biddle agrees that "service interactions were broad, deep and profound, ranging from tight integration of close air support (CAS) with ground maneuver to the use of Army logistical units to support Marine combat units inland."[137] The complaints voiced during and after Desert Storm were absent in OIF. In fact, according to one Army observer, the forces that drove on Baghdad "broke fresh ground in a number of areas, but perhaps none so important as the conduct of joint operations . . . it was the best, most efficient, most effective and most responsive air support the Air Force has ever provided any U.S. Army unit."[138]

In the final analysis, the outcome of the United States' second war against Iraq was "over determined and widely expected . . . it was never in doubt that [the] war would end Saddam's dictatorship."[139] The military assault unleashed in March 2003 overwhelmed the Iraqis at every level, even though there was no attempt to implement Wade and Ullman's *Shock and Awe*. Kagan explains that their concept called "for basically devastating the enemy country to the point where it's no longer capable of functioning as a society."[140] That was not an option in 2003. Ricks rejects this common characterization even more adamantly: "Shock and awe was a media frenzy . . . it was pure horseshit. It had nothing to do with anything. It was not a governing principle of the war."[141] In a colloquial sense, however, the Iraqis may very well have been shocked and awed by the military juggernaut that swept into their country.[142] The combination of wide-ranging aerial attacks with an extremely rapid ground advance created more problems than the Iraqis could possibly handle. In their advance on Baghdad, American "ground forces moved with such swiftness that virtually every decision the Iraqi high command made was

---

135 Kober, "Does the Iraq War Reflect a Phase Change in War?" p. 112; and Berkowitz, *The New Face of War*, p. 115.
136 Murray and Scales, *The Iraq War*, p. 247.
137 In Boot, *War Made New*, p. 400.
138 Budiansky, *Air Power*, p. 423.
139 Stephen Biddle, "Speed Kills?" p. 8.
140 Interview with Frederick Kagan, *PBS Frontline: The Invasion of Iraq* (2004). Accessed at: www.pbs.org/wgbh/pages/frontline/shows/invasion/interviews/kagan.html.
141 Interview with Thomas Ricks, *PBS Frontline: The Invasion of Iraq*.
142 See, for example, Scott Peterson and Peter Ford, "From Iraqi Officers, Three Tales of Shock and Defeat," *Christian Science Monitor* Vol. 95, No. 100 (April 18, 2003), p. 1.

already overtaken by events." And as a result of the United States' ability "to strike the enemy across the entire extent of his territory in many dimensions . . . the Iraqi high command perceived from the beginning that they [sic] were under attack everywhere."[143]

There is a very good reason why Iraqi leaders perceived that they were "under attack everywhere": they were. The sense of being overwhelmed by an assault from all angles is an essential element of parallel warfare. Originally associated with John Warden and his ideas about air power and strategic paralysis, parallel (as opposed to sequential) war involves a "simultaneous and near continuous attack against strategic, operational and tactical targets" or "the simultaneous application of force . . . across each level of war without the inhibition of geographical location."[144] Even Kagan agreed that parallel war "represented a fundamental transformation of warfare."[145] Until recently such an attack would have been impossible because it requires large amounts of detailed intelligence and reliably precise munitions. With inaccurate weapons one needs large numbers of soldiers, platforms, and munitions to attack a single target, making it impossible to attack many at once. And while Schneider (in 1998) characterized "Desert Storm as the first and only test of parallel warfare *on a total scale,*" Deptula thinks it provided only "a glimpse of its potential."[146] Thanks to technological advances since 1991 and unprecedented jointness in planning and execution, that potential was more fully realized in OIF. This is significant because in many respects "parallel warfare *is* the manifestation of the revolution in military affairs."[147]

The "Digital Divide"

Despite very real advances in information gathering and dissemination technologies, American forces in OIF remained a long way from the goal of the complete battle space knowledge envisaged by advocates of the RMA and net-centric warfare. Problems were most evident at the tactical level. The impressive range of surveillance and communications capabilities did not always provide forces on the ground critical information about the location of friendly and hostile forces. While Mahnken

[143] Murray and Scales, *The Iraq War*, pp. 245 and 248.

[144] Robert R. Soucy, *Serial vs. Parallel War: An Airman's View of Operational Art* (Fort Leavenworth, KS: School of Advanced Military Studies, 1993), p. 1; and David Deptula, "Parallel War: What Is It? Where Did It Come From? Why Is It Important?" in William Head and Earl A. Tilford, eds., *The Eagle in the Desert: Looking Back on U.S. Involvement in the Persian Gulf War* (New York: Praeger, 1996), p. 134.

[145] Kagan, *Finding the Target*, p. 123.

[146] Steven M. Schneider, *Parallel Warfare: A Strategy for the Future* (Fort Leavenworth, KS: U.S. Army Command and General Staff College, 1998), p. 28, emphasis added. Deptula, "Parallel War," p. 151.

[147] Ibid., p. 146.

correctly notes that BFT "reduced drastically fratricide," he somewhat overstates the case in claiming that "during the major combat phase of Operation Iraqi Freedom, only one soldier was killed by friendly direct ground fire."[148] Many more, however, were killed by aerial friendly fire. On March 23, for example, 18 Marines were killed when attacked by an A-10 attack aircraft during an air strike they themselves had called in. This incident alone accounted for more than ten percent of all American fatalities during the major combat phase of OIF. As is usual in such cases, a number of factors contributed to the tragedy. Part of the problem was that A-10s were equipped to identify ground vehicles by the thermal panels normally placed on their roofs but not the florescent panels that recently replaced them. The official Air Force investigation of the incident dryly cited "a lack of coordination regarding the location of friendly forces" as the "primary cause."[149] American forces also faced inevitable equipment failures and limitations. The punishing environment and speed of movement taxed the capabilities of computers and other information hardware, partly because some of the off-the-shelf equipment was not built to endure the harsh conditions of desert war. According to Adams, "one Brigade of the third ID reported that whenever the unit moved, everything would fail except the Blue Force tracking system." To get the information it needed, "every few hours the unit would stop, hoist up its antennas, log back into the network, and attempt to download whatever it could. But software and bandwidth problems would lock up the computer for 10 to 12 hours at a time, rendering it useless."[150] The ideal of "a seamless flow of information" in real time was too often not achieved as ground troops "wrestled with everything from Web browsers constantly crashing due to desert sand and heat fouling up equipment designed for use in offices, not battlefields."[151]

The most serious problems involved situational awareness at the tactical level, when American forces often lacked information about the location and the size of Iraqi forces they confronted in battle. Despite all the sophisticated sensors overhead, Boot notes that "combat units often found out where the enemy was just as soldiers have been doing for millennia: by 'movement to contact,' the military term for bumping into your foes."[152] The BFT system, which by all accounts worked extremely well, was only designed to track friendly forces, not the enemy. So even though "U.S. forces were all networked together, with 'blue force tracker' letting them know the position of all the friendly units . . . they still did not know

---

[148] Mahnken, *Technology and the American Way of War*, p. 210.
[149] Gordon and Trainor, *Cobra II*, pp. 250–51.
[150] Adams, *The Army After Next*, p. 147.
[151] Singer, *Wired for War*, p. 190.
[152] Boot, *War Made New*, p. 398.

who the enemy ('the red force') was or when and where he would be coming... as one marine joked, 'when do we get red force trackers?'"[153]

It is not surprising that American forces usually lacked information about the location of the Fedayeen until they came under attack. As irregular forces that tried to blend into the local population, they fought without the traditional, big military hardware American sensors were designed to detect (e.g., tanks and armored personnel carriers). JSTARS could locate and track a column of Iraqi Army tanks moving through the desert as it approached American forces, but a handful of Fedayeen launching an ambush in a crowded city with machine guns mounted on pickup trucks would not likely be discovered until they started firing. As a result, "situational awareness... prov[ed] to be more theoretical than actual, especially when it came to ferreting out the Fedayeen."[154] But the problem of insufficient situational awareness went well beyond the understandably difficult-to-find Fedayeen.

More troublesome were those instances when American forces lacked the very knowledge their surveillance assets should have provided. Although some of the details remain fuzzy, a case in point occurred on April 3, when elements of the third ID attempted to secure a critical bridge, dubbed "Objective Peach," crossing the Euphrates on their approach to Baghdad. With a warning that only a single Iraqi brigade was heading in his direction, Lieutenant Colonel Marcone and his troops had no idea they were about to confront one of the most significant Iraqi attacks of the war. There is some disagreement about the size of the Iraqi force they encountered. By one account, "he faced not one brigade but three: between 25 and 30 tanks, plus 70 to 80 armored personnel carriers, artillery, and between 5,000 and 10,000 Iraqi soldiers coming from three directions."[155] In a postwar interview, however, Marcone credited the Iraqis with "15 tanks and 30 to 40 armored personnel carriers reinforced with artillery mortars." Regardless of which estimate is correct, this was precisely the type of force that should have been detected. Marcone's admission that "we didn't realize how big [a] force we were fighting" certainly speaks of a lack of situational awareness.[156] Although "someone may have known above me," he claims there was "zero information getting to me."[157] This is but one example of what is commonly referred to as the "digital divide" in which "commanders at the division level and above often had an excellent view of the battlefield, [while] troops

---

[153] Singer, *Wired for War*, pp. 189–90.
[154] Gordon and Trainor, *Cobra II*, p. 300.
[155] David Talbot, "We Got Nothing Until They Slammed Into Us," *Technology Review* (November 2004), p. 36.
[156] Interview for *PBS Frontline: The Invasion of Iraq* (2004). Accessed at: www.pbs .org/wgbh/pages/frontline/shows/invasion/interviews/marcone.html.
[157] Talbot, "We Got Nothing Until ...," p. 36.

at the brigade and battalion [levels] received much less information."[158] Cebrowski's recognized the need to close this divide: "what we're seeing is essentially net-centric warfare for the joint task force commander. The next step is network-centric warfare for the warfighter–reflecting increased 'jointness' at the tactical level of war."[159]

Against the unskilled and poorly equipped Iraqis, information deficits and the lack of situational awareness were regrettable but seldom deadly. Even though Marcone knew little about the size of the Iraqi force that attacked on April 3, his troops prevailed with few loses in men or material. The outcome might have been very different had the undetected enemy been better equipped and trained than the Iraqis. In 2003, however, American advantages across the board were so great that an occasional breakdown in situational awareness was not catastrophic.

Conclusion

Twice in slightly more than a decade the United States, with varying degrees of allied support, fought, and defeated the Iraqi military quickly and with historically low levels of friendly casualties. Understandably, these victories were taken as a vindication of policy – the technologies, weapons systems, force training, and war-fighting doctrine that yielded such favorable military results. Many also saw the outcomes and conduct of the wars as confirming predictions of an RMA in which changes in technology, organization, and doctrine were altering the character of warfare, at least for those possessing the relevant technologies. In the aftermath of the 2003 Iraq War, Eliot Cohen, an analyst not usually prone to exaggeration and faddish notions, concluded that "there is... reason to think that a major change – call it transformation or not – in warfare has occurred... the RMA is here to stay."[160] Skeptics could certainly point out that the reality of war often fell short of the more grandiose predictions of some RMA theorists: claims that the fog of war can be eliminated are almost certainly hyperbolic and unlikely to ever come to pass. But clearly the United States was able to apply force and achieve military objectives in ways that were unprecedented, and attempts to portray everything that seemed revolutionary as actually orthodox and traditional were increasingly strained.

That said, in both conflicts the United States was fortunate to fight the type of war and opponent it had been preparing for since the mid-1970s – a high-intensity interstate war against a conventionally organized

---

[158] Mahnken, *Technology and the American Way of War*, p. 211.
[159] Dan Caterinicca and Matthew French, "Network-Centric Warfare: Not There Yet," *Federal Computer Week* (June 9, 2003).
[160] Cohen, "Change and Transformation in Military Affairs," p. 407.

and equipped, albeit it weaker and less competent, military. And for the most part, the wars were fought in wide open spaces where the enemy found it difficult to hide and any movement or massing led to detection and likely destruction, the only significant exception being the battles with the Fedayeen in urban environments. Given the nature of the enemy and environment, American technologies and capabilities achieved their maximum effect in the Iraq Wars. If there was a type of war they were going to revolutionize, this was it.

OIF, however, did not end with Saddam's defeat, or even his capture a few months later. More than six years later OIF continued. But even though the official name remained the same, the enemy and mission would change over the following months and years. American forces, technology, and doctrine would be tested in a mission few welcomed, anticipated or prepared for, and the RMA, at least as pursued by the United States in the 1980s and 1990s, would reveal its limits as the third Iraq War took shape in the summer and fall of 2003.

6   THE THIRD IRAQ WAR, 2003–? – A REVOLUTION DENIED?

Liberation to Occupation

On May 1, 2003, President Bush, wearing full flight gear, made a dramatic landing on the deck of the U.S.S. Abraham Lincoln off the California coast to declare the end of major combat operations in Iraq. The setting was stirring, the sailors applauded, and the infamous "Mission Accomplished" banner hung prominently in the background. Although careful to warn that work remained, Bush's message was clear: the difficult part of Operation Iraqi Freedom was over. Saddam had been deposed and few Americans lost their lives in bringing him down. There was every reason to think the troops would start to come home before long. No one on that deck would have predicted that American forces would still be fighting in Baghdad half a decade later.

Two weeks later, Paul Bremer, the former diplomat Rumsfeld tapped to head the Coalition Provisional Authority (CPA), arrived in Baghdad and began issuing a series of controversial orders. The first related to the "de-Baathification of Iraqi society" and eliminated tens of thousands of Baath Party members from positions throughout the government, regardless of whether they were oil ministry engineers, hospital administrators, or university professors. The second order followed a week later and disbanded the Iraqi Army and much of country's police and internal security forces. Although precise numbers are difficult to verify, Bremer's orders left several hundred thousand Iraqis, many with military training and weapons, jobless and angry.[1] Both orders surprised military commanders in Iraq, many of whom objected strenuously. General Petraeus reportedly told one of Bremer's aides "that the decision to leave the Iraqi soldiers without a livelihood had put American lives at risk."[2] Thus, by the end of May the regime, government, military, and police that

---

[1] Ricks, *Fiasco*, pp. 162–3.
[2] Gordon and Trainor, *Cobra II*, p. 484.

controlled Iraq for more than two decades had been eliminated by war or fiat. The CPA, which is to say the United States, had become the de facto government of Iraq, responsible for all the things people usually expect of their governments. Bremer realized that "we were the government of Iraq under international law," which made him the head of state.[3] Although the United States claimed that it came to liberate the Iraqi people, they found their new leader had an American face. This was the point when, according to one participant, "we stopped being liberators and became occupiers."[4]

When the switch to occupation began, the United States had slightly over 100,000 troops in Iraq, a country of 38 million people spread over 400,000 square miles. Given the size of the country and magnitude of the tasks it faced, this was not a large force. When compared to the police department of any major American city, whose job is arguably less demanding, the disjuncture between manpower and responsibilities becomes clear. New York City, for example, employs about 38,000 police officers to maintain order in a city of 8 million people and less than 500 square miles. Iraq's population is approximately three and half times that of New York, and its territory is almost 1,000 times larger. And unlike American forces in Iraq, the NYPD operates within a larger, functioning municipal government. The NYPD does not have to provide or restore services or protect the city's borders. As a result of the political vacuum created by the war and the CPA's early decisions on de-Baathification and the Iraqi Army, American forces would have to address the multitude of problems pretty much by themselves. Even without an insurgency, this would be a tall order. As a RAND study concluded at the time, "not since the occupation of Germany and Japan has the United States undertaken such an ambitious task: the military occupation of a sizable country and a stated commitment to wholesale political transformation."[5]

Disorder and Insurgency

For those who worried about the adequacy of force levels in Iraq, the first signs of trouble came well before the emergence of an insurgency, indeed even before Bremer's army and de-Baathification orders. While some

---

[3] Interview with Paul Bremer, *PBS Frontline: The Lost Year in Iraq* (2006). Accessed at: www.pbs.org/wgbh/pages/frontline/yeariniraq/interviews/bremer.html.

[4] Williamson Murray and Geoffrey Parker, "The Post-War World, 1945–2007," in Geoffrey Parker, ed., *The Cambridge Illustrated History of Warfare* (Cambridge: Cambridge University Press, 2008), p. 382.

[5] James Dobbins, John G. McGinn, Keith Crane, Seth G. Jones, Rollie Lal, Andrew Rathmell, Rachel M. Swanger, and Anga R. Timilsina, *America's Role in Nation-Building: From Germany to Iraq* (Santa Monica, CA: RAND, 2003), p. 168. Drawing on traditional metrics of the sort Shinseki invoked the previous year, the study concluded that more than 400,000 troops would be needed to provide security in Iraq.

Iraqis turned out to celebrate Saddam's demise in those first days after the fall of Baghdad, showing their disdain by slapping his toppled statue with the soles of their shoes, others looted government ministries, museums and hospitals. Offices were emptied of furniture, buildings stripped of copper wire and pipes, museums cleared of priceless artifacts, and even hospitals robbed of life-saving equipment. American troops largely stood by as looters did substantial damage to the nation's basic infrastructure, physically destroying the institutions of government. Iraqis saw American soldiers perched on their tanks and fighting vehicles watching looters haul off anything not bolted down, apparently unable or unwilling to intervene. With only two U.S. divisions in a city of five million, it is not clear what they could have done even if they were inclined to act. The soldiers thought they had come to Iraq to get rid of a dictator and prevent another 9/11, not to shoot civilians carrying home sofas and carpets.

The military's inaction during the postwar chaos contrasted starkly with the competence and decisiveness displayed during the war. The reaction in Washington did not improve matters. Questioned about the scenes of chaos in Baghdad and elsewhere, Rumsfeld offered one of his classically cavalier responses, portraying the looting as a sign of freedom and manifestation of pent-up rage against Saddam's despised regime. In one of the most famous moments of the war, he described the situation in Iraq as "untidy," noting that "freedom's untidy. And free people are free to make mistakes and commit crimes and do bad things. They're also free to live their lives and do wonderful things. And that's what's going to happen here."[6] The critical legacy of these first days, however, was the impression of a force that was not in control of the country, or even the cities where its troops were concentrated. The American soldiers that defeated Saddam appeared stunned and helpless when faced with unarmed civilians laying waste to the city right before their eyes. If the Americans would not ensure order and provide basic security, who would? It was a less than awe-inspiring performance.

Scattered violence and unrest continued throughout the remainder of the spring and early summer as American forces struggled to gain control of the country and restore basic services while searching for the weapons of mass destruction whose presumed existence justified the war. It did not take long before the first clashes with Iraqi civilians turned deadly. One of the earliest incidents occurred in Fallujah, a predominantly Sunni city that had been bypassed the previous month as American units raced to Baghdad. While many Iraqis adopted a wait-and-see approach to the American occupation, "denunciation of the United States and its

---

[6] "A Nation at War; Rumsfeld's Words on Iraq: 'There is Untidiness.'" *New York Times* (April 12, 2003), p. B5.

occupation emanated from Sunni mosques almost immediately." During Saddam's rule, the minority Sunnis "clearly benefited from being at the center of power and identifying themselves with a state they had helped set up . . . and had dominated ever since." The regime's collapse "constituted a massive psychological blow."[7] In many Sunni areas there were celebrations and demonstrations on Saddam's birthday, April 23, including outside a school in Fallujah. Although accounts differ as to who shot first, American forces fired into the crowd, killing fifteen and wounding may others.[8] This was only the beginning of America's troubles in Fallujah. But despite the growing turmoil, Franks surprised almost everyone when he announced plans to withdraw all but 30,000 troops by September, which even at the time struck many as excessively optimistic.

Bremer did not want to be seen as the American dictator of Iraq and felt there needed to be some move toward Iraqi self-government, no matter how symbolic. To place some Iraqi faces into the nation's governing authority, Bremer announced the creation of the Iraqi Governing Council (IGC) on July 13. Representing a fairly broad cross section of Iraqi society, its members were nonetheless handpicked by Bremer and the council had no real powers. No one took the IGC seriously. Meanwhile, protests and attacks against American forces and supportive Iraqis continued to escalate and spread. As troubling as they were, the attacks remained largely unsophisticated and seemingly uncoordinated, and thus easily dismissed as isolated outbursts of frustration or the desperate acts of regime loyalists and "dead-enders." Then in mid-summer everything changed. Although it is difficult to pick a specific date marking the beginning of the insurgency, the bombing of the Jordanian embassy on August 7 is as good as any. The Jordanian bombing was followed by increasing attacks on American and coalition forces, Iraqis helping them, and international organizations and NGOs assisting with postconflict rebuilding. Bremer, visibly shaken by the surge in violence, sensed the moment was a watershed: "we had three large terrorist attacks: the Jordanian Embassy, the smaller one; the attack on the U.N. mission; and the attack on the people in the holy city of Najaf at the end of August. Those three things clearly suggested a new order of magnitude of violence. I mean, we had certainly been losing soldiers and we'd been having some problems, but nothing on that scale."[9] Bremer might not have realized it, but the third Iraq War had begun. American troops would not be returning by September. Having retired on July 7, however, Tommy Franks was already home in the United States.

---

7 Hashim, *Insurgency and Counter-Insurgency in Iraq*, p. 21.
8 Ian Fisher, "Aftereffects: The Military; U.S. Forces said to Kill 15 at Anti-American Rally," *The New York Times* (April 30, 2003), p. A1.
9 Interview with Paul Bremer, *PBS Frontline: The Lost Year in Iraq*.

A Budding Insurgency

Bremer worried about the magnitude of the August attacks. Others were more concerned that the pattern revealed the contours of a coherent strategy against the occupation. When the bombing of embassies and NGOs was combined with attacks on oil pipelines, electrical facilities, water mains, and other essential infrastructure, it was clear that "the insurgents [had] branched out into targeting high-value and high visibility foreign targets and critical economic installations."[10] For Thomas Hammes, this was the turning point because the "choice of targets showed the strategic concept of destroying American will by attacking U.S. forces, any government or NGO supporting the United States, and any Iraqis working for or believed to be collaborating with the United States."[11] In line with classic insurgent strategies, attacks on economic infrastructure and essential services were designed to drive a wedge between the population and the governing authority by demonstrating its inability to fulfill a government's basic responsibilities. So by August the attacks were consistent with the two essential elements of successful insurgencies: first, targeting national and NGO allies to increase costs and erode their political will to remain in the conflict; and second, attacks on infrastructure that will undermine public confidence in public authorities and increase discontent.

There was tremendous reluctance to admit the existence of an insurgency or a guerilla war in Iraq. Faced with repeated questions about whether such a conflict was emerging, administration officials and military commanders offered conflicting and evasive characterizations. Many explanations have been advanced for this hesitance to acknowledge the insurgency, ranging from ambiguous facts on the ground to a deep-seated aversion to recognizing a kind of war that few wanted to fight. Any mention of insurgency and guerilla warfare, of course, would immediately raise the specter of "another Vietnam." And admitting the existence of an insurgency would have been tantamount to denying the possibility of a quick exit. And since the prospect of a protracted war was political poison, no one was anxious to touch it. Refusing to recognize the insurgency, however, did not make it go away.

Faced with more frequent and deadlier attacks, the military became starved for information – for example, who were the insurgents, where were they, what was their source of funding, and where were their weapons. Although the enemy was different than a few months before, information was still the most valuable weapon. But this was an enemy whose movements could not be tracked by JSTARS. Satellites and UAVs

[10] Hashim, *Insurgency and Counter-Insurgency in Iraq*, p. 31.
[11] Thomas X. Hammes, *The Sling and the Stone: On War in the 21st Century* (New York: Zenith Press, 2004), p. 175.

could not see into the living rooms, garages, and basements where improvised explosive devises (IEDs) were being assembled. The insurgents
enjoyed the benefit of stealth by virtue of their ability to blend into the
local environment and culture. Now it was the Americans who stood
out, whose locations were known and whose movements could be easily followed. The information needed to combat the growing insurgency
could not be obtained by national technical means. It had to be acquired
by and from people, and as Krepinevich notes, "the people who have
that intelligence are the Iraqi people. The question is, how do you get
them to give you that information?"[12] Initially, American troops fanned
out into hostile neighborhoods, conducting raids at all hours and sweeping into custody thousands of young men suspected of participating in
the insurgency or possessing information about it. The tactic was heavy-
handed. The numbers were so great that some of Saddam's prisons had
to be reopened to house and interrogate the detainees. American soldiers
with no training for the task found themselves supervising a swelling
prison population. One of those prisons on the outskirts of Baghdad, Abu
Ghraib, held more than ten thousand detainees at a time. It is unclear,
however, whether these prisoners yielded much useful information. If so,
there was little evidence on the ground as insurgent attacks declined only
slightly at the very end of 2003 before resuming their upward trajectory
in early 2004 (see Figure 6.1). Indeed, such raids "probably angered more
Iraqis than they captured, leading to an aggregate increase in support for
the insurgency."[13]

Between the summer of 2003 and spring of 2004 there was no unified
strategy to fight the burgeoning insurgency throughout Iraq, and for better
or worse, local commanders had a great deal of leeway in how they
responded. Biddle was struck by "how much variation there [wa]s in the
tactics and methods employed by U.S. combat units in Iraq in that period
['03 and '04]. You had these methods kind of bubbling up from below
rather than being directed from above ... You had all sorts of variation
locally."[14] This helps to explain why "it was common for observers
of U.S. military operations in 2003–4 to note that each division's area
of operations felt like a different war."[15] One place where things went
relatively well was the northern city of Mosul, where the 101st Airborne
Division "conducted what was generally seen as a thorough and effective
operation, balancing war fighting and nation building."[16] In contrast to

[12] Interview with Andrew Krepinevich, *PBS Frontline: Endgame* (2007). Accessed at: www
.pbs.org/wgbh/pages/frontline/endgame/interviews/krepinevich.html.
[13] Metz, *Iraq & the Evolution of American Strategy*, p. 156.
[14] Quoted in *PBS Frontline: Endgame, Timeline* (2007). Accessed at: www.pbs.org/
wgbh/pages/frontline/endgame/cron/.
[15] Ricks, *Fiasco*, p. 227.
[16] Ibid., p. 227.

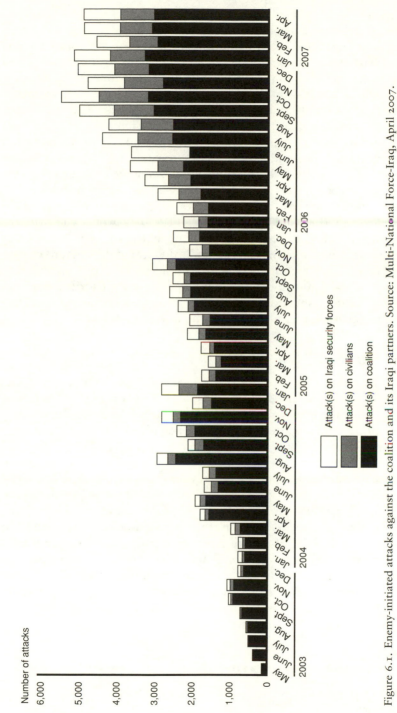

Figure 6.1. Enemy-initiated attacks against the coalition and its Iraqi partners. Source: Multi-National Force-Iraq, April 2007.

the rest of Iraq, in Mosul "U.S. soldiers walked beats like police officers and were stationed in local patrol bases, the equivalent of precinct houses. They were instructed to treat the Iraqis with respect. Knocking down doors was replaced by knocking on doors."[17] Posters in barracks asked "what have you done to win Iraqi hearts and minds today?"[18] Perhaps it is no coincidence that in Mosul informants revealed the whereabouts of Saddam's sons Qusay and Uday, who were then dispatched in a shootout on July 22. Interestingly, the 101st Airborne Division in Mosul was under the command of a relatively unknown Army Major General who would later become a household name, David Petraeus.

Politically and militarily the United States muddled through the winter of 2003–2004 as the security situation festered. Bremer and the CPA made futile attempts to create an effective Iraqi security force that could fight the insurgency and allow American forces to withdraw. Tensions and suspicions between Sunnis and Shiites continued to mount, foreign militants streamed into the country, and Al-Qaeda did its best to exacerbate the conflict. With a hotly contested presidential election underway in the United States, the disconnect between a hopeful rhetoric and a deteriorating security situation grew ever larger. As winter turned to spring, the situation took a decided turn for the worse.

April 2004: A Very Bad Month

Until the spring of 2004, southern Iraq was relatively calm as violence was centered in the so-called Sunni triangle. This was not too surprising because the south was dominated by the Shiites, who had borne the brunt of Saddam's oppression. Although southern Shiites did not greet the Americans and British as liberators as many had hoped, they did not actively resist the invasion or oppose the occupation. Shiite clerical leaders, unlike their Sunni counterparts, were divided and more moderate in their views of the British, who were largely stationed in the south, and Americans. And because the Shiites formed the majority in Iraq with approximately sixty percent of the population, they expected to be the chief beneficiaries of a more democratic political order, whereas the Sunnis feared their influence would diminish. With Sunni insurgents, ex-Baathists, foreign fighters, and Al-Qaeda wreaking havoc elsewhere in Iraq, the calm in the Shiite south was the sole bright spot. This was about to change as several influential Shiite clerics and their militias entered the fray to challenge the occupiers.

[17] Joe Klein, "Good General, Bad Mission," *Time* (January 12, 2007). Accessed at: www.time.com/time/columnist/klein/article/0,9565,1587186,00.html. On Mosul, see also Ricks, *Fiasco*, pp. 228–32.
[18] Rick Atkinson, *In the Company of Soldiers: A Chronicle of Combat* (New York: Holt, 2005), p. 304.

The critical figure in the "Shiite uprising" that began in April was Moqtada al-Sadr, one of the more radical Shiite clerics who opposed the occupation from the start. Prior to April 2004, however, al-Sadr's opposition was primarily rhetorical. Neither he nor his supporters were active participants in the insurgency. When the CPA shut down and banned al-Sadr's newspaper after it published a series of incendiary editorials, al-Sadr unleashed his militia, the Mahdi Army. Probably 10,000 strong, the Mahdi Army was a formidable paramilitary organization that al-Sadr founded immediately after Saddam's ouster. Beginning April 4, the Mahdi Army moved against coalition forces in several cities across southern Iraq and the Shiite-dominated suburbs of Baghdad. Largely because American forces were preoccupied elsewhere in Iraq, the Mahdi Army made significant advances against the handful of Spanish, Polish, and Ukrainian troops stationed in the area. A small number of poorly trained Iraqi security forces working with coalition forces were worthless, offering no meaningful resistance. More alarming were signs of cooperation between Sunni insurgents and Shiite militants. In the suburbs of Baghdad, for example, "Sunni insurgents... joined with Shi'a [Shiite] insurgents... to launch attacks on the US presence."[19] And in battle for Fallujah as well other places where American and British forces counterattacked, "Sunni Arab insurgents Shiite militias openly coordinated for the first time."[20] Because the Shiites and Sunni represented almost eighty percent of Iraq's population, this was the last thing the United States needed.

Fallujah, located just forty miles to the west of Baghdad, had been relatively calm until the end of March, perhaps deceptively so. As part of the largest troop rotation since the invasion, Marines took over from the Army's 82nd Airborne Division and adopted a more aggressive posture toward combating the city's foreign fighters and insurgents. But it was not a clash between the Marines and the insurgents that sparked a crisis, but rather the ambush of a convoy of private contractors heading into the city. After the insurgents fired on the convoy and disabled its vehicles, crowds descended on it, dragging several men from their trucks and vans, beating, killing, and dismembering them before hanging their remains from the bridge and throwing the corpses onto a pile of burning tires. The gruesome images were captured on tape and broadcast around the world and on the Internet. Comparisons to Mogadishu were unavoidable, and outrage created intense pressure to respond forcefully.

On April 5, the Marines launched a full-scale incursion into the city, determined to get those responsible for the attack and wrestle control of the city from insurgents and foreign fighters. It was a battle of the sort many feared when the Army first entered Baghdad exactly a year

[19] Hashim, *Insurgency and Counter-Insurgency in Iraq*, p. 37.
[20] Metz, *Iraq & the Evolution of American Strategy*, p. 165.

before. The Marines met well-organized resistance as "hundreds of insurgents . . . well-armed and motivated . . . dug in and decided to make a stand in this city of 300,000."[21] The Marines were battered from all directions by machine gun fire, mortars, and RPGs as they tried to navigate the city's streets and narrow alleys. They returned fire and called in a limited number of precision air strikes against suspected insurgent strongholds.[22] It was the most deadly battle since the end of major combat operations: forty Americans and hundreds of Iraqis were killed and many more injured. But under political pressure from Baghdad and the IGC, a unilateral ceasefire was declared even though none of the original objectives had been accomplished. The Marines in Fallujah were livid that their mission was terminated as result of political pressure. After negotiations, control of Fallujah was handed over to the so-called Fallujah Brigade, a group widely seen as dominated by the very insurgents the Marines had been fighting. Despite the best attempts to portray Fallujah as a victory, the city's residents knew better and turned out to celebrate the American defeat.[23] Krepinevich describes the battle for Fallujah as:

A kind of Iraqi Alamo . . . the world's greatest military power certainly would appear to be capable of taking Fallujah. For some reason they don't. The news agencies that get access to Fallujah are agencies like Al Arabiya or Al Jazeera. They show photographs of wounded children and women in the city's hospital, and the impression is that the Americans are going in and wantonly killing civilians along with the insurgents. So in just about every respect, this is a black eye for the United States.[24]

The "black eye" of Fallujah was soon to be overshadowed by a cascade of bad news, and the world would soon be exposed to images that would make the pictures from Fallujah's hospitals pale in comparison.

There had been rumors of abuse at American-run prisons in Iraq as released detainees related their experiences to friends, family, media, and human rights organizations. Their stories, however, were consistently denied, dismissed as baseless anti-American propaganda designed to stoke the insurgency. Then came the photographs of abuse at Abu Ghraib. Taken by American soldiers stationed at the prison and leaked to the press, the damning pictures became public when the American television newsmagazine *60 Minutes* ran the story on April 27 with devastating results. Military commanders in Iraq and representatives on Capitol Hill were quick to express their disgust at pictures of American soldiers

[21] Hashim, *Insurgency and Counter-Insurgency in Iraq*, p. 37.
[22] Pamela Constable, "Troops Gaining Grip in Sections of Fallujah," *Washington Post* (April 7, 2004), p. A1.
[23] Rajiv Chandrasekaran and Naseer Nouri, "We Won: Fallujah Rejoices in Withdrawal," *Washington Post* (May 2, 2004), p. A1.
[24] Krepinevich interview, *PBS Frontline: Endgame*.

gloating and giving the thumbs-up as they subjected Iraqi prisoners to a seemingly endless variety of sadistic and humiliating abuse. Bush and Rumsfeld joined the chorus of outrage. The image of a hooded prisoner subjected to a mock execution would be the following week's cover for the *Economist, Der Spiegel,* and countless other magazines and newspapers around the world, becoming the defining image of the war. That the abuse occurred at the very prison where Saddam's own enemies were tortured added an element of unfortunate irony. The scandal was a strategic disaster of the highest order for the United States, a gift to the insurgency and a pictorial indictment of the occupation. It confirmed every Iraqi's worst fears, which was catastrophic in a conflict whose outcome would require winning the people over. Ricks relates the story of Maj. Gen. John Mattis encountering a group of soldiers in Iraq watching television as the Abu Ghraib story was breaking. When he asked what was happening, a private supposedly turned and told him that "some assholes have just lost the war for us."[25] It was an ignominious way to mark the end of the United States' first year in Iraq.

Summer 2004: Finally, a Strategy

By May 2004, when even the most reluctant were forced to start using the "i" word, there was still no coherent, nationwide strategy for combating the insurgency. The United States simply muddled through as the insurgency intensified and spread. In Washington there was little stomach for a counterinsurgency campaign that would leave American troops tied down in Iraq for years. Given the presidential campaign underway in the United States and declining support for the war among the public at large and in the halls of Congress, there had to be some light at the end of a not-too-long tunnel. But since successful counterinsurgency wars tend to last about a decade, what was the alternative to a protracted military commitment? The administration's answer in the summer of 2004 was the so-called light footprint strategy.

The basic goal of this new strategy was to shift responsibility for fighting the insurgency to the Iraqis as soon as possible. Politically, this entailed the transfer of authority to an elected Iraqi government in the near future. Militarily, it meant training an Iraqi Army and security forces that could replace American troops. No one thought the Iraqis were ready for any of this that summer. Although there were a handful Iraqi forces of questionable quality that could assist, the United States would continue to shoulder the bulk of military responsibilities for some time. But how would American forces be deployed and utilized? Based partially on the plausible assumption that the American troop presence itself was one of

---

[25] Ricks, *Fiasco,* p. 290.

the factors creating resentment and fueling the insurgency, the plan called for minimizing their day-to-day visibility by remaining largely confined to a handful of central bases from which operations would be launched. At the same the United States would implement a more concerted plan for training Iraqi troops and security forces. The formulation of the new strategy, which administration officials repeated ad infinitum, was that American troops would be able to "stand down" and come home as the Iraqi's "stood up." Political transition and military disengagement were the critical elements of the light footprint.

The political transition began in June 2004 when the CPA was dissolved, Bremer left the country, and formal sovereignty was transferred to an interim Iraqi government. The more critical step would take place in January 2005, when nationwide elections for an Iraqi national assembly were scheduled. Militarily, a new Multi-National Security Transition Command-Iraq (MNSTC-I), led by General Petraeus, was also created in June to bring unity and order to the somewhat helter-skelter military and police training effort of the previous year. The command's "mission was to train and equip ten divisions of Iraqi soldiers as quickly as possible ... to create a force to which the U.S. military could turn over the country and depart." This was a daunting mission given the situation in Iraq. Robinson explains that "the challenge of building an entire military institution in the middle of a rapidly worsening insurgency was staggering." Given sectarian hostilities and suspicions, one of the major difficulties was creating military and security forces representative of Iraqi society as a whole that would be seen as legitimate and impartial rather than merely militias of the Shiite majority. As of that summer, however, insurgents were doing all they could to prevent the creation of effective military and security forces: "Sunni Arabs were leaving the Iraqi security forces due to intimidation of their families, kidnapping, and murder.... [while] busloads of recruits were killed by improvised explosive devices and ambushes."[26] For a Sunni there were few things as dangerous as cooperating with the occupiers.

Interestingly, in his role as commander of MNSTC-I (more commonly referred to as "min-sticky"), Petraeus became part of a larger counterinsurgency strategy almost totally at odds with the one he adopted in Mosul the previous year. With neighborhood bases and foot patrols, Petraeus tried to establish a "heavy footprint" in Mosul that would provide the military visibility and persistent presence required for establishing the security upon which all else depended. In addition to pointing out that the light footprint strategy flew in the face of everything known about fighting insurgencies, critics derided it as "war tourism." Ricks explains

---

[26] Linda Robinson, *Tell Me How This Ends: David Petreaus and the Search for a Way Out of Iraq* (New York: Public Affairs, 2008), pp. 73–4.

that the light footprint involved "units based in big forward operating bases – FOBS, going out and doing patrols from Humvees, usually not foot patrols, but mounted patrols, and then coming back to their base. If that's the way you're operating, you're not in the war. You're simply a war tourist."[27] Others referred to this style of operations as "drive-by" counterinsurgency.[28] The so-called green zone or emerald city in Baghdad, complete with air conditioning, pools, game rooms, and fast food restaurants came to symbolize the almost surreal military cocoons associated with the light footprint.[29] A critical problem with war tourism is that isolation leads to ignorance, which David Kilcullen explains in terms any good RMA advocate can appreciate:

Because troops did not live in the *muhalla*, the Iraq neighborhoods, they saw very little of the locals, did not know them, had no notion of who to trust and how far... Partly because of this lack of *situational awareness*, some units... tended to take an extremely "kinetic" approach to completing their mission... because of their lack of *situational awareness* and personal relationships with the people, [they] tended to treat all Iraqis as a potential threat and thus adopted a high-handed approach that alienated the population. This exacerbated the backlash against their presence, discouraged people from coming forward with information about the insurgents, and thus further reduced the units' *situational awareness*, leaving them trapped in a vicious cycle of intervention and rejection.[30]

The strategy of keeping Americans in forward bases was motivated in part by the understandable and laudable desire to minimize casualties, and there is no doubt that in 2004 and 2005 American troops were safer in their bases than patrolling the streets of Iraqi cities. But if an escalating insurgency beyond the walls and barbed wire resulted, American forces might be in greater danger in the long run. In military operations the primary goal should never be force protection per se, for if this were true and the most important objective is minimizing the loss of American lives, then best not to go to war in the first place. As Kalev Sepp of the Naval Postgraduate School puts it, "If you *really* want to reduce your casualties, go back to Fort Riley."[31] The goal has to be the minimal loss of life consistent with the achievement of the nation's strategic objectives. And in Iraq in 2004 this required defeating the insurgency.

---

[27] Ricks interview, *PBS Frontline: Endgame.*
[28] Neil Smith and Sean McFarland, "Anbar Awakens," *Australian Army Journal* Vol. 2, No. 2 (Winter 2008), p. 8.
[29] See Rajiv Chandrasekaran, *Imperial Life in the Emerald City: Inside Iraq's Green Zone* (New York: Vintage, 2007).
[30] David Kilcullen, *The Accidental Guerilla: Fighting Small Wars in the Midst of a Big One* (Oxford: Oxford University Press, 2009), p. 124, emphasis added.
[31] George Packer, "The Lesson of Tal Afar: Is It too Late for the Administration to Correct Its Course in Iraq?" *The New Yorker* Vol. 82, No. 8 (April 10, 2006), p. 52.

As 2004 came to end, "insurgents had near control over important parts of central Iraq, especially the cities of Fallujah, Ramadi, Samarra and Baquah." Less than an hour's drive from Baghdad, "Fallujah was particularly worrisome and was seen by both the insurgents and counterinsurgents as the epicenter of the resistance."[32] Indeed, some went so far as to describe the city as the IED and "car-bomb capital of Iraq" from which "insurgents would plan attacks, and then ex-filtrate with weapons and personnel only to return to their safe haven in Fallujah."[33] With elections scheduled for January 2005, Fallujah could not remain an insurgent and Al-Qaeda stronghold. Despite claims of progress in training Iraqi forces, however, the Iraqis were clearly not ready to take on Fallujah. American forces would have to do the heavy lifting. After several weeks of aerial attacks on suspected insurgent targets and warnings for civilians to leave the city, the second battle for Fallujah in 2004 began in the evening of November 7, only five days after the U.S. presidential elections. The battle's first seventy-two hours would witness the most intense fighting American forces had seen since the Vietnam War. It was brutal, house-to-house urban warfare. Ricks paints a vivid picture:

I talked to a lot of Marines about Fallujah II . . . It's astonishing, the narratives. Hand-to-hand combat. One Marine comes into a room, and he's got his weapon up in front of him. He comes around a corner, and there's an insurgent with his weapon up in front of him. . . . Both pull the triggers almost simultaneously. The Marine had pulled his trigger a split second before the other guy, and so his bullet goes into the insurgent. The insurgent's bullets just go right over his shoulder because it knocks the weapon up. . . . You have Marines killing insurgents with knives, fighting on the ground. You have guys biting each other sometimes. It was really rough fighting in Fallujah.[34]

American forces regained control of the city within two weeks, but victory came at a high cost. Fifty-one Americans were killed and more than five hundred seriously wounded. Although reliable figures are impossible to obtain, local and Arab media portrayed the battle as an indiscriminate assault that left scores of civilians dead. The U.S. military, however, claimed that less than five hundred civilians remained in the city on November 7. Damage to the city and its infrastructure was extensive with thousands of buildings completely or partially destroyed. But the immediate military objective had been achieved. What impact this might have on the impending election and overall level of violence in the country or the Sunni triangle remained to be seen.

[32] Metz, *Iraq & the Evolution of American Strategy*, p. 169.
[33] Herspring, *Rumsfeld's Wars*, p. 176.
[34] Ricks interview, *PBS Frontline: Endgame*.

2005: Elections, Governance, and Insurgency

The United States was always looking for the silver bullet, a military or political event that would finally halt the escalating violence and turn the corner on the insurgency – for example, the capture of Saddam in December 2003, the dissolution of the CPA and handover of sovereignty in June 2004, and recapture of Fallujah in November 2004. Each time expectations were dashed and the violence continued to worsen. As 2004 came to an end, there were hopes that upcoming elections would accomplish what none of these previous events could, and the initial signs were encouraging.

On January 30, 2005, Iraqis went to the polls to elect a transitional National Assembly to draft a new constitution. Many feared that widespread violence would mar the election as insurgents attempted to derail the democratic process. Although thirty Iraqi civilians were killed in scattered attacks, the voting went more smoothly than almost anyone expected. Images of long lines at polling stations and enthusiastic Iraqis waving their ink-stained index fingers as proof that they voted were met with jubilation back in Washington. At long last the promise of Iraqi democracy appeared within reach. There were, however, reasons to worry. The overall turnout was decent at fifty-eight percent (higher than the recent U.S. presidential election), but in some areas it was as low as two percent. The Kurds and majority Shiites showed up to vote in large numbers while the Sunnis did not. Whether their absence reflected insurgent intimidation or a hesitance to legitimize a process that would formalize their minority status, the Sunnis largely sat this one out. This was reflected in the result. Although Sunnis were about twenty percent of Iraq's population, the most significant Sunni party participating in the election garnered less than two percent of the vote, translating into just five of the National Assembly's 275 seats.[35] Since bridging Iraq's sectarian divisions and suspicions was essential to unifying a democratic state, it did not bode well that Sunnis were turning their backs on the political process.

Insurgent attacks and civilian deaths decreased slightly in the election's immediate aftermath, but the reduction was by no means dramatic. By the summer of 2005, violence exceeded its preelection levels. There was no indication of a major turning point. Hopes were dashed again, and the insurgency continued unabated. Not surprisingly, even commanders on the ground began to question the effectiveness of existing strategy. One of these was Col. H.R. McMaster, whose third Armored Cavalry Regiment (ACR) had finished its first tour of duty in March 2004 and was

[35] See Kenneth Katzman, *CRS Report for Congress: Iraqi Elections and New Government* (Washington, DC: Congressional Research Service, April 7, 2005), pp. 4–5. Accessed at: www.digital.library.unt.edu/govdocs/crs/permalink/meta-crs-6354:1.

preparing return to Iraq early in 2005. With a Ph.D. in military history from the University of North Carolina, McMaster knew that this was not the first time the United States had dealt with an insurgency: "the Army has a lot of experience to draw on," he noted, "but it hadn't really been institutionalized in terms of counterinsurgency operations, because the Army was biased in favor of conventional wars . . . that didn't involve a protracted commitment and a complex state-building counterinsurgency environment."[36] His previous experience in Iraq and understanding insurgencies led McMaster to reject the light footprint in favor what would become known as "clear, hold and build," which was really just a new and clever label for traditional counterinsurgency doctrine.

McMaster and his regiment were deployed to the area around Tal Afar, a city of 250,000 in the northwest province of Ninawa, about 50 miles from the Syrian border. Despite previous efforts to clear the city, it was "a hotbed of insurgent activity and a transit point for foreign fighters entering from Syria."[37] McMaster describes the situation upon his arrival as "very bleak . . . the enemy had essentially established control over the city. This was sort of a franchise operation of Al-Qaeda in Iraq."[38] His goal was to clear the city of insurgents and terrorists, retain control after their departure, and then build the infrastructure and institutions to enable and empower the Iraqis and eventually allow American troops to leave. Conceptually, this was not completely at odds with operations elsewhere in Iraq. The difference was that in the rest of Iraq American forces would come out of their bases to do the clearing and leave the holding and building to the Iraqis. Unfortunately, the Iraqis were unable and/or unwilling to do the holding and building. As a result, cleared areas quickly reverted to insurgent control once the Americans left. For McMaster, the only short-term solution was for American forces to do the clearing, holding, and building until the Iraqis were ready to take over, and in 2005 they were not ready.

Upon arrival in Tal Afar, the first order of business was purging the city of insurgents, foreign fighters and, most importantly, Al-Qaeda operatives who were terrorizing the local population and using the city as base for operations throughout the region. This involved some heavy fighting, resulting in twenty-one American fatalities. Once this was accomplished, McMaster's troops remained and lived in the city, patrolling the streets from neighborhood outposts. They did not retreat into isolated and more

---

[36] Interview with H.R. McMaster for *PBS Frontline: Endgame* (2007). Accessed at: www .pbs.org/wgbh/pages/frontline/endgame/interviews/mcmaster.html. McMaster's doctoral dissertation on the Vietnam War was eventually published as *Dereliction of Duty: Johnson, McNamara, the Joint Chiefs of Staff, and the Lies That Led to Vietnam* (New York: Harper Perennial, 1998).

[37] Metz, *Iraq & the Evolution of American Strategy*, p. 175.

[38] McMaster interview, *PBS Frontline: Endgame*.

comfortable accommodations. Implicitly criticizing what was being done elsewhere, McMaster explained that although "you would think that's kind of risky, putting soldiers in the middle of a city . . . actually the riskiest course of action would have been to consolidate our forces on one big base and feel safe but really not know what is going on."[39] Troops needed to interact regularly with the community and treat people with respect to build trust, elicit cooperation, and acquire the intelligence that only locals could provide. "Every time you treat an Iraqi disrespectfully," McMaster warned his troops, "you are working for the enemy."[40] His was "a different approach based on understanding the intricacies of local culture and political power, sustaining the U.S. presence in areas cleared of insurgents, and treating detainees with all possible dignity to avoid dishonoring them and inspiring them (or their families) to seek revenge."[41] In Packer's view, McMaster and the troops of the third ACR were "rebels against an incoherent strategy that had brought the American project in Iraq to brink of failure."[42]

Undoubtedly several unique factors worked to McMaster's advantage. Compared with Baghdad, Fallujah or Mosul, for example, Tal Afar had a relatively small population of a quarter million people, so he was able to hold and build with the roughly one thousand troops that remained after Tal Afar was cleared. Implementing a similar strategy in a sprawling city of millions would be more challenging and require much higher force levels. McMaster was also honest enough to admit that "the enemy [also] deserves credit for their own defeat." The campaign of intimidation and violence, especially by Al-Qaeda, turned the city's population against the insurgents, creating an opening for the Americans. This was critical because in insurgencies the side that alienates the people tends to lose. So it "was not just the way we were treating the population," McMaster explains, "but the brutality of the enemy worked against them."[43] The strategy worked. By the end of 2005, Tal Afar was relatively calm and peaceful, something that could not be said for the rest of Iraq.

The end of 2005 also offered a few glimmers of hope on the political front. The constitution drafted by the transitional National Assembly was approved in an October national referendum with 77.7 percent of the vote, though an alarming 96.9 percent of voters in the Sunni Arab province of Al Anbar voted against it. The successful constitutional referendum set the stage for new National Assembly elections in December. This time there was no Sunni boycott, since by this point, "many Sunni

---

39 Ibid.
40 Thomas Ricks, *The Gamble: General David Petraeus and the American Military Adventure in Iraq, 2006–2008* (New York: The Penguin Press, 2009), p. 60.
41 Metz, *Iraq & the Evolution of American Strategy*, p. 175.
42 Packer, "The Lesson of Tal Afar," p. 49.
43 McMaster interview, *PBS Frontline: Endgame.*

Arabs acknowledge[d] that it was a failure of historic proportions that they did not vote" in the earlier election.[44] Sunni clerics who instructed their followers to stay home in January urged them to turn out in December. The outcome of the election was something of a mixed bag. On the one hand, the willingness of all groups to participate in this round was taken as a sign of progress, however modest. On the other hand, it was somewhat discouraging that the Iraqis voted almost completely along sectarian lines, with Shiite parties garnering about sixty percent of the vote and Sunni Arab parties slightly more than twenty percent.[45] Overall, however, in a country with little to be happy about, the election process and outcome instilled a limited sense of optimism. But as was becoming the pattern in Iraq, the optimism did not last long.

2006: Insurgency and Civil War?

Until the end of 2005 the conflict in Iraq was viewed primarily as a Sunni insurgency with smaller elements of Shiite militancy and Al-Qaeda terrorism. In February 2006, however, many began to worry about an even more frightening prospect, an outright civil war between Sunnis and Shiites that could rip the country apart.[46] On February 22, 2006, this fear threatened to become a reality as Iraq erupted in a spasm of sectarian attacks and reprisals following the bombing and near destruction of one of the holiest Shiite sites, the "Golden Mosque" in Samarra, about sixty miles north of Baghdad. Most suspect the attack was the work of Al-Qaeda, specifically intended to ignite and foment sectarian violence and prevent any meaningful political reconciliation. The reaction was probably exactly what Al-Qaeda hoped for as the bombing:

ignited a nationwide outpouring of rage... Shiite militia members flooded the streets of Baghdad, firing rocket-propelled grenades and machine guns at Sunni mosques as Iraqi Army soldiers... stood helpless nearby. By the day's end, mobs had struck 27 Sunni mosques in the capital, killing three imams and kidnapping a fourth... In the southern Shiite city of Basra, Shiite militia members destroyed at least two Sunni mosques, killing an imam, and launched an attack on the headquarters of Iraq's best-known Sunni Arab political party.[47]

While there had been sectarian violence before the Golden Mosque attack, it grew to unprecedented levels over the course of 2006, which would see the highest civilian casualty levels of the war (see Figure 6.2). Hundreds

[44] Hashim, *Insurgency and Counterinsurgency in Iraq*, p. 51.
[45] See www.voanews.com/english/archive/2005-12/2005-12-20-voa9.cfm.
[46] See James Fearon, "Iraq's Civil War," *Foreign Affairs* Vol. 86, No. 2 (March/April 2007), pp. 2–15.
[47] Robert E. Worth, "Blast Destroys Shrine in Iraq, Setting Off Sectarian Fury," *New York Times* (February 22, 2006).

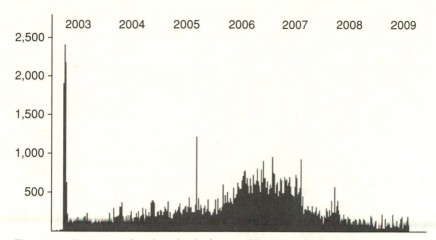

Figure 6.2. Documented civilian deaths from violence. Source: Iraq Body Count (www .iraqbodycount.org/database downloaded on October 28, 2009).

of roadside bombs and IEDs exploded every week. Neighborhoods in Baghdad and elsewhere were ethnically cleansed. Death squads and militias took their grizzly revenge at night, leaving bodies scattered on the side of the roads to be collected every morning like trash. Suicide bombers targeted civilians in markets and mosques. The violence and insecurity paralyzed ordinary Iraqis. Normal day-to-day life in large parts of Baghdad ceased. The combination of an insurgency and low-grade sectarian civil war brought Iraq to the edge of an abyss by the end of the year as "civilian deaths peaked between September 2006 and January 2007, with between 2,700 and 3,800 killed per month."[48]

The compelling question is: Why could no one stop the violence more than three years after the fall of Saddam? After all, more than three years had passed since General Petraeus and "min-sticky" received orders to rebuild and train the Iraqi Army and security forces. In September 2004, Petraeus penned an editorial for the *Washington Post* detailing the "tangible progress" already made, noting that "six battalions of the Iraqi regular army and the Iraqi Intervention Force are now conducting operations . . . Within the next 60 days, six more regular army and six additional Intervention Force battalions will become operational. Nine more regular army battalions will complete training in January."[49] Nonetheless, a year and a half later Iraqi soldiers and police were apparently "helpless" to protect Sunni mosques from Shiite attacks in the nation's capital. Since American strategy called for transferring responsibility for internal security to the Iraqis as soon as possible, this was not a good sign. But many

---

[48] Kilcullen, *The Accidental Guerrilla*, pp. 125–6.
[49] David H. Petraeus, "Battling for Iraq," *Washington Post* (September 26, 2004), p. B7.

suggested an even more troubling explanation of Iraqi "helplessness": Iraqi soldiers and police stood by because they did not want to stop the attacks. Their inaction reflected a lack of desire to help and sympathy with the attackers, not a lack of ability. The Sunnis had long suspected that the Iraqi government, army and police did the bidding of the Shiite majority. If democracy means the majority rules, the Shiites would rule. The Sunnis were not alone in their suspicions. According to Krepinevich, "2006 was supposed to be the year of the police in Iraq. They proved to be woefully inadequate. They are not loyal to the government. They are prone to sectarian violence."[50] Kilcullen was even stronger in his indictment, arguing that by 2006 Iraqi governmental institutions "were heavily penetrated by Shi'a [Shiite] extremists who used them to deny services to members of the Sunni community, or to actively kill or drive out Sunnis."[51] "The core of the Iraqi state was rotten," explains Ricks, "The Iraqi Army was heavily Shiite," and even worse, "the National Police was thoroughly infiltrated by Shiite militias."[52] Indeed, the situation was so bad that the "the government was a sectarian combatant in the civil war that started after Samarra, not a politically neutral 'honest broker' that governed in the interests of all Iraqis."[53]

While not many were willing to characterize the conflict in Iraq as a full-fledged sectarian civil war, few could disagree with Kilcullen's judgment that "Samarra was a disaster that had fundamentally and irrevocably changed the nature of the conflict."[54] More than three years had passed since the American invasion. More than three thousand U.S. soldiers were dead. Thousands more were seriously injured. Tens of thousands of Iraqis had also lost their lives. And after all of this, the prospect of a unified and democratic Iraq appeared more elusive than ever.

The Rise of Counterinsurgents[55]

As the situation in Iraq deteriorated during the first half of 2006, it appeared as if the United States was on the verge of losing the war. Hollow rhetoric about progress in battling the insurgency and encouraging statistics on the number of Iraqi soldiers and police trained could no longer be reconciled with the dire facts on the ground. No good news was coming out of Iraq. The existing strategy was inexorably leading to failure.

---

50 Krepinevich interview, *PBS Frontline: Endgame*.
51 Kilcullen, *The Accidental Guerrilla*, p. 125.
52 Ricks, *The Gamble*, p. 46.
53 Kilcullen, *The Accidental Guerrilla*, p. 125.
54 Ibid., pp. 121–2.
55 See Spencer Ackerman's excellent series, "The Rise of the Counterinsurgents," *The Washington Independent* (March 2008). Accessed at: www.washingtonindependent .com/426/series-the-rise-of-the-counterinsurgents.

Such was the conclusion of a growing and increasingly active of group of what Ricks describes as "sympathetic war critics" – retired military officers, civilian defense analysts and counterinsurgency theorists – who argued in public and lobbied in private for one last reorientation of strategy that they hoped might snatch victory from the jaws of impending defeat. They were, however, swimming against the political current, largely because their strategy called for sending more American forces at a moment when support for the war was collapsing and Congressional elections approached. Prevailing opinion, embodied in the conclusions of the Iraq Study Group, favored a more rapid transfer of authority to the Iraqis, not expanding and prolonging the American military presence.[56] Although public debate focused on the easy to comprehend issue of troop levels, this was not the critical element of the proposal. There was no point in sending more troops to do the same thing. Additional troops were needed to implement an inherently more manpower intensive strategy, one in line with traditional counterinsurgency doctrine. The goal was to combat the *insurgency*, not just the *insurgents*, by providing the Iraqi people with what they wanted most, security and safety. It was a "bottom up" strategy in which security for the population was assumed to be a prerequisite for elite political accommodation.

As the counterinsurgents were pushing their case in Washington, General Petraeus was at Fort Leavenworth, Kansas, where he was stationed after his tour as commander of MNSTC-I ended in 2005. Here he led the Army's Combined Arms Center, offering counterinsurgency courses and training to mid-career officers. More importantly, he guided the effort to write the military's first new counterinsurgency field manual in more than two decades. Drawing on his knowledge and experience as well as the expertise of a wide range of advisors, some of whom were active in the effort to change American strategy, the result was *FM 3–24: Counterinsurgency*, the final draft of which was circulated in the summer of 2006. The manual distilled the lessons of the twentieth century's successful counterinsurgency campaigns, emphasizing that "at its core," counterinsurgency is "a struggle for the population's support" which requires "a mix of offensive, defensive, and stability operations conducted along multiple lines of operations . . . a mix of familiar combat tasks and skills more often associated with nonmilitary agencies. Soldiers and Marines are expected to be nation builders as well as warriors."[57] It pointed to

---

[56] James A. Baker, Lee H. Hamilton, Lawrence S. Eagleburger, Vernon E. Jordan, Edwin Messe, Sandra Day O'Connor, Leon Panetta, William J. Perry, Charles S. Robb, and Alan K. Simpson, *The Iraq Study Group Report* (2006). Accessed at: www.usip.org/isg/iraq_study_group_report/report/1206/iraq_study_group_report.pdf.

[57] *FM 3–24: Counterinsurgency* (Washington, DC: Department of the Army, 2006), pp. 1–28 and forward.

paradoxes of counterinsurgency operations that make them "counter-intuitive to the traditional U.S. view of war." Echoing concerns about "war tourism" and aggressive raids, the manual noted that in counterinsurgency campaigns "the more you protect your force, the less secure you may be" and "the more force is used, the less effective it is."[58] McMaster's "clear, hold and build" strategy in Tal Afar was highlighted as an example of an effective counterinsurgency operation.[59] It did not take much reading between the lines to see the manual as an indictment of American strategy in Iraq since 2003. Against this backdrop of spiraling sectarian violence in Iraq, an organized campaign to change American strategy, and the appearance of the new counterinsurgency field manual, the unfortunately labeled "surge" took shape in the fall of 2006.

Less than twenty-four hours after Republicans took a beating in the 2006 midterm elections, losing control of both the House and Senate, President Bush announced that he had accepted Rumsfeld's resignation and would replace him with Robert Gates, a moderate who had expressed no opinion about the war while serving as president of Texas A&M University. By this time Richard Perle, Paul Wolfowitz, Douglas Feith and other architects of the war had already left. Rumsfeld's departure was a signal. President Bush realized the war was at a critical juncture and only new leadership could extract the United States from the quagmire. Continuing the current approach was not a feasible option. The real choices were either an accelerated transfer of power to the Iraqis and pullback of American forces, as the Iraq Study Group recommended, or an increase in troop levels accompanied by a new strategy. Bush chose the latter, announcing his "surge" in a nationally televised address on January 10, 2007. In addition to increasing troop levels by more than 20,000, Bush explained that "America will change its strategy to help the Iraqis . . . put down sectarian violence and bring security to the people of Baghdad . . . to help the Iraqis clear and secure neighborhoods, to help them protect the local population, and to help insure that the Iraqi forces left behind are capable of providing the security that Baghdad needs."[60] This strategy, in Kilcullen's judgment, "finally began to reflect counterinsurgency best practice as demonstrated over dozens of campaigns in the last several decades."[61] More troops would stream into Baghdad over the next few months. They would be accompanied by new leaders, including General Petraeus, who would return for his third tour, this time as commander of all forces in Iraq. But was this all too little, too late?

[58] Ibid., pp. 1–27, 28.
[59] Ibid., pp. 5–22, 23.
[60] Kilcullen, *The Accidental Guerrilla*, p. 128.
[61] Ibid., p. 129.

One Last Try, with a Little Help

American forces in Iraq were already receiving some help from an unexpected source even before the surge began as the so-called Sunni Awakening was transforming the conflict in Sunni areas of Iraq. Within the Sunni triangle the United States was increasingly able to exploit growing disenchantment with Sunni Islamic extremists and Al-Qaeda, which had portrayed itself as an ally of Sunnis fearful of Shiite domination. But as McMaster discovered in Tal Afar, Al-Qaeda had a tendency to overplay its hand by attempting to assert political dominance, imposing strict religious rules of conduct, and using widespread violence against those who opposed its agenda.[62] The violence of Al-Qaeda and extremist insurgents eventually alienated local leaders and population, causing a shift in attitudes that the United States exploited. Smith and McFarland, who were involved in the Sunni Awakening in Ramadi, note that by 2006 "tribal leaders were...fed up with Al Qaeda's violence and frustrated by their own loss of prestige and influence in their traditional heartlands."[63] In addition to furnishing actionable intelligence on Al-Qaeda members and their locations, tribal leaders provided the names of men willing to serve in local militias that became known by a number of names, including "Sons of Iraq," "awakening councils," or, as Petraeus preferred, "local concerned citizens." The men were armed and paid by United States to serve as de facto police/security forces in Sunni neighborhoods.

Some effort was made to screen the volunteers, although since only previously captured insurgents could be identified with the biometric filters employed, there were undoubtedly a good number of former Sunni insurgents among them. This meant that the United States was paying, arming and working alongside men who had been trying to kill Americans the year before. While the eventual goal was to incorporate the councils into the Iraqi Army or national security forces, the Iraqi government had no control over the councils and their ultimate loyalty remained in question. The awakening was clearly an alliance of convenience to defeat Al-Qaeda and the more extremist elements of the Sunni insurgency. But no one thought Sunni volunteers were motivated by a love for the United States or the Iraqi government. The United States was, as Ricks explains, in "the dangerous and complex new territory of supporting an armed group that was opposed to the government in Baghdad that the United States also supported."[64] In the short term, however, the

---

[62] See Steven Simon, "The Price of the Surge," *Foreign Affairs* Vol. 87, No. 3 (May/June 2008), pp. 57–76.

[63] Smith and McFarland, "Anbar Awakens," p. 82. This is an excellent essay on the origins, and process of recruiting, the Awakening Councils.

[64] Ricks, *The Gamble*, p. 67.

Sunni Awakening was "a great success story after its spread from Sunni tribes in Anbar Province to become an ad-hoc armed force of 65,000 to 80,000 across the country in less than a year. A linchpin of the American strategy to pacify Iraq, the movement has been widely credited with turning around the violence-scarred areas where the Sunni insurgency has been based."[65]

Despite the intense public debate, the troop surge of 2007 was actually quite modest – fewer than 30,000 additional forces deployed to a nation of more than 30 million people. Even after the surge, there would only be about 150,000 American troops fighting in Iraq, well below what most counterinsurgency metrics suggest was necessary. The plan, however, did not envisage a nationwide counterinsurgency campaign. The renewed effort would be focused on Baghdad and, to a lesser degree, Anbar province. According to Jack Keane and Frederick Kagan, the two most important figures behind the surge, "bringing security to Baghdad . . . [was] the essential precondition for political compromise, national reconciliation and economic development." But even in the narrow context of Baghdad alone, 20,000 additional troops were a mere drop in the bucket given the city's population and level of violence. Surge advocates were quick to point out that because the violence was not equally distributed, American forces could concentrate on "clearing and holding the Sunni and mixed Sunni-Shiite neighborhoods in the center of Baghdad, which are the keys to getting the overall levels of violence down." Bringing security to these neighborhoods would "require around nine American combat brigades . . . [which] would require a surge of at least four additional combat brigades – some 20,000 combat troops."[66] Only by limiting the scope of the surge to select neighborhoods was it possible to implement an extremely manpower intensive counterinsurgency effort with very limited forces. Kilcullen is not exaggerating when he notes that "we had barely sufficient troop numbers, in classical counterinsurgency terms, to pursue the operations we conducted."[67]

When the surge began in February 2007, no one knew if it would work, if surge troop levels would be sufficient, or if the situation on the ground had already spiraled beyond the point of no return. Few expected instant gratification as American forces left their forward bases in the spring and summer to clear and hold some of Baghdad's most dangerous neighborhoods. Their bases had been designed to reduce the

---

[65] Alissa J. Rubin and Damien Cave, "In a Force for Iraqi Calm, Seeds of Conflict," *New York Times* (December 23, 2007), p. 1.

[66] Jack Keane and Frederick Kagan, "The Right Type of 'Surge,'" *Washington Post* (December 27, 2006), p. A19. For a detailed presentation of Kagan's proposal, see Frederick Kagan, *A Plan for Success in Iraq*, December 13, 2006. Accessed at: http://www.realclearpolitics.com/RCP_PDF/ChoosingVictory.pdf.

[67] Kilcullen, *The Accidental Guerrilla*, p. 147.

American footprint and keep casualties low. Leaving them was certain to increase both the footprint and casualties. To be successful, the new approach "required soldiers to be among the people, where they would form new relationships."[68] This is how they would provide security and gain valuable intelligence. To this end, American forces and their Iraqi counterparts deployed to a string of Joint Security Stations once neighborhoods were cleared of insurgents. Soldiers were "now living in their area rather than visiting it – they could simply step out the front door and be at work."[69] Although expected to bring long-term benefits and security, in the short run, "it also exposed them to hellacious new levels of violence."[70] As a result, the situation for American soldiers would worsen before it got any better. And get worse it did.

Throughout the spring and much of the summer, there were few tangible signs of progress. American military and Iraqi civilian casualties remained high. Surge skeptics in the United States were quick to declare it a failure. Criticism even came from unexpected quarters. In August 2007, for example, five members of the 82nd Airborne Division wrote an editorial for the *New York Times* as their tour in Iraq was coming to an end. They minced no words:

To believe that Americans, with an occupying force that long ago outlived its reluctant welcome, can win over a recalcitrant local population and win this counterinsurgency is far-fetched . . . we see that a vast majority of Iraqis feel increasingly insecure and view us as an occupation force. . . . we need to recognize that our presence may have released Iraqis from the grip of a tyrant, but that it has also robbed them of their self-respect. They will soon realize that the best way to regain dignity is to call us what we are – an army of occupation – and force our withdrawal.[71]

Perhaps not coincidentally, only three weeks earlier, on the same editorial page, defense analysts Michael O'Hanlon and Kenneth Pollack pointed to largely anecdotal evidence (e.g., better morale) that the surge was beginning to work. Conceding that "the situation in Iraq remains grave," they were nonetheless "surprised by the gains . . . [and saw] the potential to produce not necessarily 'victory' but a sustainable stability that both we and the Iraqis could live with."[72] In the summer of 2007, this passed for wild optimism. Although these editorials set off an intense debate, it was too early to offer anything other than premature judgment

---

[68] Ricks, *The Gamble*, p. 178.
[69] Kilcullen, *The Accidental Guerrilla*, p. 139.
[70] Ricks, *The Gamble*, p. 178.
[71] Buddhika Jayamaha, Wesley D. Smith, Jeremy Roebuck, Omar Mora, Edward Sandmeier, Yance T. Gray, and Jeremy A. Murphy, "The War as We Saw It," *New York Times* (August 19, 2007), p. 11.
[72] Michael E. O'Hanlon and Kenneth M. Pollack, "A War We Just Might Win," *New York Times* (July 30, 2007), p. 17.

about the surge, even in military/tactical terms, never mind the ultimate strategic/political objectives.

The situation remained unclear when General Petraeus and Ambassador to Iraqi Ryan Crocker made their highly anticipated appearance before House and Senate Committees in September to testify about the surge's progress. With the 2008 presidential campaign in its early stages and the controversial "General Betray Us" moveon.org advertisement drawing heated criticism, the atmosphere was charged. Petraeus and Crocker noted signs of improvement in Iraq and urged patience, warning against an early pullback or firm timetable for withdrawal.[73] Critics were not persuaded. Senator (and presidential candidate) Hillary Clinton (D-NY) got the sound bite of the day, claiming that accepting their testimony required a "willing suspension of disbelief." Politically, however, Petraeus's appearance was widely deemed a success that bought the administration some time.

By the end of 2007 the security situation was clearly much improved. Compared with a high of 126 American casualties in May 2007, the downward trend was unmistakable with 66 in July, 55 in August and 14 in December.[74] These declines occurred despite more Americans being in harm's way. This was certainly welcome for obvious reasons. But trends in American casualties may not be the most revealing metric of success. The goal of the surge, after all, was to make Iraq a safer place for the Iraqis, not American soldiers. Iraqi civilian deaths declined from more than 2,700 in May 2007 to fewer than 1,000 in December and only 742 in January 2008, the lowest total in almost three years (see Figure 6.2). While the next three months witnessed a slight increase, after April 2008 Iraqi civilian casualties would remain well below 1,000 a month. So, when Petraeus returned to testify on Capitol Hill on April 2008, he finally had some good news.

Although supporters of the surge could point to these trends as tangible indications of at least temporary success, a few hundred civilian casualties constituted "good news" only in the sense that it was better than thousands. Iraq remained a dangerous and violent place, and not everyone credited the surge for the improvement. Biddle, for example, agreed that "the strategic landscape in Iraq is now much more favorable than it was in 2006." He thought this was "due *partly* to the surge and *largely* to fortunate events beyond our control."[75] What were these "fortunate events"? The first was the emergence of spontaneous factional ceasefires unrelated to the surge, the most important being Moqtada al-Sadr's unilateral ceasefire declaration in August 2007. The second was the Sunni

---

[73] Petraeus's statement can be accessed at: www.defenselink.mil/pubs/pdfs/Petraeus-Testimony20070910.pdf.

[74] Ricks, *The Gamble*, p. 240.

[75] Stephen Biddle, "After the Surge," Statement to the Committee on Armed Services, U.S. House of Representatives (January 23, 2008), emphasis added.

Awakening, which began in 2006 and spread throughout Anbar and into Baghdad by the summer of 2007. A few go so far as to deny that the surge played any role in improving the situation. According to Colonel Gian Gentile, "the two factors overwhelmingly responsible and demonstrably accountable for the diminished violence haven't depended on the surge at all. The first was the 2006 decision . . . to pay large sums of money to our former enemies to ally themselves with us . . . the second factor was Muqtada al-Sadr's decision to stand down."[76] In the final analysis, however, it is difficult to believe that the surge in troops and change in strategy was irrelevant to reducing the violence, even if it is nearly impossible to assess with any precision the relative contribution of various factors.[77]

The surge, like the American military presence generally, was supposed to be temporary. Diminished violence, whatever its cause, was a means to an end, not an end in itself. As Fred Kaplan explains, "the point of the surge was to create 'breathing space' that might allow Iraq's political leaders to reconcile their differences and form a viable central government. If the Iraqis didn't take advantage of this breathing space, the most brilliant strategy and the most successful operations would ultimately be for naught."[78] The big uncertainty in 2008 involved the relationship between military success at the tactical level and political progress at the strategic level. For advocates of the surge, reducing violence was a *necessary*, not a *sufficient*, condition for movement on the political front. But what would the Iraqis do with the breathing space provided? The issues were daunting, none more so than establishing competent and genuinely national army and security forces. Neither the "concerned citizen councils" of the Sunni Awakening nor the Shiite militias could be allowed to continue as armed, independent competitors of the central government. Many feared that the Shiite-dominated government would not incorporate the Sunni volunteers or take on the Shiite militias. And this was only the beginning of the thorny issues that needed to be resolved. For the United States, the critical question was how best to facilitate the requisite political accommodations. The administration, military commanders in Iraq and most surge advocates warned that a premature withdrawal or firm timetables risked a resurgence of violence that would derail the political process.[79] Others argued that an open-ended military commitment was an invitation

---

[76] Gian P. Gentile, "A (Slightly) Better War: A Narrative and Its Defects," *World Affairs* Vol. 171, No. 1 (Summer 2008), p. 64.

[77] For a range of opinions see Dylan Matthews and Ezra Klein, "How Important Was the Surge? Ten Iraq Experts Weigh in on the Effectiveness of the Surge," *The American Prospect*, online only (July 28, 2008). Accessed at: www.prospect.org/cs/articles?article=how_important_was_the_surge.

[78] Fred Kaplan, "Three Possible Post-Surge Scenarios for Iraq," *Slate* (December 24, 2007). Accessed at: www.slate.com/id/2180798/.

[79] See, for example, Stephen Biddle, Michael E. O'Hanlon, and Kenneth M. Pollack, "How to Leave a Stable Iraq," *Foreign Affairs* Vol. 87, No. 5 (September/October, 2008), pp. 40–58.

to procrastination, an excuse for the Iraqis to avoid tough political choices and compromises.[80] Either way, the eventual outcome was now a primarily political, not military matter.

Evaluating the Third Iraq War

Whatever the eventual political outcome in Iraq, the United States' failures and frustrations after 2003 will always stand in stark contrast to the stunningly successful campaign that deposed Saddam. But rather than view success and failure in isolation, common wisdom treats both as results of the same war plan, a plan brilliantly crafted and executed for one task but completely inadequate for another. The tree of failure grew out of the initial success. According to Ricks, "it was a plan... [whose] incompleteness helped *create* the conditions for the difficult occupation to follow."[81] In military terms, the most frequently voiced criticism focuses on the lack of sufficient forces to deal with the myriad of foreseeable challenges that arose in the political vacuum created by the regime's demise. There were simply not enough troops to keep order in the cities, secure weapons sites, guard the nation's borders, and protect critical infrastructure. In those critical days after the fall of Baghdad large parts of the country were devoid of any U.S. military presence. *The Economist* reflects the common wisdom: "the light, mobile force that smashed its way to the centre of Baghdad was plainly inadequate for the task of garrisoning the country, securing the borders and arms dumps, confronting the insurgency and preventing the slide to sectarian war."[82] The United States was an occupier that did not actually occupy much of the country, a de facto government without the capacity to govern. The war plan's manpower problems were, of course, exacerbated by early decisions to disband the Iraqi Army and security forces. The end result was that "Rumsfeld limited the number of American troops in Iraq, and Bremer limited the number of Iraqi troops that were immediately available. The two decisions combined to produce a much larger security vacuum."[83] These gaps in functions unfulfilled and territory unpoliced fueled the insurgency, or at least allowed it to fester, organize, and grow unopposed. This was the plan's original sin, so to speak.

With the benefit of hindsight, it is difficult to read Paul Wolfowitz's cavalier dismissal of General Shineski without wincing. Recall his response to the General's claim that hundreds of thousands of troops would be

[80] See, for example, Mark Lynch, "Politics First: Why Only U.S. Withdrawal Can Spur Iraqi Cooperation," *Foreign Affairs* Vol. 87, No. 6 (November/December, 2008), pp. 52–5.

[81] Ricks, *Fiasco*, p. 116, emphasis added.

[82] "The Hobbled Hegemon," *The Economist* Vol. 383, No. 8534 (June 30, 2007), p. 28.

[83] Gordon and Trainor, *Cobra II*, p. 483.

needed in Iraq: "it is hard to conceive," Wolfowitz replied, "that it would take more forces to provide stability in post-Saddam Iraq than it would take to conduct the war itself. . . . hard to imagine." Unfortunately, no one pressed Wolfowitz about *why* he found this inconceivable. In fact, one can easily imagine why it might require more troops to stabilize Iraq than defeat Saddam's army. The basic point is simple: defeating a national military force is a fundamentally different enterprise than conducting postwar political and economic rebuilding and stabilization. What *is* difficult to imagine is why anyone would think there was a connection between the number of troops needed to oust Saddam and what was required to secure the country. There is no reason to assume, for example, that merely because new technologies reduce the manpower requirements for some missions that they reduce it for all missions. Even if technology was driving a military revolution changing the character of warfare, RMAs do not revolutionize every task a military might have to perform. RMAs do not even revolutionize every type of war a military might have to fight. The United States learned this lesson the hard way in Iraq.

The puzzle is why those who created the war plan failed to see the need for more forces for postwar tasks. With well over a year to evaluate options, time pressures certainly cannot be blamed for the lack of adequate foresight or preparation. Even Rumsfeld admitted that unlike the somewhat rushed war in Afghanistan, "in Iraq, there has been time to prepare."[84] There was ample time for many within the government to warn about the likely problems of the immediate postwar period. Within the State Department the Future of Iraq Project produced a series of reports on everything from maintaining law and order to rebuilding Iraq's crumbling infrastructure.[85] A study by the Army War College's Strategic Studies Institute also detailed the variety of missions the military would need to carry out in the postconflict phase.[86] Such warnings were largely ignored. Paul Bremer indicated that he did not even know about the Future of Iraq Project until after arriving in Baghdad. It is difficult to avoid the conclusion that those planning the war were simply not interested in analyses suggesting the need for a larger force or a more

---

[84] Jacob Heilbrunn, "The Rumsfeld Doctrine," *New York Times Book Review* (April 30, 2006), p. 9.

[85] Eric Schmitt and Joel Brinkley, "State Department Study Foresaw Problems Now Plaguing Iraq," *New York Times* (October 19, 2003), p. 1; and David Rieff, "Blueprint for a Mess," *New York Times Magazine* (November 2, 2003), pp. 28–33, 44, 58, 72, and 77–8. The now unclassified reports of the Future of Iraq Project can be accessed from the National Security Archives at: www.gwu.edu/~nsarchiv/NSAEBB/NSAEBB198/index.htm.

[86] Conrad Crane and W. Andrew Terrill, *Reconstructing Iraq: Insights, Challenges, and Missions for Military Forces in a Post-Conflict Scenario.* Accessed at: www.strategicstudiesinstitute.army.mil/pubs/display.cfm?pubID=182.

protracted presence. But why? The question remains as posed by James Fallows: "How could the Administration have thought that it was safe to proceed in blithe indifference to the warnings of nearly everyone with operational experience in modern military occupations?"[87]

An extremely uncharitable explanation would highlight crass political calculation. Determined to invade Iraq and aware that it was a tough sell, the administration had an incentive to emphasize anything to increase public support and downplay whatever would diminish it. Much has already been written elsewhere about the possibility of threat inflation, but the flip side of the coin is cost minimization, which was manifested in attempts to sweep aside any notion that the war would cost tens or hundreds of billions of dollars as well as confident assertions that Iraqi oil revenues would more than cover the cost of reconstruction.[88] Since larger deployments, lengthy commitments, or even any mention of "occupation" would likely decrease support domestically and internationally, planning for such eventualities was avoided.

There is also another, simpler explanation for failures to prepare for the occupation: administration officials actually believed all the optimistic scenarios they presented to the public. They did not send more troops to deal with problems they never thought would arise. The Iraqis would welcome the Americans as liberators, embrace a new and democratic government, and use their oil revenues to quickly get about the business of rebuilding their country after American forces started to return home in a matter of months. Whether one characterizes it as myopic self-delusion or naïve wishful thinking, the administration may have genuinely expected postwar problems to be minor and transitory, challenges that could be managed with a little more than 100,000 troops. The failures of planning may simply reflect a series of colossal misjudgments about the political dynamics of post–Saddam Iraq.

The Third Iraq War and Military Transformation

Few are content, however, to attribute the shortcomings in planning to mere political calculation or mistakenly rosy assessments of Iraqi politics. Most see something deeper at work. The more common explanation is that the administration was led astray not by political expediency or ignorance but by misguided notions of military transformation and the RMA. Lewis, for example, claims that "the insurgency war was primarily a function of Rumsfeld's flawed vision of war."[89] In Kagan's view,

[87] James Fallows, "Blind into Baghdad," *The Atlantic* Vol. 293, No. 1 (January/February 2004), p. 74.
[88] Jeff Gerth, "Report Offered Bleak Outlook About Iraq Oil," *New York Times* (October 4, 2003), p. 1.
[89] Lewis, *The American Culture of War*, p. 437.

"transformation is not at all separate from the problems that U.S. has encountered...It is, on the contrary, one of the most basic causes of those problems."[90] Max Boots asks, "Why did the Defense Department not invest in more linguists, more MPs, more civil affairs specialists, more soldiers in general, rather than more JDAMs and JSTARS?" "The answer," he argues, "is that senior leaders, such as Donald Rumsfeld, believed that the future of warfare lay in high-tech informational systems, not in lowly infantrymen."[91] And John Mearsheimer sees an administration guided by a "faith in the so-called revolution in military affairs" that would allow the United States to "rely on stealth technology, air-delivered precision-guided weapons, and small but highly mobile ground forces...[to] swoop down out of the sky, finish off a regime, pull back and reload the shotgun for the next target." "A large-scale occupation of Iraq" was anathema because it "would undermine the Bush administration's plan to rely on the RMA to win quick and decisive victories."[92]

The basic argument here is that transformation, and the underlying vision of the RMA that drove it, left the American military unprepared for the challenges it faced after the fall of Saddam. Fixated on technology, it was unable to conceive of wars and missions that were not primarily about guiding munitions to targets with incredible precision from great distances, and the military was ill-equipped and poorly trained for anything other than high-intensity inter-state warfare. According to Kagan, the United States' difficulties in Iraq and Afghanistan were rooted in a conception of military transformation that "defines *the* basic problem of war as identifying and destroying the correct targets to force the enemy to capitulate." Unfortunately, this "misses the point of war *entirely*...War is not about killing people and blowing things up. It is purposeful violence to achieve a political goal...The focus on controlled destruction helped *blind* military and political leaders to a serious focus on the political objective of the war."[93] As a result, the moment the military mission in Iraq shifted to something that was not fundamentally about targeting and destruction, the problems began. The American military was unable and/or unwilling to engage in postwar stabilization or implement an effective counterinsurgency strategy because it was in the grips of a technological spell that reduced war to nothing but controlled destruction. The perfected reconnaissance-strike complex that decimated the Iraqi military proved decidedly less useful for stopping looters, preventing foreign fighters from crossing the border, or making the people of

---

[90] Kagan, *Finding the Target*, p. x.
[91] Boot, *War Made New*, p. 467.
[92] John Mearsheimer, "Hans Morgenthau and the Iraq War: Realism versus Neo-conservatism," *openDemocracy* (May 19, 2005). Accessed at: www.opendemocracy.net/democracy-americanpower/morgenthau_2522.jsp.
[93] Kagan, *Finding the Target*, pp. 358–9, emphasis added.

Iraq feel safe and secure from insurgents, terrorists and religious zealots. And it was completely useless for rebuilding Iraq's political and economic infrastructure.

Kagan identifies the war plan's crucial shortcoming correctly – the failure to relate military plans to political objectives. He traces this failure to a transformational agenda derived from NCW and other variants of the RMA that were based on a narrow conceptualization of war as a targeting drill, thus blinding American leaders to the essentially political nature of warfare. The problem with this explanation is that the inclination to divorce military and political issues seems to be a long-standing, if regrettable, feature of American military history. In his study of American counterinsurgency policy in Vietnam, for example, Shafer notes that "the armed forces, long-resistant to involvement in politics, believe in drawing a clear boundary between military and political affairs. As an explicitly *politico*-military doctrine, counterinsurgency violated this distinction."[94] John Nagl sees this as deeply ingrained in the American military culture. Again with reference to Vietnam, he explains that "the focus on large wars, fought with the American advantages of high technology and firepower, but without an appreciation for the political context in which they were fought, would not work in the favor of the United States Army when it faced a revolutionary insurgency."[95] And Jeffrey Record refers to "the American tendency to separate war and politics – to view military victory as an end in itself, ignoring war's function as an instrument of policy."[96]

Interestingly, Kagan recognizes that this trend "was already present in the military even before transformation." But if this is so, in what sense can transformation be singled out as "one of the most basic causes" of the failures in Iraq? The answer for Kagan is that while the tendency to separate war and politics may have been *present*, "transformation made it *dominant*."[97] This is the critical move in Kagan's argument that allows him to focus on transformation as the source of American woes in Iraq. There is, however, no reason to believe that the tendency to pursue military actions unconnected to political objectives was any more dominant in 2003 than in 1965 or 1939.[98] A more persuasive argument

---

D. Michael Shafer, *Deadly Paradigms: The Failure of U.S. Counterinsurgency Policy* (Princeton: Princeton University Press, 1988), p. 24.

John A. Nagl, *Learning to Eat Soup with a Knife: Counterinsurgency Lessons from Malaya to Vietnam* (Chicago: University of Chicago Press, 2002), p. 49.

Quoted in Kurt Campbell and Michael E. O'Hanlon, *Hard Power: The New Politics of National Security* (New York: Basic Books, 2006), p. 44.

Kagan, *Finding the Target*, p. 358.

Russell Weigley finds even deeper historical roots for this. He claims that throughout most of its history "the United States was not involved in international politics continuously enough or with enough consistency of purpose to permit the development of a coherent national strategy for the consistent pursuit of political goals by diplomacy in combination with armed force. A not unfortunate corollary of this situation was its contribution to civilian predominance over the military in the American government; when the military themselves *regarded strategy as narrowly military in content*, their

is that prevailing concepts of transformation and the RMA reflected and reinforced this preexisting tendency.

The military's reluctance to conduct stability operations and fight counterinsurgencies, after all, was evident long before anyone heard of the RMA, net-centric warfare or military transformation. "The U.S. military," Ucko explains, "has typically paid little attention to the nature and requirements of counterinsurgency and stability operations."[99] It has always focused on decisive military campaigns emphasizing maneuver and firepower in high-intensity wars against other states. "Lesser" tasks and missions have consistently been a low priority. So rather than seeing the major failures in Iraq as the result of a narrow and apolitical view of warfare inherent in relatively recent notions of an RMA, NCW or transformation, it makes more sense to focus on a long-standing and very restrictive vision of the military's role and missions. Such a vision was reflected in Bush's 2000 presidential campaign. Asked in his foreign policy debate with Al Gore whether he supported the intervention in Somalia, Bush noted that what "started off as a humanitarian mission . . . changed into a nation-building mission, and that's where the mission went wrong. The mission was changed. And as a result, our nation paid a price." Bush then used Somalia as an opportunity to express his general approach to the use of military power: "I don't think our troops ought to be used for what's called nation-building. I think our troops ought to be used to fight and win wars. . . . Our military's meant to fight and win war. That's what it's meant to do."[100] According to Brooks, Bush's stance resonated with prevailing sentiment within the military: "The Bush administration's pledges to 'stop nation-building,' in particular, were well received by many in the uniformed services who questioned Clinton's interventions in Somalia, Bosnia, Kosovo and Haiti in the 1990s."[101]

One need only look to the parallels between American counterinsurgency efforts in Iraq and Vietnam to see an enduring historical pattern, not a recent phenomenon. Krepinevich explains that "the Army's attitude on Vietnam was one of general disinterest in applying counterinsurgency principles, particularly when they conflicted with more traditional military operations . . . priority was given to the destruction of guerrilla forces through large scale operations."[102] Fast-forward a few decades, and one sees the same lack of interest. Ricks observes that "McMaster's successful campaign in Tall Afar in late 2005 . . . seemed to be largely ignored by

temptations to intervene in the making of national policy were proportionately small." *The American Way of War: A History of United States Military Strategy and Policy* (Bloomington, IN: Indiana University Press, 1960), p. xix.

[99] David Ucko, "Innovation or Inertia: The U.S. Military and the Learning of Counterinsurgency," *Orbis* (Spring 2008), p. 290.

[100] Accessed at: www.cbsnews.com/stories/2000/10/11/politics/main240442.shtml.

[101] Risa Brooks, *Shaping Strategy*, p. 234.

[102] Andrew F. Krepinevich, *The Army and Vietnam* (Baltimore: Johns Hopkins University Press, 1986), p. 56.

top commanders, or dismissed as irrelevant. Despite the attention given
to Tall Afar by the media, there seemed to be no concerted effort in the
Army to discern if the success there might be replicated elsewhere."[103] A
change in strategy was eventually brought about by retired officers and
civilian analysts lobbying the administration directly in Washington. As
in Vietnam, "the DoD leadership largely opposed applying counterinsurgency methods in Iraq in the first place. This change was driven by
the White House and imposed upon the Pentagon ... The commanders of
both CENTCOM and of MNF-I opposed this change in strategy, pushing
instead for a *reduction* in the presence and visibility of U.S. troops."[104]
The transformational agenda may have done nothing to challenge or
lessen this resistance to counterinsurgency operations, but it can hardly
be blamed for creating it.

The Third Iraq War and the RMA

The military transformation agenda of the 1990s was largely an attempt
to exploit what many saw as an emerging revolution in military affairs
in which technological advances were creating the potential for significant changes in the character of warfare. Properly understood, there
was nothing about the RMA to suggest that military missions should be
restricted to high-intensity warfare or that all potential wars and missions
are being revolutionized. In this sense, "revolution in *military affairs*" is
a somewhat unfortunate and misleading description. *Warfare* is being
revolutionized, not *military affairs*. Indeed, it is not even clear what "military affairs" means. But even "revolution in warfare" would not suffice
because it implies that war is a generic, undifferentiated phenomenon, as
if all wars are the same. If the Iraq Wars demonstrate that the military
needs to think about its missions in more expansive terms, they also show
that RMA advocates need to think in more restrictive terms, recognizing
the RMA's limitations as well as its promises. Breathless generalizations
about information technologies changing warfare do not help in understanding the complexities of military change. In reality, there are different
kinds of wars waged against different types of opponents. We need more
clarity about what aspects and types of war are being revolutionized and
which are not, and the American experience in Iraq since 2003 offers
some valuable insights.

The contemporary RMA is often portrayed as the military manifestation of the larger information revolution. The ability to gather, transmit,
and use unprecedented amounts of information is central to the RMA and

---

[103] Ricks, *The Gamble*, p. 160.
[104] David Ucko, "Innovation or Inertia," p. 302.

is reflected in concepts such as dominant battlespace knowledge or situational awareness. Combined with radically improved munitions guidance technologies, the RMA promises to fundamentally alter the character of warfare by lifting the fog of war and solving the problem of target acquisition. Kagan correctly explains that the current RMA is largely about improvements in targeting – sensors identifying targets and munitions destroying them. This is the reconnaissance-strike complex. But as Lawrence Freedman notes, "the setting for military operations will determine the advantage provided [by] access to new technology."[105] Technologies and weapons that provide an advantage in some settings might be less useful or even completely useless in others. For our purposes we might also propose a corollary of Freedman's basic insight: the setting for military operations will determine if the impact of new technologies will be revolutionary or not. New technologies might help revolutionize some wars but not others. This is a useful starting point for thinking about the promise and limits any military revolution.

In the current RMA, information or intelligence is largely synonymous with detection via national technical means – for example, satellites, aerial radar, and UAVs. Battlespace awareness refers to knowledge of the location and movement of friendly and hostile forces. There is and can be no such thing as completely lifting of the fog of war because crucial information cannot be gathered by such means. The opponent's actions, for example, may be knowable but his intentions are not. Almost everything else about the RMA depends on the information gathered through technical means. If something cannot be detected, there is no knowledge to communicate or targets to strike. As a result, the impact of the technologies associated with the RMA will be most significant or revolutionary in settings and wars in which the most important military assets can be identified by national technical means. This describes modern, industrial age, conventional warfare that pits masses of forces equipped with large distinguishable weapons and platforms against each other. As Rupert Smith notes, "in industrial war the equipment is the critical item in war-making and it is manned by people: if you know where the equipment is, you therefore know where the people are."[106] It is this equipment that is most susceptible to technical detection, and if it can be found, it can be targeted and destroyed. But this is not the case in every war.

In some wars, the critical military assets are much less susceptible to military detection, and for military missions the ability to find and strike targets is not particularly relevant. The impact of technologies depends on the setting and mission. This helps explain why Rumsfeld's vision of transformation and the RMA was both vindicated *and* repudiated by the

[105] Freedman, *The Revolution in Strategic Affairs*, p. 43.
[106] Rupert Smith, *The Utility of Force*, p. 330.

experience in Iraq. On the one hand, as Schaubelt observes, "the initial phases of OIF appeared to validate the ability of U.S. (and coalition) forces to rapidly defeat a much larger military."[107] "Rumsfeld proved his point," Benjamin and Simon argue, "the force that deployed to Iraq was a fraction of what 'old think' commanders would have used, and it was sufficient to topple the Iraqi regime in no time."[108] On the other hand, this war (or phase of the war, if one prefers) was only beginning. In the immediate postwar period, American forces would face challenges that detection and targeting technologies could not solve. An appreciation of the limits as well as the promise of RMA technologies would have made that evident. In this case, Rumsfeld and others responsible for postwar planning either ignored those limitations, did not expect there to be many security problems, or hoped that someone else would take care of them. There should have been a recognition that postwar tasks might require more forces than were needed to overthrow the regime because the tasks were fundamentally different and potentially manpower intensive. To the extent that failures in the postwar phase reflect flaws in Rumsfeld's vision, it was primarily in terms of his inability to recognize the limits of transformations and the RMA.

The limitations were even more glaring when the United States found itself fighting the growing insurgency, a type of conflict that presents a very different set of military problems than traditional interstate wars. The first major difference with counterinsurgencies goes right to the heart of the RMA – information. As Corum explains, "the role of intelligence in counterinsurgency is fundamentally different from its role in conventional war. Conventional military intelligence is about looking for things we can see and count." By contrast, "in counterinsurgency, the first mission of the intelligence agencies is to understand the context of the conflict, which means collecting information about the whole society, understanding local conditions, monitoring public opinion, and analyzing social and political relationships and networks."[109] This kind of information or situational awareness cannot be gleaned from JSTARS and UAVs. It comes from a knowledge of local culture and regular interaction with the local populations. Petraeus and McMaster learned what they needed to know by sitting down with local tribal leaders and drinking endless cups of tea. When American forces battled Saddam's military, technology created an information gap in the United States' favor. As the insurgency grew, the tables were turned. As just one example, Martin Van Creveld explains that "whereas hundreds of thousands of Iraqis knew at least

---

[107] Christopher M. Schnaubelt, "Wither the RMA," *Parameters* (Autumn 2007), p. 100.
[108] Daniel Benjamin and Steve Simon, *The Next Attack* (New York: Holt, 2006), p. 187.
[109] James Corum, "Getting Doctrine Done Right," *Joint Force Quarterly* (2nd Quarter, 2008), p. 95.

some English, hardly any American personnel could speak, read or write Arabic.... Yet in any sort of organized human activity, war included, language is the most important tool by far.... what 'information dominance' existed went not to the Americans but to their enemies."[110] In counterinsurgencies the most important information must be gathered by people, not machines.

The technologies associated with the RMA have been harnessed to provide smaller forces with greater lethality. In 1991 and 2003, the combination of situational awareness and precision targeting provided the United States with an unprecedented ability to attack a wide swath of tactical and strategic targets with devastating effect. Although there is certainly more to war than killing people and blowing things up, the ability to do so can be decisive in conventional wars. This is not the case in all wars, especially counterinsurgencies. The United States' problems in Iraq began when the task shifted from bringing down a hostile regime to building a friendly government and battling the forces determined to prevent it. In fighting an insurgency, destructive capacity is not very useful. In counterinsurgency campaigns the goal is to defeat the insurgency, not kill the insurgents. This will inevitably entail some military actions against the insurgents, but these are secondary to the more fundamental challenge of securing popular support by providing security, creating political institutions perceived as effective and legitimate, and promoting economic reconstruction and development. Lethality and firepower can be decisive in conventional wars that are enemy-centric but not in counterinsurgencies that are population-centric rather than insurgent-centric.

The lesson here is not that the technologies and weapons associated with the RMA are useless outside the realm of high-intensity inter-state warfare. Buchan explains that even though "the current RMA may not have as much relative impact on low intensity and lesser operations as on major conflicts... that is not to say... that the new information based technologies and other tools of the RMA might not be useful in low intensity conflicts."[111] Although counterinsurgencies may not be *primarily* military in nature, they are at least *partially* military operations. For those aspects of a counterinsurgency that resemble more traditional warfare many RMA technologies can be extremely valuable. Guided munitions and sensitive aerial sensors, for example, are almost always useful, even when one's opponent lacks easily detectable weapons platforms and massed forces. When American troops moved on Fallujah the ability to call in precision strikes against insurgent strongholds certainly made the

[110] Van Creveld, *The Changing Face of War*, p. 250.
[111] Glenn A. Buchan, "Force Projection: One-and-a-Half Cheers for the RMA," in Gongora and von Riekhoff, eds., *Toward a Revolution in Military Affairs?* (Westport, CT: Greenwood Press, 2000), pp. 146–8.

job of clearing the city easier than it otherwise might have been. Although an aerial precision strike capability did not eliminate the need for close combat, it might help explain why American casualties, though heavy by recent standards, were fairly low in historical terms for similar operations. UAVs with visual and/or infrared sensors can accompany military convoys as aerial escorts, scanning wide areas in search of insurgents laying in wait to ambush. If equipped with laser-guided missiles they can even pursue the attackers, identifying them by their body heat and the warmth of their recently fired weapons as they flee. Ricks even points to the proliferation of UAVs as an important element of the surge's success:

> One of the reasons that redeploying the troops into small outposts could work better in 2007 than it would have in previous years was that brigade commanders had far more aerial surveillance assets available.... During 2007 the number of these drone reconnaissance aircraft operating in Iraq would increase tenfold.... This made it far easier, for example, for a commander to keep an eye on potential threats to his outposts.[112]

Given the nature of the tasks associated with counterinsurgency, however, technology may be more of a manpower enabler than multiplier. RMA technologies may not change the fact that "when it comes to reorganizing or building political, economic and social institutions, there is no substitute for human beings in large numbers."[113] So, while technologies may revolutionize some forms of warfare, they may just have a significant impact on others.

Conclusion

The American experience in Iraq after 2003 is hardly unique or unprecedented. The United States is by no means the first great military power to make quick work of some opponents but then struggle almost immediately or even simultaneously against seemingly lesser adversaries. Nor is America's military revolution the first to reveal its limitations when faced with enemies and modes of warfare different from those expected. Looking back at previous military powers and their revolutions, Thomas Graves explains that, "however [an] RMA is defined, many defense professionals agree that the period of Napoleon and the French Revolution, and the German innovation of Blitzkrieg achieved substantial success in integrating military capabilities that gave them a marked advantage over their opponents. In both cases, the development of new formations, doctrine, and tactics allowed them to dominate their opponents on the

---

[112] Ricks, *The Gamble*, p. 192.
[113] Frederick Kagan cited in Singer, *Wired for War*, p. 215.

battlefield for a significant period."[114] But this is only partly true. Even these RMAs had their limits. France and Germany's innovations, real though they were, did not always allow them to dominate opponents. Germany's blitzkrieg, for example, may have been incredibly effective against Poland, the Low Countries, and France, but it was decidedly less so in Russia, whose vastness created operational and logistical challenges that ultimately worked against the Germans.[115] Germany was also neither the first nor the last to learn the limits of conventional military power against unconventional opponents. Van Creveld notes that "faced with armed resistance on the part of occupied populations the Germans soon discovered that it was precisely the most modern components of their armed forces that were most useless . . . confronted with small groups of guerillas who did not constitute armies, did not wear uniforms, did not fight in the open, and tended to melt away . . . they found themselves almost entirely at a loss."[116] Substitute "Americans" for "Germans" and Van Creveld's observation could easily be mistaken for a passage lifted from Thomas Ricks' *Fiasco*.

An even earlier and more striking parallel to the American experience in Iraq can be found in the war that gave the world the term "guerrilla." After almost a decade of war in which French armies routed some of Europe's major military powers, including Prussia, Austria, and Russia, to gain control of much of continental Europe, Napoleon's power and prestige reached a peak by 1807. Although his invasion of Russia in 1812 would seal Napoleon's fate, his decline actually began several years earlier. It was France's invasion of Spain and the so-called Peninsular War (1808–1814) that followed that marked the beginning of the end for Napoleon. "Prior to 1808," Gates explains, Napoleon's "forces had only been pitted against the professional armies of other monarchs."[117] Against this type of military opposition, France's mass conscript army organized into highly mobile corps consisting of infantry, cavalry, and artillery that lived off the land they conquered and occupied fared well. Initially, the result in Spain was similar as the abysmal Spanish army proved no match for Napoleon's forces. King Charles was

[114] Thomas C. Graves, *Al Qaeda, RMA, and the Future of Warfare* (Carlisle, PA: U.S. Army War College, 2008), p. 8.
[115] Boot, *War Made New*, p. 417. Omar Bartov, "From Blitzkrieg to Total War," in Ian Kershaw and Moshe Lewin, eds., *Stalinism and Nazism: Dictatorships in Comparison* (Cambridge: Cambridge University Press, 1997), p. 165; Harold A. Winters, *Battling the Elements: Weather and Terrain in the Conduct of Warfare* (Baltimore: Johns Hopkins University Press, 2001), pp. 86–94; and Thomas B. Buell, John H. Bradley, Clifton R. Franks, and John A. Hixson, *The West Point Military History Series: The Second World War, Europe and the Mediterranean* (New York: Square One Publishers), pp. 123–5.
[116] Martin Van Creveld, *The Rise and Decline of the State* (Cambridge: Cambridge University Press, 1999), pp. 397–9.
[117] David Gates, *The Spanish Ulcer: A History of the Peninsular War* (New York: W.W. Norton, 1986), p. 468.

quickly deposed and Napoleon's brother Joseph was coronated as Spain's new monarch.[118] Napoleon no doubt expected the general population to accept French occupation passively as had generally been the case elsewhere. Gradually, however, popular resentment of French occupation turned to rebellion as locally organized resistance grew and spread in the form of small bands of insurgents or guerrillas that opportunistically harassed French forces throughout the country. The French had encountered popular resistance elsewhere but nothing like they faced in Spain.[119] Aided by the British, the Spanish guerillas were a problem for which the French had no answer other than to respond to cruel and barbarous attacks in kind. The war on the Iberian Peninsula, commonly referred to as Napoleon's "Spanish ulcer," became "constant lesion which drained French blood and resources for five years."[120] In the end and despite losing 300,000 men, Napoleon failed to gain control of Spain. Not surprisingly, in the wake of his 1815 defeat Napoleon regretted most his ill-fated attempt to conquer Spain: "That unfortunate war destroyed me; it divided my forces, multiplied my obligations, undermined my morale... All the circumstances of my disasters are bound up in that fatal knot."[121] Perhaps 200 years later others will express a similar sentiment about a different war.[122]

[118] Gunther E. Rothenberg, *Napoleon's Great Adversaries: The Archduke Charles and the Austrian Army, 1792–1814* (Bloomington: Indiana University Press, 1982), p. 121.

[119] See Milton Finley, *The Most Monstrous of Wars: The Napoleonic Guerrilla War in Italy, 1806–1811* (Columbia, SC: University of South Carolina Press, 1994).

[120] John A. Lynn, "Nations in Arms," in Geoffrey Parker, ed., *The Cambridge Illustrated History of Warfare* (Cambridge: Cambridge University Press, 2008), p. 204.

[121] John Lawrence Tone, *The Fatal Knot: The Guerrilla War in Navarre and the Defeat of Napoleon in Spain* (Chapel Hill: University of North Carolina Press, 1994), p. 6.

[122] For an interesting discussion of the parallels between Iraq and the guerrilla war in Spain see George W. Smith, "Avoiding a Napoleonic Ulcer: Bridging the Gap of Cultural Intelligence (Or, Have We Focused on the Wrong Transformation?)" in *Essays 2004: Chairman of the Joint Chiefs of Staff Strategy Essay Contest* (Washington, DC: National Defense University Press, 2004), pp. 21–38.

CONCLUSION: THE FUTURE OF AMERICA'S MILITARY REVOLUTION

Almost two decades have elapsed since the Gulf War provided the first glimpse of a range of technologies and weapons heralding the revival of American military power and a possible revolution in the conduct of warfare. The war publicized and intensified the debate about a contemporary revolution in military affairs in which technological advances were supposedly leading to profound changes in warfare on par with some of history's great military transformations such as the introduction of gunpowder weapons, the Napoleonic reforms, and Germany's mechanized blitzkrieg. The debate has proceeded along two intertwined tracks. On a theoretical level, there were broad, general, and even grandiose predictions about the emergence of new forms of war reflecting the information revolution sweeping the society as a whole. On a policy level, the focus was on exploiting these new technologies to solve the United States' most pressing military and strategic challenges. Desert Storm appeared to confirm predictions of an RMA while validating the direction of the American defense policy since Vietnam. Recent experience in Iraq, however, has taken the shine off the RMA and called into question much of American defense policy derived from such notions. Some have even come to view the RMA with nostalgia, the military equivalent of the hula-hoop, which has little relevance for post–Iraq debates about warfare and defense policy. "Ah, the 'revolution in military affairs,'" Frank Hoffman begins wistfully before dismissing it as "a blast from the past, a piece of pre-9/11 prehistory."[1]

Instead of rushing to consign the RMA to the dustbin of history, perhaps it is better to step back to consider what the totality of the American military experience in Iraq and elsewhere over the past two decades tells us about the RMA in both theoretical and policy terms. Ironically, this experience simultaneously muddies and clarifies important issues surrounding

---

[1] Frank Hoffman, "New Ideas that Look Old," *Armed Forces Journal* (July 2006). Accessed at: www.armedforcesjournal.com/2006/07/1853779.

the RMA. The debate has been muddied in that more ambiguous conflicts and less decisive outcomes have discredited the more extravagant
claims of exuberant RMA advocates and raised questions about whether
the American military is well-equipped and prepared for the wars and
missions it will most likely face. But the debate has also been clarified in
that we now better understand the limits as well as the promises of the
RMA, and this clarity provides a more realistic basis for thinking about
the future of American defense policy.

The Nature and Limits of the RMA

Have the Iraq Wars and other conflicts of the last two decades provided
evidence of a new RMA? Are technological advances combining with
changes in military doctrine and organization to alter the character of
warfare? Will future generations look back upon the Iraq Wars as turning points in military history? These remain the critical theoretical and
conceptual questions in the RMA debate. The experience of the last two
decades suggests that although the answers are complex on balance the
case for a contemporary RMA is persuasive, if not definitively compelling.
If we are in the midst of an RMA, it is one driven largely by advances
in information gathering, communications, and targeting technologies.
Some prefer to characterize it as an *information revolution* in which the
proliferation of better sensors is substantially reducing the fog of war.
In Cohen's assessment, it is "the information technologies above all that
underpin the transformation of war, and it may be precisely because they
are so familiar that we fail to see how much change they have brought
about."[2] Others see it as a *precision revolution* because the military benefits of situational awareness would not be nearly as great without precision targeting. Krepinevich, for example, suggests that "precision warfare
may itself represent a military revolution. Certainly it has dramatically
changed the character of military competitions."[3] A handful of others
talk in terms of an *air power revolution* in which an improved ability to
strike tactical and strategic targets from standoff range has dramatically
increased the leverage and contribution of aerial forces.

  Although the exact emphasis varies, the tendency is to focus on precision strike as the defining feature of the RMA. It is precision strike that
provides much of the force multiplier enabling fewer troops to achieve
equal or greater lethality. It is precision strike that permits a reasonably sized force to attack an unprecedented number of targets in a short
period. It is precision strike that eliminates the age-old trade-off between
distance (and thus vulnerability) and accuracy. It is precision strike that

---

[2] Cohen, "Change and Transformation in Military Affairs," p. 399.
[3] Andrew F. Krepinevich, *Operation Iraqi Freedom: A First-Blush Assessment* (Washington, DC: Center for Strategic and Budgetary Assessments, 2003), p. 14.

greatly reduces collateral damage. It is difficult to imagine an argument for the existence of an RMA in the absence of precision-strike capabilities. Thus, Kagan argues that "the RMA the transformation enthusiasts are chasing so eagerly has already arrived. It is the precision-strike RMA."[4] And although Watts recognizes that each analyst is "free to reach his or her own judgment concerning the degree of transformation associated with the guided-munitions era into which the American military has been moving," he concludes that "what does not appear debatable . . . is that in terms of how wars are fought, the era of guided munitions is quite different – qualitatively different – from that of unguided munitions and aimed fires."[5] In what sense, however, is warfare in the guided munitions era *qualitatively different*? This question is best answered in terms of Hundley's conceptualization of RMAs as paradigm shifts in warfare resulting from new technologies that either create new core competencies and/or render previous competencies obsolete. His test is straightforward: "If a development in military technology does not *either* render obsolete a core competency of a dominant player *or* create a new core competency, it is not an RMA. If it does, it is."[6]

The contemporary RMA rests on suite of technologies combined to form a genuine reconnaissance-strike complex able to identify and attack a wide range of tactical, operational, and strategic assets reliably and almost simultaneously with fewer soldiers, weapons, and platforms as well as less destruction. Advances in surveillance, communications, and munitions guidance make it possible to wage war in a manner that was not feasible in the pre–guided munitions era. This constitutes a core competency that has given rise to a new conceptual approach for applying force commonly referred to as parallel warfare. As Kurtis Lohide explains, "the intent of parallel warfare is to *reconfigure the basic elements of warfare* by distributing mass along a time line that is narrow but a space continuum that is broad. This configuration allows mass to become concentrated in time but not in space."[7] Without using the term, Jeffrey Cooper sees this new core competency as critical to American success against Iraq:

Desert Storm demonstrated that a key advantage for the U.S. forces was the ability to exercise complex, orchestrated, high tempo, simultaneous, parallel operations that overwhelmed the enemy's ability to respond. The advantage was built not only on sensors and smart weapons, but perhaps more importantly on forces supported by modern C4I systems and technologies that allowed the United States to collapse previous spatial and temporal constraints on simultaneous operations, whether combined or joint.[8]

---

[4] Kagan, *Finding the Target*, p. 391.
[5] Watts, *Six Decades of Guided Munitions and Battle Networks*, p. 265.
[6] Hundley, *Past Revolutions, Future Transformations*, p. 11.
[7] Kurtis D. Lohide, "Desert Storm's Siren Song," *Airpower Journal* (Winter 1995), p. 5, emphasis added.
[8] Cooper, "Another View of the Revolution in Military Affairs," pp. 125–6.

While the conceptual roots of parallel warfare can be traced to notions of deep battle that have been part of military theorizing for decades, it was simply impossible to realize such visions as long as mass was required to compensate for the inaccuracy of weapons and/or information. Although operational and strategic targets have been vulnerable since aircraft first leaped over the battlefield, the scale and breadth of attacks in such a short period in both Desert Storm and Operation Iraqi Freedom (OIF) was something new in the annals of warfare. Drawing a comparison to World War II, Deptula notes that "the Gulf War began with more targets in one day's attack plan than the total number of targets hit by the entire Eighth Air Force in all of 1942 and 1943 – more separate target air attacks in 24 hours than ever before in the history of warfare."[9] And this was only the beginning. It is easy to imagine in the very near future a war plan involving coordinated attacks by armed UAVs, cruise missiles, fighters, and bombers against several hundred targets over thousands of square miles in the span of an hour or even minutes. This shift toward parallel as opposed to linear, serial, or sequential operations represents a potentially revolutionary change in the character of war. While it may be true that as applied against Iraq in 1991 and 2003 parallel attacks failed to achieve all the objectives its more enthusiastic proponents hoped for or expected, there can be little doubt that this new capability contributed significantly to the favorable outcomes for the United States.

This new core competency did not render existing competencies irrelevant or obsolete, which is simply another way of saying that the contemporary RMA is not revolutionizing everything. A radically improved ability to conduct parallel attacks did not completely eliminate the need for more traditional military operations in either Desert Storm or OIF. At a very general level Biddle is correct in observing important continuities in conventional land warfare stretching back almost a century to the origins of the modern system. In ground combat effective employment of modern system tactics remains essential. If anything, the technologies associated with the RMA have dramatically improved the ability of the United States to implement the modern system: advances in force tracking and communication technologies make it easier for commanders to follow and coordinate troop movements; GPS guidance and night vision permit maneuver under the cover of darkness; and new sensors complicate an opponent's efforts at concealment.

But even those inclined to describe these changes as revolutionary must recognize that this RMA, like all revolutions, has its limits. No military revolution has ever changed all aspects of every type of war, never mind every mission for which military forces might be used. Even in the

---

[9] David A. Deptula, *Effects-Based Operations: Change in the Nature of Warfare* (Arlington, VA: Aerospace Education Foundation, 2001), p. 2.

midst of profound change important elements of continuity remain, and highlighting these in no way denies the magnitude and significance of the changes underway. The current RMA is driven by technologies for identifying, locating, tracking, and targeting certain types of militarily relevant assets. The RMA's limitations derive from the fact that what constitutes militarily relevant assets varies by conflict and opponent, as does the value of destroying those targets. In some wars against certain opponents there will be massed forces, large weapons platforms, and military installations that can be easily detected and reliably targeted. An effective exploitation of new technologies may very well revolutionize these wars. But in other wars against different opponents such targets may be scarce or nonexistent, and as a result these wars may not be revolutionized. Similarly, in some wars the ability to inflict lethal and destructive violence may be decisive, while in others it may be less useful or even counterproductive. It is a matter of understanding the impact of new capabilities in different contexts. As Colin Gray notes, "the US military machine, even when further down its impressive transformation road could be frustrated in strategic contexts wherein firepower, agile manoeuvre, and the warrior spirit are not at a premium."[10] An appreciation of strategic context is critical for understanding both the promises and limitations of the RMA.

As the 1991 and 2003 Iraq Wars illustrate, the precision-strike RMA manifests itself most clearly in high-intensity interstate wars that pit conventionally organized and equipped militaries against each other. These conflicts are rich in the sort of targets that new sensor technologies can detect, and the destruction of these targets is often decisive for outcomes. The RMA's disproportionately high impact on these wars reflects the nature of the conflicts and their participants, the technological capabilities at the heart of the RMA, and the manner in which the United States has exploited and channeled these technologies. Steve Metz argues that:

The idea that armed conflict evolves through periodic revolutions did not imply the direction that the revolution of the 1990s should take. Several were feasible – a revolution focused on irregular conflict, on robotic warfare, and so forth. RMA advocates harnessed the idea of military revolutions to a view of global security focused on force projection for conventional conflict against aggressive states. In other words, the RMA did not provide an alternative to the idea of military strategy built on major regional contingencies but was merged with it. The result was a peculiarly American notion of the ongoing military revolution.[11]

Metz suggests that the RMA's disproportionate impact on conventional warfare results from American strategic and military priorities rather than the technologies themselves. That is, the RMA as pursued by the

[10] Gray, *Another Bloody Century*, p. 54.
[11] Metz, *Iraq & the Evolution of American Strategy*, p. 59.

United States may not have revolutionized irregular and unconventional conflicts, but it could have and may yet still. But given the nature of such conflicts, it is difficult to see how RMA technologies could have been harnessed to bring about a similar revolution in irregular warfare. Remote sensors, for example, will almost certainly never be able distinguish insurgents from ordinary civilians. This would require some technological innovation well beyond anything available or even conceivable at the moment. As a result, sensor technologies cannot have nearly the impact on situational awareness in irregular conflicts that they have in more conventional contests. None of this is to say that irregular wars are unaffected by the RMA, and perhaps more thought should be given to how RMA technologies can be exploited for these conflicts. But overall, the information gathering and targeting technologies that define the RMA are by their very nature better suited to revolutionizing conventional war. Kober is blunt on this point. In arguing that the 2003 Iraq War marked a "phase change in warfare," he notes that his analysis "does not deal with the low-intensity, protracted conflict (LIC) in which the Coalition has been engaged since the high-tech war came to an end" because at this point the war was transformed into "a conflict that does not represent any significant change in warfare, and cannot be won with precision strikes and a slim ground component."[12] This is perhaps the most significant limitation of the contemporary RMA: a reconnaissance-strike complex is going to have only a limited impact on conflicts in which detection of critical targets remains difficult and the value of lethal force is diminished.

As a result, many have been quick to argue that the RMA is having its greatest impact on a form of warfare that appears to be declining in significance, especially since the end the Cold War. Jeffrey Record reflects common wisdom, claiming that "Clausewitzian great-power clashes have been superseded by smaller, politically messy wars, many of them fought by irregular forces within failed states. Policing such states has become more time-consuming and force-consuming than preparing to refight the Korean and Gulf Wars. . . . Mastery of the RMA is mastery of a war that likely will never be fought."[13] In this analysis, the 1991 and 2003 Iraq Wars were aberrations or anachronisms, remnants of a world order in which wars were decisive contests of arms between states. Indeed, the declining significance of conventional wars is often portrayed as a reaction to American dominance. Since no opponent has any chance of even competing with the United States on a conventional battlefield, the rational response is to resort to irregular forms of the conflict that minimize

---

[12] Kober, "Does the Iraq War Reflect a Phase Change in Warfare?" p. 122.

[13] Jeffrey Record, "Operation Allied Force: Yet Another Wake-up Call for the Army?" *Parameters* Vol. 29, No. 4 (Winter 1999–2000), p. 20. Kober notes that high-intensity interstate wars "constitute only some five percent of post-Cold War conflicts." See "Does the Iraq War Reflect a Phase Change in Warfare," p. 122.

American advantages and magnify its weaknesses (e.g., an assumed political unwillingness to accept casualties in protracted conflicts). As Colin
Gray argues, "enemies of America who cannot afford to emulate US
investment in, say, space systems, long range air power, or networked
communications, will be obliged to pursue Brodie's logic and seek strategic behavior that works well enough, be it ever so inelegant and probably
decidedly irregular."[14] Whatever the explanation offered for the declining frequency of conventional wars, the argument is that the RMA may
have brought significant change but to an increasingly insignificant phenomenon, like a cure for disease afflicting fewer and fewer people.

Of course, no one knows if the decline in conventional warfare is
a short-term anomaly or a long-term trend. Predicting the shape and
dynamics of world politics by assuming that present patterns will be
reflected in future developments is notoriously dangerous. Horowitz and
Shalmon highlight the difficulties of anticipation by asking us to "consider how well the typical analyst would have done in predicting the future
security environment twenty years hence, once every decade starting in
1900." They think the results would not have been encouraging: "focusing on twenty-year increments, a futurist projecting linearly from 1900 to
1920, 1910 to 1930, and so on, would have done quite poorly."[15] More
recently, one wonders whether a single analyst in 1981 came even close to
anticipating the strategic environment of 2001. Given the sketchy record
of strategic predictions, some measure of modesty is in order before dismissing the RMA on the grounds that large-scale conventional war is on
its way out.

A final limitation of the RMA is that most wars will continue to be
waged by nations and other actors that possess few if any RMA capabilities. The United States is not the world and its wars do not exhaust the
category of modern warfare. At the moment the wars being revolutionized are those that happen to involve the United States. But how long is
this likely to remain the case? Will the *American* RMA become a broader
phenomenon? Historically, other major powers and many lesser powers
were quick to copy the technologies and innovations that defined RMAs.
This is part of the process by which the "first-adopter's advantage" erodes
and changes in warfare become generalized. Some are convinced that this
dynamic will be repeated with the current RMA. Since "the end result
of every RMA to date has been the possession by all major powers of
the technology and capabilities originally pioneered by one," Kagan predicts confidently that "this RMA will be no different."[16] In the very long

[14] Gray, *Another Bloody Century*, p. 52.
[15] Michael C. Horowitz and Dan A. Shalmon, "The Future of War and American Military
Strategy," *Orbis* Vol. 53, No. 2 (Spring 2009), p. 308. They credit Alan Stam for
clarifying this point.
[16] Kagan, *Finding the Target*, p. 390.

run Kagan may be correct. The likelihood of an indefinite "lockout" in which the United States alone possess RMA capabilities seems remote. But the lag time between American innovation and widespread emulation may be much longer for this RMA. To cite just one example, it has been almost two decades since the United States unveiled its F-117 stealth fighter, and yet no other nation has deployed anything comparable. As Lambeth explains, "despite much ongoing activity in air power enhancement among developed nations of the world . . . only the United States can afford to pursue such high-end stealth applications as those currently embodied in the F-117, B-2 and F-22 combat aircraft."[17]

This lag in emulation is one reflection of what may be a historically unprecedented gap in military technology and power. "In the early years of the twenty-first century," Boot observes, "the United States enjoys a preponderance of military power greater than that of any other nation in history." American military spending nearly surpasses that of the rest of the world combined, and its research and development expenditures alone are greater than any other nation's entire military budget.[18] Historian Paul Kennedy judges that "nothing has ever existed like this disparity of power; nothing."[19] And Freedman sees little reason to expect the gap to narrow because "it is almost impossible to identify any country or group of countries that would have the resources to match the US in RMA capabilities, even if inclined to do so."[20] Watts make a similar point with respect to reconnaissance- and precision-strike capabilities, highlighting how the dynamics of the current and previous RMAs differ:

Reconnaissance-strike complexes have proven far more challenging and costly for other nations to emulate than armored divisions and *Blitzkrieg* tactics were during 1939–1945 . . . From a hardware perspective, it was not that difficult for industrial powers such as the United States, Great Britain, and the USSR to field symmetric responses to the German *Blitzkrieg* during World War II. The resource and technical barriers to matching American capabilities for global precision strike, however, appear considerably steeper. . . . The costs of maintaining worldwide GPS coverage, like those of operating a fleet of electro-optical and radar reconnaissance satellites, go far to explain why no other nation is presently even close to replicating the full range of US capabilities for reconnaissance and precision strike.[21]

Some RMA capabilities are less costly and thus more easily copied. UAVs, for example, are relatively inexpensive and thus likely to proliferate quite

[17] Lambeth, *The Transformation of American Air Power*, p. 8.
[18] Boot, *War Made New*, pp. 429 and 431.
[19] Michael Kelly, "The American Way of War," *The Atlantic* Vol. 289, No. 6 (June 2002), p. 18.
[20] Freedman, *The Revolution in Strategic Affairs*, p. 70.
[21] Watts, *Six Decades of Guided Munitions and Battle Networks*, pp. xiv and 88.

rapidly. But in contrast to previous RMAs, it will be some time before even major powers possess the technology and capabilities pioneered by the United States.

Emulation, however, is not the only means by which potential competitors erode the first adopter's advantage. When emulation is neither technologically feasible nor cost-effective, the preferred option will be countering rather than copying. Given the high costs of entry for the current RMA, this may be the more likely option as nations unable to create their own reconnaissance-strike complexes attempt to disable the United States, Wrage makes a fairly persuasive case that "long before rival countries can match the Americans' technological feats with precision weapons... they will develop devices to neuter them." He speculates that "it cannot be too difficult to produce jamming devices to block or alter the weak signals broadcast by Global Positioning System satellites." And once "GPS signals are blocked, Joint Direct Attack Munitions (JDAMs)... will stray from their targets and produce unacceptable damage and deaths. Commanders will have no choice but to suspend their use."[22] Berkowitz agrees: "our opponents will work on countermeasures – GPS jammers, devices that dazzle laser seekers, and the like. If we depend heavily on smart bombs and our opponents find the right countermeasures, the result could be really, really bad."[23] So, while Kagan laments that "military thinkers and force planners have devoted far less effort to figuring out how to defeat enemies with similar capabilities," there may be a very good reason why they have not done so – the prospect of facing an opponent with similar capabilities in the near future is extremely remote.[24]

In previous RMAs the process of emulation eventually resulted in wars in which all the major participants possessed RMA capabilities. This is how the French RMA of the early 1800s and German RMA of the 1930s were generalized. There may come a day when the United States faces an opponent with equivalent reconnaissance- and precision-strike capabilities. Such a war would certainly look very different than the 1991 and 2003 Iraq Wars, and there is no guarantee that the outcome will be either low cost or favorable. But it is by no means clear that this is inevitable. Historical patterns provide a useful starting point for thinking about the possible course of a contemporary RMA, but we should not implicitly assume the existence of iron laws destined to be repeated. Thus so far, the reconnaissance- and precision-strike RMA has been largely an American affair. Others may dabble in the RMA by acquiring some of its

---

[22] Stephen D. Wrage, "Prospects for Precision Air Power," *Defense & Security Analysis* Vol. 19, No. 2 (2003), p. 105.
[23] Berkowitz, *The New Face of War*, p. 99.
[24] Kagan, *Finding the Target*, p. 391.

less complex and expensive capabilities, but at present the United States is the only full participant in the contemporary RMA.

The Iraq Wars and the Future of American Defense Policy

Although the last American combat forces left Vietnam more than a generation ago, the war continues to cast a long shadow. Much of the discussion of American defense policy in the wake of Iraq continues to reach back to the post–Vietnam era. Nagl provides a representative example:

> The story of how the Army found itself less than ready to fight an insurgency goes back to the Army's refusal to internalize and build upon the lessons of Vietnam. . . . The Vietnam hangover resulted in American unwillingness to think about and prepare for future counterinsurgency campaigns, a failure that led to a 40-year gap in comprehensive American counterinsurgency doctrine and con-tributed to the American military's lack of preparedness for fighting insurgencies in Afghanistan and Iraq.[25]

This has become a standard analysis of the roots of the United States' trou-bles in Iraq: the Army failed to learn and/or institutionalize the lessons of the Vietnam, West Point cadets were not required to take courses on counterinsurgency strategy, and soldiers trained to wage war against opponents that fought as the United States preferred. The legacy of this failure became all too evident as the mission in Iraq switched from depos-ing Saddam to rebuilding the government and defeating the insurgency. As a description of what happened, there is little objectionable in this account. As a historical policy judgment, however, it is unclear that the decision to refocus on conventional warfare after Vietnam was mistaken. A very plausible case can be made that involvement in Vietnam's insur-gency was an unnecessary distraction from the greater strategic threat posed by the Soviet Union. Given scarce resources and geopolitical real-ities, it may not have been possible to prepare adequately for every con-tingency, in which case it made perfect sense to prioritize the existing conventional threat.

In thinking about the future of American defense policy, historical experience should be seen as a diagnostic test yielding critical informa-tion about the military's relative competencies. Analysts may debate, for example, the reasons for American failure in Vietnam, but the war demon-strated that counterinsurgency was not the military's forte. The Iraq Wars and other engagements over the past two decades provide similarly useful information about American military strengths and weaknesses. But the

---

[25] National Press Club Roundtable on "Counterinsurgency and Modern Warfare," The National Press Club, July 22, 2008. Transcript available at: www.cna.org/documents/Counterinsurgency%20Transcript.pdf.

connection between past performance and future policy is not straightforward. Previous experience can only tell us what the military does well, not what it *needs* to do well. The military lessons of the last two decades can support a range of future defense policies depending on predictions about the future strategic environment as well as assessments of American interests and likely threats to those interests. Unless there are sufficient resources to prepare for all conceivable threats to every interest, choices need to be made and priorities set on the basis of these assessments. This is why the decision to concentrate on conventional warfare after Vietnam may very well have been the correct strategy. If resources were limited and the primary threat to America's most important interests was conventional, preparing to counter that threat should have been the focus of the military policy.

Of course, the world of 2010 is very different than the world of 1975. The Cold War is over, the Soviet Union has disappeared, and no peer military competitor has emerged to take its place. In purely conventional terms, no nation comes close to rivaling American power. There may be a handful of conventional threats (e.g., North Korea), but nothing comparable to the Soviet Union in the late 1970s and early 1980s. In this environment there may be a much stronger case for reorienting American defense policy toward unconventional threats and counterinsurgencies than in the aftermath of Vietnam. Nonetheless, there also appears to be a consensus that the United States must maintain the full spectrum of military capabilities, an ability to fight any kind of war and carry out any mission, whether it is peacekeeping, stabilization, counterinsurgency, or conventional high-intensity warfare. Recommendations for change are portrayed as shifts in emphasis rather than eliminating any class of capabilities. In short, the United States needs to be able to do everything. This is reflected, for example, in recent statements by Secretary of Defense Robert Gates seeking to chart a "balanced" course for American defense policy which includes:

doing everything we can to prevail in the conflicts we are in, and being prepared for other contingencies that might arise elsewhere, or in the future... institutionalizing capabilities such as counterinsurgency and stability operations, as well as helping partners build capacity, and maintaining our traditional edge – above all, the technological edge – against the military forces of other nation states; and... retaining those cultural traits that have made the United States armed forces successful by inspiring and motivating the people within them, and shedding those cultural elements that are barriers to doing what needs to be done.[26]

---

[26] Robert Gates, Presentation at the National Defense University, September 28, 2008. Accessed at: www.defenselink.mil/speeches/speech.aspx?speechid=1279.

Within this general consensus on maintaining full spectrum capabilities, debate focuses on three central issues: prioritizing contingencies and missions, the fungibility of military forces, and the extent of institutional reforms needed.

Priorities

In terms of potential missions, formulations such as Gates' appear to be all addition and no subtraction: new tasks are constantly included without others being jettisoned. The demands on the military grow ever greater even though its human and financial resources are clearly not. The uncomfortable question, seldom tackled head-on, is whether the military must, or even can, achieve not only full spectrum *competence* but also full spectrum *excellence*. Although Kevin Reynolds, for example, agrees that "the military must acquire capabilities which allow it to fight effectively across the full spectrum of conflict," he also cautions that "this does not mean the military should prepare for all contingencies equally. Rather, it should weigh its capabilities in light of future policies and prioritize the tasks it most likely will have to accomplish."[27] That is, the military must be *able* fight in any conflict, but not equally so: the military should prepare for some contingencies more than others. The need for prioritization in the abstract is easy to accept. It is an essential element of a grand strategy. More difficult is identifying what should be emphasized and de-emphasized. Prioritization is partly an intellectual exercise involving judgments and predictions about the likelihood and significance of threats years and even decades into the future. This intellectual task is complicated enough. Unfortunately, prioritization is also an intensely political process with important consequences for the allocation of resources among powerful interests and institutions.

It is the counterinsurgents who most welcome talk of changing priorities as a long overdue recognition that the military's traditional emphasis on technology, air power, and decisive victory achieved through rapid maneuver and overwhelming firepower is largely irrelevant to the security challenges the United States will face in coming decades. The call for shifting priorities reflects "a growing realization that the most likely conflicts of the next fifty years will be irregular warfare in an 'Arc of Instability' that encompasses much of the greater Middle East and parts of Africa and Central and South Asia ... [where] many of our enemies will be insurgents."[28] The counterinsurgents are heartened, for example,

---

[27] Kevin Reynolds, *Defense Transformation: To What? For What* (Carlisle, PA: U.S. Army War College Strategic Studies Institute, 2006), p. 54.

[28] Nagl, *Learning to Eat Soup with a Spoon*, p. XVI.

when Gates expresses support for "institutionalizing counterinsurgency skills, and our ability to conduct stability and support operations," seeing this as an encouraging sign that the United States will not repeat the mistakes it supposedly made after Vietnam. McMaster sees a belated triumph of practice over theory, a rejection of "fantastical" and "faith-based" notions such as the RMA, transformation, and net-centric warfare that rested on "the dangerous and seductive illusion that technology can solve the problem of future conflict."[29] But despite promising indications to the contrary, many who favor a new emphasis on irregular conflict continue to worry that the temptation to retreat into more comfortable and familiar terrain might prove irresistible. Colonel Peter Mansoor, a member of Petraeus' advisory team in Iraq, worries that "our senior leaders [will] allow our newly developed counterinsurgency capabilities to lapse... [and] focus instead on preparing the Army to fight the next 'big one.' After all, why worry about fighting real wars in the Middle East and South Asia when we can instead keep our military forces in the United States to fight imaginary ones?"[30] Similarly, Hammes laments "the fact that the Pentagon is still structuring forces to fight a near-peer competitor, 17 years after the last one disappeared."[31]

Not everyone is convinced, however, that the United States *should* focus on fighting "real wars" in the Middle East and South Asia for the next fifty years, and to characterize the alternative as preparing for "imaginary wars" is a bit of rhetorical excess. Those who would rather maintain the emphasis on conventional capabilities emphasize the *significance* of future threats, not their *likelihood*. While the irregular conflicts Nagl worries about may be more common over the next few decades, they will rarely involve genuinely vital American interests. Most would be, to use a familiar formulation, wars of choice rather than necessity. Over the long term the United States still needs to worry about the possible emergence of a peer strategic competitor. It needs to be prepared to either fight a challenger or remain so dominant in conventional capabilities as to deter its emergence in the first place. Freedman, for example, argues that "eventually, a serious 'peer competitor' will emerge, ready to challenge the benign hegemony of the US. The penalties could be severe if investment for this moment has been neglected because a distracting preoccupation with recent trends in civil disturbance has led to a chase after minor

---

[29] H.R. McMaster, "On War: Lessons to Be Learned," *Survival* Vol. 50, No. 1 (February–March 2008), pp. 19, 21, and 26.

[30] Peter Mansoor, "Misreading the History of the Iraq War," *Small Wars Journal* (blog), posted on March 10, 2008. Accessed at: www.smallwarsjournal.com/blog/2008/03/misreading-the-history-of-the/.

[31] T.X. Hammes, "How Will We Fight," *Orbis* Vol. 54, No. 3 (Summer 2009), p. 383.

irritants."[32] Retired Army General Barry McCaffrey makes the similar argument, identifying the future strategic threat by name:

> The looming challenge to U.S. national security... in the coming 15 years will be posed by the legitimate and certain emergence of the People's Republic of China... In less than one generation, China will have the military capacity to pose a national survival threat to America.... There is little likelihood of U.S. smart engagement power having adequate deterrence impact on Chinese unilateral military capabilities unless we maintain the enormous technological lead to command air and sea operational maneuver areas surrounding our regional allies.[33]

Michael Mazarr also warns against the "folly" of reorienting American defense policy toward counterinsurgency and other asymmetric conflicts that "represent less of the threat to the United States than has become fashionable to assume." A shift along the lines the counterinsurgents advocate "promises to keep the United States involved in conflicts in which it is often counterproductive to become militarily embroiled." Mazarr prefers that American defense policy continue to focus on "the much more important global role for U.S. military power: deterring and responding to major conventional aggression." To the extent that insurgency, asymmetric conflicts, and state failure do threaten American interests, it is better to "shore up institutionalization and governance in critical states... by relying on an expanded and deepened set of *nonmilitary* tools."[34]

So, just as Mansoor fears the United States will again fail to learn the lessons of its experience with counterinsurgency, others worry it will overlearn those lessons, treating Iraq and Afghanistan as templates for future conflicts while ignoring more significant strategic threats until it is too late or relying on military responses for essentially nonmilitary problems. Ideally, of course, the United States would prepare for all contingencies. The ability to do so, however, depends in part on the fungibility of military capabilities – that is, can a military trained and equipped to fight irregular conflicts also deal with conventional threats and vice versa? In other words, is it possible to create an all-purpose force?

Fungibility

It would be easier to excel at the full spectrum of operations if military forces were fungible. The military has typically assumed that they were. As Gates notes, "the prevailing view for decades was that weapons

[32] Freedman, *The Revolution in Strategic Affairs*, p. 73.
[33] Barry R. McCaffrey, "Rebuilding Global Airpower," *Joint Force Quarterly* No. 49 (2nd Quarter, 2008), p. 77.
[34] Michael Mazarr, "The Folly of 'Asymmetric War,'" *The Washington Quarterly* Vol. 31, No. 3 (Summer 2008), p. 35.

and units designed for the so-called high-end could also be used for the low." This was a very convenient assumption because it reinforced the bias toward conventional conflict and obviated the need for specialized training for other types of missions. That the experience in Vietnam did not seem to justify such a view was somehow overlooked. The military's experience in Iraq, however, has led many to rethink this traditional view. After serving in Iraq, for example, Nagl concluded that he "underestimated the challenge of adapting the army for the purposes of defeating an insurgency while simultaneously maintaining the army's ability to fight a conventional war."[35]

It was not just an issue of having the right weapons and hardware, though that was certainly part of it. The more important obstacle is that counterinsurgency also requires different "software." Adaption may require not merely new tools but possibly a completely different mind set and ethos. Commanders and soldiers need to change how they think about conflict, the requirements for victory, and their role in achieving it. Whereas conventional warfare stresses massive firepower and killing the enemy, in counterinsurgencies massive firepower is often counterproductive, and minimizing civilian casualties is more important than maximizing enemy deaths. Rather than searching for and killing insurgents, soldiers need to spend the bulk of their time walking the streets, listening to complaints, becoming familiar with the ebb and flow of local life, and establishing the social and political relationships that yield information and cooperation. The conventional war mindset and its negative consequences were evident early on in Iraq. According to Bing West, "in 2003–2004, the Americans were robo-cop outsiders, tough in battle but not understanding the environment."[36] They may have won all their battles, but the United States was still in danger of losing the war. Sometimes robo-cops are exactly what are needed, but Iraq in 2004 was not one of those times. The aggressive ethos usually valuable in conventional warfare is inconsistent with many of the tasks needed for counterinsurgency. The eventual switch to counterinsurgency in Iraq was more difficult than even Nagl expected because it involved "an entirely different way of thinking about combat – a different level of professional knowledge about a different kind of war."[37]

[35] Nagl, *Learning to Eat Soup with a Spoon*, p. xiv.
[36] Bing West, "Decency, Toughness....and No Shortcuts," *The Atlantic: Dispatches* (online). Posted on September 24, 2008. Accessed at: http://www.theatlantic.com/doc/200809u/iraq-lessons.
[37] Nagl, *Learning to Eat Soup with a Spoon*, pp. xiv and xii. On the need for a distinct culture in dealing with counterinsurgencies, see also Robert M. Cassidy, "The British Army and Counterinsurgency: The Salience of Military Culture," *Military Review* Vol. 85, No. 3 (May–June 2005), pp. 53–9.

It is, however, possible to overstate the difficulty of such an adaptation. This argument suggests that the major obstacle in Iraq was the inability of forces trained for conventional war to get their minds around the dynamics and requirements of counterinsurgency. If this is so, how does one account for the early successes of Petraeus in Mosul or McMaster in Al Anbar? There is no reason to think their troops were trained any differently than all the others in Iraq, yet they proved perfectly capable of implementing counterinsurgency best practice. They did not behave as the robo-cops West refers to. In Mosul in 2003, American forces combined aggressive actions against insurgents with the less kinetic aspects of counterinsurgency.[38] The critical factor was local commanders who understood and appreciated the nature of counterinsurgency and how it differed from conventional warfare. And despite complaints that the military virtually ignored counterinsurgency in the decades between Vietnam and Iraq, once political and military leaders decided to adopt a counterinsurgency strategy in 2007, the results were pretty good. As Metz observes, "while the military was not optimized for counterinsurgency, it seemed flexible enough to be tolerably effective at that mission."[39] Gates makes the same point, noting that "in Iraq, we've seen how an army that was basically a smaller version of the Cold War force can over time become an effective instrument of counterinsurgency."[40]

More recently, some have even begun to worry that the pendulum has already swung so far in the direction of counterinsurgency that conventional war-fighting skills are suffering. As the military is preoccupied with fighting two insurgencies and training centers retool to prepare troops for these missions, skills that do not play much of a role in these conflicts are taking a back seat. No one has been more vocal in expressing these concerns than Colonel Gian Gentile, a somewhat contrarian figure in debates about American counterinsurgency strategy in Iraq. Although he agrees "the U.S. Army needs to be able to conduct stability operations, to combat insurgencies, [and] to keep the peace," he argues that "after six years of performing almost nothing but counterinsurgency operations . . . the army is 'out of balance.' And the balance, such as it is, ought to be weighted more heavily toward the requirements of conventional warfare."[41] Gentile draws parallels to the Israeli experience, claiming that after years of low-intensity operations in the occupied territories, it was no surprise the Israeli Defense Force performed so poorly against Hezbollah in its invasion of Lebanon in 2006. Bacevich sides with Gentile:

[38] See Jarett D. Broemmel, Shannon E. Nelson, and Terry L. Clark, *An Analysis of Counterinsurgency in Iraq: Mosul, Ramadi and Samarra from 2003–2005* (Monterey, CA: Naval Postgraduate School Thesis, December 2006), pp. 17–28.
[39] Metz, *Iraq & the Evolution of American Strategy*, p. 158.
[40] Speech to the National Defense University, September 29, 2008.
[41] Gentile, "A (Slightly) Better War: A Narrative and Its Defects," p. 64.

The concern is not idle.... The officer corps itself recognizes that conventional-warfare capabilities are already eroding. In a widely circulated white paper, three former brigade commanders declare that the Army's field-artillery branch – which plays a limited role in stability operations, but is crucial when there is serious fighting to be done – may soon be all but incapable of providing accurate and timely fire support. Field artillery, the authors write, has become a "dead branch walking."[42]

Gentile cites the same report but takes it one step further, arguing that "Iraq bids to transform the entire force into a 'dead army walking.'"[43]

Whatever the merits of Gentile's argument with regard to the par-ticulars, he raises a larger issue relevant to the problem of fungibility. Creating a force able to carry out the full spectrum of military missions requires more than fostering the right mindsets and providing the nec-essary equipment. One of the most important elements in the revival of American military power after Vietnam was the emphasis on realistic training. In the absence of real-world experience, such training is the only effective way to hone essential skills. But training time and facilities are also limited resources. The question is whether it is possible to create a military force that has the mindset, equipment as well as the training and skills it needs to fulfill such a wide range of potential missions, a tall order indeed. Krepinevich highlights the key challenge (or biggest danger): "the Army's leadership has rightly concluded that it needs a force capable of performing across the full spectrum of conflict at a high level of effec-tiveness. But in its attempts to become equally effective across a range of conflict types, it risks becoming marginally competent in many tasks, and highly effective at none."[44]

Institutions

Reflecting on the United States' security challenges in light of the expe-rience in Iraq, the *Economist* notes correctly that "counterinsurgency, insurgency, and foreign military training... are operations that require technological systems and force structures different from those needed

---

[42] Andrew J. Bacevich, "The Petraeus Doctrine," *The Atlantic* Vol. 302, No. 2 (October 2008), p. 20. Secretary Gates also appears to agree, noting in his National Defense University speech, "as a result of the demands of Afghanistan and Iraq, the ground forces have not been able to stay proficient in specialties such as field artillery in the Army, and amphibious operations in the Marine Corps. We must remedy this as soon as we can through growing the ground forces, and increasing dwell time and opportunities for full spectrum training."

[43] Gentile, "A (Slightly) Better War," p. 64.

[44] Andrew F. Krepinevich, "The Future of U.S. Ground Forces," *Testimony Before the U.S. Senate Armed Services Committee: Airland Subcommittee* (March 26, 2009), p. 12. Accessed at: www.csbaonline.org/4Publications/PubLibrary/T.20090326.The_Future_of_US_G/T.20090326.The_Future_of_US_G.pdf.

for high-intensity conventional combat." Given these differing requirements, "the dilemma *for the Pentagon* is how to improve its ability
to fight today's insurgencies while preparing for tomorrow's conventional threats."[45] If anything, the *Economist* underestimates the challenge
by omitting a number of potential missions, such as peacekeeping and
humanitarian intervention, that may have little to do with either counterinsurgency or conventional warfare. But what if the Pentagon is unable
to reconcile the conflicting demands of so many different missions? And
why is it assumed that this is the *Pentagon's* dilemma? James Ellsworth
discusses the same issues with a critical difference in emphasis, asking
"How can the United States shape its power projection to be decisive in
the operations most critical in the war on terrorism while retaining and
honing the 'sharp edge of the sword' that will be decisive in the next conventional conflict, which history reminds us is lurking down the road?"[46]
The subtle but important difference is that the *Economist* presents the
problem as one for *the Pentagon* to solve, whereas Ellsworth formulates
it more broadly as a problem for *the United States*. Ellsworth suggests
that the solution might not be found within the Pentagon, which hints at
a more fundamental rethinking of how the United States provides for its
varied security needs.

Arguing that it is impossible to maintain a single force able to excel
at such disparate missions as peacekeeping, stabilization, reconstruction,
counterinsurgency, and conventional warfare, a handful of analysts suggest the most radical of solutions to the problem of force fungibility –
creating distinct and separate forces with different core competencies.
Thomas P.M. Barnett has long been a prominent advocate of a radical
"force-structure solution" to the challenges arising from the military's
constantly expanding missions.[47] He argues that an all-purpose force
with core competencies in everything is unattainable. An organization
designed to defeat conventional threats cannot be expected to take the
lead in establishing effective governance, either as a stand-alone mission
or in the aftermath of war. The inclusion of such wide-ranging tasks will
inevitably degrade the military's ability to carry out its core mission –
fighting and deterring conventional military threats. And while such
threats might temporarily appear in short supply, it is unwise to assume
that the era of state-on-state conventional warfare is gone for good. The
United States needs to retain a military force whose focus on conventional
warfare remains undiluted. Barnett argues that this requires two forces,

---

45 "The Hobbled Hegemon," p. 29, emphasis added.
46 James B. Ellsworth, *SysAdmin: Toward Barnett's Stabilization and Reconstruction Force*
    (Arlington, VA: The Institute of Land Warfare, September 2006), p. 3.
47 Thomas P.M. Barnett, *The Pentagon's New Map: War and Peace in the Twenty-First
    Century* (New York: Putnam, 2004) and *Blueprint for Action: A Future Worth Creating*
    (New York, Putnam, 2005).

one to wage war and another to wage peace, a department of war and a department of everything else.[48] One force fights war and the other carries out those military operations other than war. In Iraq, the United States lacked a discrete follow-on force to perform basic stabilization functions and build a successor regime. In this view, the problem was not just a lack of sufficient forces per se, but rather the absence of forces trained to perform critical postwar tasks with the same level of skill displayed by those who fought the war. Two hundred thousand extra troops ill-prepared for postwar tasks might not have made things much better.

A study of the U.S. Army War College's Strategic Studies Institute examining how other militaries, particularly the French and the British, adjusted to meet unconventional threats reaches much the same conclusion as Barnett:

the military cannot focus at the same time on both conventional and unconventional warfare...one or the other inevitably will suffer. Good infantrymen can do many things well, but in relying only on them and good infantry thinking, the best we are likely to manage in unconventional warfare is muddling along. The requirements for each kind of warfare are distinct and rarely complementary. The issue here is not so much budgetary (our unconventional warfare capability should be low-tech, for example) as it is cultural. The two kinds of warfare require two different ways of thinking and evaluating. There is no reason to believe that any organization or the people within it will be equally good at both.[49]

Concrete proposals for this kind of far-reaching reform are rare and usually quite vague, ranging from a modest reorganization within the Department of Defense to carve out a special niche for forces specializing in irregular warfare to more radical plans to create an entirely new cabinet-level department bridging the space between the Departments of Defense and State. Barnett sees his "department of everything else" beginning in the Department of Defense but eventually migrating to independent status.

Whatever the intellectual merits of a two-force solution, it is difficult to see any political will or institutional support for such a radical reorganization. Even within the counterinsurgency community, there does not appear to be much support, especially for the more radical force-structure solutions. In a roundtable discussion including such notables as John Nagl and David Kilcullen, the prospect of creating an entirely different force for stability and counterinsurgency operations was dismissed almost out of hand. "In my opinion," Carter Malkasian predicted, "the bulk of our

[48] See "The Pentagon's New Map: A Conversation with Thomas P.M. Barnett," accessed at: www.globetrotter.berkeley.edu/people5/Barnett/barnett-con5.html. A video of Barnett's presentation on "The Pentagon's New Map: A Force to Wage War; Another to Wage Peace," is available at: www.ted.com/index.php/talks/thomas_barnett_draws_a_new_map_for_peace.html.
[49] Tucker, *Confronting the Unconventional*, p. 68.

forces can probably be expected to adapt. The bulk of infantry battalions and regiments and brigades can be expected that [sic] they are going to have to adapt to one force or another, because *we are not going to have an army for counterinsurgency and an army for regular warfare."*[50] No one on the roundtable challenged his conclusion. Instead, the general predisposition is to work within existing institutional structures to improve the capacity of the military and other government agencies to conduct counterinsurgencies as well as broader state-building and reconstruction missions requiring expertise that simply cannot be contained completely with the Department of Defense. As McMaster argues, "military forces, their governments and coalitions need...to develop improved interdepartmental capabilities for...protracted counter-insurgency and state-building efforts that require population security, security-sector reform, reconstruction and economic development, development of governmental capacity, and the establishment of rule of law."[51]

Horowitz and Shalmon sketch out what may be the most likely solution to creating a military with full spectrum capabilities, a so-called division of labor within the Department of Defense. Accepting the prevailing assumption "that the United States must be ready for future irregular wars but must also maintain and strengthen its conventional warfighting capacity," they argue that "it is perfectly possible to have parts of the Army and Marine Corps optimized for COIN [counterinsurgency] while optimizing the Navy and Air Force for higher intensity engagements." This division of labor with the existing institutional framework would nonetheless require the Army and Marines to perform both tasks. They note that "*adding* crowd control and civil-military operations to the list of basic skills for infantry would never mean not training them to operate against other conventionally trained infantry."[52]

Conclusion: "Re-Balancing" American Defense Policy?

It is too soon to predict with any certainty how the experience in Iraq and Afghanistan will shape American defense policy in the coming years. The wars are far from over, and the debate over their lessons and policy implications is just beginning. A critical moment in what is sure to be a long process of debate and adjustment occurred in April 2009, when Secretary Gates unveiled a defense budget that represented the first comprehensive attempt to rethink and reorient defense policy in light of the Iraq and Afghan wars. Although Gates presented his proposals in calm tones with

---

[50] National Press Club Roundtable on "Counterinsurgency and Modern Warfare," emphasis added.
[51] McMaster, "On War: Lessons to be Learned," pp. 24–5 and 27.
[52] Horowitz and Shalmon, "The Future of War and American Strategy," p. 316.

measured rhetoric, knowledgeable observers were quick to see the potential significance of his effort to "re-balance" defense priorities. In general terms, his budget was seen as a "bid to shift military spending from preparations for large-scale conventional war against traditional rivals to the counterinsurgency programs...likely to dominate conflicts in the coming decades."[53] Gates framed his budget as an attempt to "re-balance this department's programs" and "ruthlessly separate appetites from real requirements" in order to "institutionalize and finance our capabilities to fight the wars we are in today and the scenarios we are most likely to face in the years ahead." Anticipating opposition to his cuts in a number of politically popular programs, he warned that "every defense dollar spent to overinsure against a remote or diminishing risk or, in effect, to run up the score in capabilities where the United States is already dominant is a dollar not available to take care of our people, reset our force, win the wars we are in, and improve in areas where we are underinvested." And while acknowledging the need to prepare for future threats, "goals should be tied to the actual and prospective capabilities of known future adversaries – not by what might be technologically feasible for a potential adversary given unlimited time and resources."[54]

Since budgets reflect priorities, one needs only to follow the money to get a sense of direction in which Gates wanted to take American defense policy. One of the big losers in his budget was the F-22 Raptor stealth fighter, a critical element of the Air Force's modernization program designed to replace the aging F-117. The original plan called for more than 600 F-22s, though this number has been steadily reduced since the program began in the early 1990s. As of April 2009, 183 planes had been purchased. The F-22 was a high priority for the Air Force and those who wanted to maintain the United States' unquestioned dominance in air power with an eye toward the emergence of China as a strategic threat. Barry McCaffrey, for example, argued that there was "*no single greater priority* in the coming 10 years than for the Air Force to fund, deploy, and maintain at *least 350* F-22A Raptor aircraft to ensure air-to-air total dominance of battlefield air space in future contested areas." For its supporters, the F-22 was a technological marvel that would guarantee American superiority in the air well into the future. To its opponents, the F-22 was an expensive Cold War relic ideally suited to major conventional wars against peer competitors but of little use against the enemies the United States actually faces. Although the first F-22s entered service in 2006, critics point out that they have yet to fly a single

---

[53] R. Jeffrey Smith and Ellen Nakashima, "Gates Planning Major Changes in Programs, Defense Budget," *The Washington Post* (April 4, 2009), p. A1.

[54] Robert Gates, News Briefing Transcript (April 6, 2009). Accessed at: www.defenselink .mil/transcripts/transcript.aspx?transcriptid=4396.

mission in either Iraq or Afghanistan. Even McCaffrey concedes that "the aircraft has minimal value in low intensity ground-air combat operations such as Iraq and Afghanistan."[55] On this point Gates would no doubt agree, which is why he proposed halting production of F-22s. Asked if his decision to halt to a program McCaffrey identified as the Air Force's *single greatest priority* was "a close call or a no-brainer," Gates replied, "for me, it was not a close call." Given his general comments about defense priorities, either American dominance in the air is already so great that the F-22 would merely be "running up the score," or the threat it counters is too remote to warrant the expenditure in the face of more immediate needs.

Gates also proposed substantial cuts in the so-called Future Combat System (FCS), long a favorite of RMA and defense transformation advocates. An ambitious program to apply the principles of net-centric warfare, the Army launched the FCS in 2003 as the centerpiece of its modernization program. At a projected cost of $200 billion, the FCS has been described as "the largest weapons procurement in history...at least in this part of the galaxy."[56] The goal was nothing less than to "remake the largest war machine in history."[57] The system envisaged the creation of new brigades built around a networked collection of sensors, drones, and weapons as well as manned and unmanned combat vehicles. One of the supposed benefits of the FCS was increased mobility – its combat and personnel vehicles would be lighter, making them easier to deploy to distant battlefields and faster in combat once they arrived. They would become lighter largely by stripping them of armor that made existing forces heavy and slow. The problem, however, was that eliminating armor increased not only mobility but also vulnerability. Armor, after all, is what protects vehicles and soldiers from enemy fire, so removing it solves one problem only to create another. The FCS substituted technology for armor as protection: sensors would detect enemy forces when they were still far away, and standoff precision weapons would attack long before the enemy was in position to do any harm. There would no longer be any need for heavy armor.

Although the FCS was portrayed as versatile, capable of full spectrum operations, it really only made sense for conventional warfare when the enemy could be detected and targeted from a safe distance in traditional battles.[58] In the context of wars such as those in Iraq and Afghanistan, where personnel and combat vehicles can be attacked with roadside bombs and improvised explosive devices without an insurgent in sight, the

55 McCaffrey, "Rebuilding Global Airpower," p. 78, emphasis added.
56 Singer, *Wired for War*, p. 114.
57 Alec Klein, "The Army's $200 Billion Makeover," *The Washington Post* (December 7, 2007), p. A1.
58 See Yang and Vocke, "US Army Transformation: Where Is the Future," pp. 391–5.

system would be worse than useless. In these settings armor protection is essential and cannot be sacrificed in a quest for greater speed without placing lives in greater danger. As Gates explained, "the FCS vehicles – where lower weight, higher fuel efficiency and greater situational awareness are expected to compensate for less armor – do not adequately reflect the lessons of counterinsurgency and close-quarters combat." Consequently, he proposed canceling the vehicle component of the FCS, thus "ripping the heart" out of the entire program.[59]

The message of these cuts seemed clear. Whereas in Rumsfeld's Pentagon anything that did not contribute to transformation was in danger of being axed, under Gates any system with little or nothing to offer in counterinsurgencies and irregular conflicts was viewed with skepticism. At the same time, his budget called for increased spending on systems and forces that have proven their value for irregular warfare and counterinsurgency operations, particularly special operations forces, Predator and Reaper class surveillance and attack drones, helicopter maintenance, and littoral combat ships.

Reaction to Gates's budget announcement was mixed. Although Gates gave no indication of supporting a two-army solution, Thomas P.M. Barnett could barely contain his enthusiasm, portraying the budget as a "shot across the bow of the big-war camp" in which Gates "came down – quite explicitly – on the side of the small-wars Army and Marines, stating he would no longer tolerate big-war demands for ruinously expensive ships from the Navy and aircraft from the Air Force." Claiming "this Gates-led rebalancing constitutes only the second such momentous shift in American history," Barnett expressed relief that Gates appeared to be "the seminal figure I hoped he would become."[60] Most observers were a bit more restrained, characterizing the budget as somewhere between "a sweeping overhaul" and the beginning of "much-needed process of rethinking American defense strategy after the Cold War."[61] Others were decidedly less unenthusiastic. Senator Saxby Chambliss (R-GA), for example, charged that Gates's spending cuts betrayed a willingness "to sacrifice the lives of military men and women for the sake of domestic programs favored by President Obama."[62] In a similar vein, Senator James Inhofe (R-OK) criticized proposed cuts in the FCS, arguing that "without

---

[59] See Noah Shachtman, "Pentagon Chief Rips Heart Out of the Army's 'Future,'" *Wired* (April 9, 2009). Accessed at: www.wired.com/dangerroom/2009/04/gates-rips-hear/.

[60] Thomas P.M. Barnett, "Inside the War Against Robert Gates," *Esquire* (April 14, 2009). Accessed at: www.esquire.com/the-side/richardson-report/robert-gates-new-defense-budget-041409.

[61] August Cole and Yochi J. Dreazen, "Pentagon Pushes Weapons Cuts," *Wall Street Journal* (April 7, 2009), p. A1; and Fareed Zakaria, "Is Robert Gates a Genius?" *Newsweek* Vol. 153, No. 16 (April 20, 2009), p. 29.

[62] Michael Gerson, "A War Fighter's Budget," *The Washington Post* (April 10, 2009), p. A1.

it, we risk sending our sons and daughters into combat in vehicles that are second-rate and are less survivable and effective in combat."[63]

Rhetoric aside, how much of a shift in priorities did Gates's budget really represent? There is no question it contained important and controversial recommendations to eliminate or substantially scale back major weapons systems that have little relevance for counterinsurgencies and irregular war. But once one moves beyond headline-grabbing proposals, it is not clear that the shift in priorities was that momentous or sweeping. Even after cuts in the F-22 and FCS programs, for example, Gates breaks down his budget as "about 10 percent for irregular warfare, about 50 percent for traditional, strategic and conventional conflict, and about 40 percent for dual-purpose capabilities." Although Gates failed to explain how he arrived at these figures, this distribution hardly seems like much of a shot across the bow of the big-war camp. If devoting ten percent of the defense budget exclusively to meeting the needs of irregular warfare constitutes the second greatest defense reorientation in American history, previous changes could not have been very large. Gates himself repeatedly emphasized that his budget "is not about irregular warfare putting conventional capabilities in the shade. Quite the contrary, this is just a matter ... of having the irregular-war constituency have a seat at the table for the first time when it comes to the base budget." Again, it is difficult to see how merely giving the irregular war constituency a "seat at the table" rises to the level of a momentous shift in priorities. Even in the unlikely event that the Congress agrees to everything in Gates's budget, defense resources will remain overwhelmingly focused on preparations for conventional conflict, with counterinsurgency and irregular war claiming only a small share the defense budget.

The bias toward conventional conflict is evident in the details as well as the overall distribution of resources. While halting production of the F-22 may indicate an unwillingness to waste money on a "ruinously expensive" aircraft in search of an enemy or plausible threat, Gates nonetheless proposed spending in excess of $1 trillion over the next decade to acquire more than 2,000 F-35 fighters for the Air Force (F-35A), Marines (F-35B), and Navy (F-35C). Slightly less expensive than the F-22, at least according to current estimates, this is still an awful lot of money for an aircraft whose potential contribution to counterinsurgencies and irregular warfare appears as limited as the F-22. The F-35 program alone would probably consume more than the ten percent of the budget Gates devotes to irregular warfare. Zakaria also points to the fate of the Navy's carrier battle groups as a sign that Gates's shift is extremely modest, not momentous. Although he applauds Gates for ending the Navy's stealth destroyer program, Zakaria wonders why the Navy is slated to lose just one of its eleven aircraft carrier battle groups, and this not until 2040. Maintaining carrier battle groups is an extremely expensive commitment, and Zakaria sees no reason why the United States needs ten when its only plausible strategic competitor, China, does not have a single carrier battle group.

Ideally, American defense policy should be the product of a coherent strategic analysis. In reality, of course, political and institutional interests inevitably intrude. Even the modest rebalancing represented by Gates's proposed budget may not survive. Although some analysts focused on the strategic implications of his recommendations, others emphasized their economic and political dimensions. The day after Gates unveiled his budget, the *Wall Street Journal*'s lead story, subtitled "New Focus on Unconventional Conflicts; Defense Contractors Gird for Political Battle," noted that "Mr. Gates's proposed shake-up is expected to stoke debate about the importance of weapons manufacturing jobs and appears to mark a turning point for an industry that enjoyed record business during the Bush administration." The International Association of Machinists and Aerospace Workers, for example, was among the first to denounce the decision to halt F-22 production, claiming that "we simply cannot afford to cannibalize our national security to repair damage caused by reckless financial institutions and greed-crazed corporate executives."[64] In the end, Gates prevailed on this issue when the Senate voted 58–40 to halt production of the F-22 at 187.[65] Nonetheless, McMaster worries that "institutions and corporations that stand to benefit from a flawed concept of future conflict [will] find it difficult to divest themselves of a marketing concept that has been successful and profitable in the past."[66] Gates's budget and early battle over the F-22 were only opening salvos in what will certainly be a contentious struggle to identify the lessons of the United States' most recent wars and reorient American defense policy. His budget represented a particular vision of the capabilities and resources needed to defend the nation's interests, and one possible balancing of the defense requirements for meeting immediate and more distant threats. The initial response to his proposals was a reminder that alternative visions and other considerations will also shape American defense policy and, thus, the future of America's military revolution.

---

[64] Cole and Dreazen, "Pentagon Pushes Budget Cuts," p. A1.

[65] Mark Thompson, "Defense Secretary Downs the F-22," *Time* (July 22, 2009). Accessed at: www.time.com/time/nation/article/0,8599,1912084,00.html.

[66] McMaster, "On War: Lessons to Be Learned," p. 26.

INDEX